P9-DGW-389

THOMAS EDISON

Titles in the
People Who Made History Series

Adolf Hitler
Charles Darwin
Cleopatra
John F. Kennedy
Martin Luther King Jr.
Napoléon Bonaparte
Thomas Edison

**PEOPLE
WHO MADE
HISTORY**

THOMAS EDISON

Carol Cramer, *Book Editor*

Bonnie Szumski, *Editorial Director*
Stuart B. Miller, *Managing Editor*
David M. Haugen, *Series Editor*

Greenhaven Press, Inc., San Diego, CA

Every effort has been made to trace the owners of copyrighted material. The articles in this volume may have been edited for content, length, and/or reading level. The titles have been changed to enhance the editorial purpose. Those interested in locating the original source will find the complete citation on the first page of each article.

$m\omega$

Library of Congress Cataloging-in-Publication Data

Thomas Edison / Carol Cramer, book editor.
      p.   cm. — (People who made history)
    Includes bibliographical references and index.
    ISBN 0-7377-0427-6 (pbk. : alk. paper) —
ISBN 0-7377-0428-4 (lib. bdg. : alk. paper)
    1. Edison, Thomas A. (Thomas Alva), 1847–1931—In literature. 2. Inventors—United States—Biography. 3. Electric engineers—United States—Biography.
I. Cramer, Carol. II. Series.

TK140.E3 T53   2001
621.3'092—dc21   00-056048
[B]   CIP

Cover photo: © Hulton-Deutsch Collection/Corbis
Library of Congress, 31, 71, 83, 110, 130, 144, 158, 201
U.S. Department of the Interior, 48, 58

No part of this book may be reproduced or used in any form or by any means, electrical, mechanical, or otherwise, including, but not limited to, photocopy, recording, or any information storage and retrieval system, without prior written permission from the publisher.

Copyright © 2001 by Greenhaven Press, Inc.
PO Box 289009
San Diego, CA 92198-9009
Printed in the U.S.A.

CONTENTS

3. The American Myth of Thomas Edison

FOREWORD

In the vast and colorful pageant of human history, a handful of individuals stand out. They are the men and women who have come variously to be called "great," "leading," "brilliant," "pivotal," or "infamous" because they and their deeds forever changed their own society or the world as a whole. Some were political or military leaders—kings, queens, presidents, generals, and the like—whose policies, conquests, or innovations reshaped the maps and futures of countries and entire continents. Among those falling into this category were the formidable Roman statesman/general Julius Caesar, who extended Rome's power into Gaul (what is now France); Caesar's lover and ally, the notorious Egyptian queen Cleopatra, who challenged the strongest male rulers of her day; and England's stalwart Queen Elizabeth I, whose defeat of the mighty Spanish Armada saved England from subjugation.

Some of history's other movers and shakers were scientists or other thinkers whose ideas and discoveries altered the way people conduct their everyday lives or view themselves and their place in nature. The electric light and other remarkable inventions of Thomas Edison, for example, revolutionized almost every aspect of home-life and the workplace; and the theories of naturalist Charles Darwin lit the way for biologists and other scientists in their ongoing efforts to understand the origins of living things, including human beings.

Still other people who made history were religious leaders and social reformers. The struggles of the Arabic prophet Muhammad more than a thousand years ago led to the establishment of one of the world's great religions—Islam; and the efforts and personal sacrifices of an American reverend named Martin Luther King Jr. brought about major improvements in race relations and the justice system in the United States.

Each anthology in the People Who Made History series begins with an introductory essay that provides a general overview of the individual's life, times, and contributions. The group of essays that follow are chosen for their accessibility to a young adult audience and carefully edited in consideration of the reading and comprehension levels of that audience. Some of the essays are by noted historians, professors, and other experts. Others are excerpts from contemporary writings by or about the pivotal individual in question. To aid the reader in choosing the material of immediate interest or need, an annotated table of contents summarizes the article's main themes and insights.

Each volume also contains extensive research tools, including a collection of excerpts from primary source documents pertaining to the individual under discussion. The volumes are rounded out with an extensive bibliography and a comprehensive index.

Plutarch, the renowned first-century Greek biographer and moralist, crystallized the idea behind Greenhaven's People Who Made History when he said, "To be ignorant of the lives of the most celebrated men of past ages is to continue in a state of childhood all our days." Indeed, since it is people who make history, every modern nation, organization, institution, invention, artifact, and idea is the result of the diligent efforts of one or more individuals, living or dead; and it is therefore impossible to understand how the world we live in came to be without examining the contributions of these individuals.

INTRODUCTION: A PASSION FOR INVENTING

Almost everyone is familiar with the inventor Thomas Edison and his major contributions to society: the incandescent lightbulb with its distribution system, the phonograph, the motion picture, and his most abstract invention, the industrial research laboratory. Edison is the embodiment of the American dream of rags to riches through hard work. Born into the era of buggies and gas lights, he transformed the world around him and lived long enough to contemplate the problem of harnessing and using atomic energy. He came along too late to invent the telegraph so he had to be content with improving it. Another man beat him to the telephone, but Edison went on to build a better one.

Some say he was ineffectual as a businessman, yet Edison was an astute promoter who, to gain acceptance for his electric light, had to invent dynamos, cables, insulators, conductors, voltage regulators, junction boxes, meters, fuses, and fittings—everything necessary to turn his invention from a curiosity into a practical, inexpensive, and safe tool. Electric light for the world was his primary objective—creating an industry followed. And that is how Edison the inventor and Edison the entrepreneur came together to achieve success.

Touted as America's first true native-born genius, this Wizard of Menlo Park was probably the most famous inventor of all time. Whether by fate or circumstance, it had fallen to Edison, as remarkable an inventor as he was a shrewd businessman, not only to define the meaning of progress but to chart the path by which he would lead the country toward it. Edison was the product of an era that straddled two centuries. On the far side lay the technological revolution of the twentieth century—the birth of the modern era.

THE EARLY YEARS

Born in Milan, Ohio, on February 11, 1847, Thomas Alva Edison was the seventh and youngest child of Samuel and Nancy Elliott Edison. Thomas Edison's father fled from Canada during the Rebellions of 1837 and worked in Milan, Ohio, as a shingle maker and land investor. When Alva, as his family called the youngster, was seven years old, the Edisons moved to Port Huron, Michigan. There his father ran businesses in lumbering and land investing.

Despite his many illnesses, young Edison was filled with curiosity and had a knack for getting into trouble. He managed to survive setting a fire in his father's barn and almost suffocating after falling into a grain elevator, yet his curiosity was never dampened. His curiosity irritated and amused adults, and he would ask endless questions until his victim was reduced to admitting he didn't know the answer. Then Alva would demand, "*Why* don't you know?"[1]

Coming from a simple background and being plagued by a loss of hearing since the age of twelve, Edison overcame great difficulties to achieve all that he did. He was inspired by his mother, Nancy, who homeschooled Alva and gave him lessons that were more stimulating than those he had during his brief time at public school. She encouraged him to read on his own, and he was influenced early on by an elementary science book, *A School Compendium of Natural and Experimental Philosophy* by Richard Green Parker. The experiments explained in the book were easily performed by Edison, who set up his first laboratory in his bedroom. The chemicals made such a mess that his parents insisted he move them to the cellar, and Alva labeled them all "poison" to keep them out of others' hands.

When he was nearly a teenager, Edison worked at odd jobs to pay for the materials he needed to conduct experiments in telegraphy, his first passion. Samuel Morse's invention of the telegraph was the biggest advancement in communications since carrier pigeons, and it fascinated young Alva. He and a friend rigged a crude telegraph running house-to-house lines so that they could tap messages to each other late at night. At twelve, he became a candy butcher selling foodstuffs and newspapers to passengers on the new Grand Trunk Railway line. With nothing to do during the daily layovers, Alva came up with an idea to set up a laboratory in a baggage car. He got a trainman to agree to this, and all his free time was now filled experimenting with test tubes, batteries, and bottles of chemicals. This lasted a couple of years until some of the chemicals eventually caught fire and he was told the laboratory had to go. He quickly replaced the baggage car lab with a secondhand printing press and briefly published a small newspaper known as the *Weekly Herald* that he sold to passengers.

AN ACT OF HEROICS SETS HIS COURSE

At fifteen, Edison's interest in the telegraph was again revived. When the stationmaster's toddler had wandered onto the train tracks and Edison snatched the boy to safety, the grateful father rewarded Alva by teaching him how to transmit the Morse code. The telegraphy lessons paid off, and Edison obtained his first telegraphy position at a salary of $25 a month (good money for 1860). This fateful lifesaving incident set Edison on a course that would change his life. He joined the ranks of the wandering telegraph operators and quickly became the fastest operator on the Western Union system.

In 1863, Edison began work as a telegrapher in Port Huron. During the following four years, he worked as an itinerant telegrapher in numerous Midwest cities, sometimes behind the battlefronts of the Civil War. Edison learned much about the mechanical, electrical, and chemical elements of telegraphy. He read scientific and telegraph journals and books and experimented with telegraph equipment.

OVERCOMING LIMITATIONS

By this time, Edison had developed severe hearing problems. His condition worsened as he grew older, and late in life he could only hear people if they shouted directly into his ear. Young Edison didn't allow this challenge to keep him from pursuing his interests and actually used it to his advantage. Ronald W. Clark, an acclaimed British author of best-selling biographies, mentions that when Edison became a telegrapher, he was able to completely focus on his work and could hear the loud ticking of the equipment without being distracted by other sounds. An older Edison also credits his deafness for being responsible for the extensive experimentation that perfected his phonograph invention.

Despite Edison's hearing difficulties, he mastered the art

of receiving news reports by telegraph. He used a skill common among hearing-impaired people called "filling the gaps," or guessing based on relevant knowledge. Many telegraph operators used this skill to finish interrupted and incomplete messages when the gist of the information was known. Edison used it for even more. He read newspapers in his spare time to gather information that might help him complete messages about current events. As a telegraph operator, Edison learned of news and information that helped him develop a keen awareness of political and business matters throughout the nation.

At age twenty-one, Edison moved to Boston as a telegraph operator. While there, he made improvements on a town fire alarm system, on printing telegraphs for stockbrokers, and on a device to transmit images over telegraph lines. He also applied for his first patent—for an electric vote recorder for legislatures. Although the efficient invention worked well when exhibited before a committee of Congress, the unwanted electric vote recorder sparked no interest and was never purchased. It was then that Edison decided to always identify a market before creating an invention.

The following year, 1869, Edison moved to New York City. There he met the leaders of the telegraph industry and important people in the financial community. He also developed improvements in stock tickers, telegraph devices used to report the purchase and sale of stocks. One such improvement yielded him a profit of $40,000 when all rights were purchased. This provided Edison the revenue he needed to strike out on his own and start a manufacturing shop.

Edison was inspired by the works of British scientist Michael Faraday. Of Faraday, Edison said, "I am now twenty-one. I may live to be fifty. Can I get as much done as [Faraday] did? I have got so much to do, and life is so short. I am going to hustle."[2]

Becoming a Freelance Inventor

In 1870, Edison moved again to Newark, New Jersey. In partnership with a machine shop operator, he started a stock ticker manufacturing company. To keep the business successful, Edison continually tried to improve the devices he sold. Charles Batchelor and other mechanically talented associates joined the new manufacturer in developing a steady stream of inventions.

Western Union, then owned by the Vanderbilts and J.P. Morgan, ranked as America's leading electrical enterprise at the time. Edison joined a group of talented inventors, including Elisha Gray and J.B. Stearns, and helped develop several electrical devices for the company. Their knowledge of the field, like Edison's, flowed from an evolving technological environment. The young inventor's skill in eliminating problems, or "bugs," became legendary. He obtained permission to work all night at Western Union headquarters, and the company's operating chief noticed Edison's drive and genius. But Edison was not a Western Union employee; he was a freelance agent who contracted to the highest bidder. When financier Jay Gould set up a rival telegraph company to compete with Western Union, Edison sometimes served under him, acting as a scientific soldier of fortune in the camps of the warring robber barons. It was obvious that Edison's loyalty was not to the companies but to the work they offered. He was fascinated by problem solving, and it was irrelevant who "owned" the problem.

MARRIAGE

Although his work schedule was demanding, Edison did find time for other important things in life. There are different accounts of his courtship with Mary Stilwell, his first wife, but one thing was certain, he was obviously attracted to the sixteen-year-old girl working in his shop. He asked her parents' permission to call on her and soon afterward asked Mary's father for her hand in marriage. He was told he must wait a year since Mary was still young. Edison accepted the condition, and they married on December 25, 1871, when Edison was twenty-four. Their first child, Marian, was born in 1873, and was nicknamed "Dot" by her father (after the Morse code). She was followed by Thomas Jr., born in 1876, who was dubbed "Dash," and a third child, William Leslie, was born in 1878.

THE INVENTION FACTORY IS BORN

In 1874, Edison completed the design of the quadruplex—his most ingenious invention. This improved telegraph was faster and more efficient than the regular telegraph and could send four messages at a time on a single wire instead of just one message. This important invention doubled the capacity of the existing duplex of Stearns and strengthened Edison's reputation as an inventor in the telegraph community.

In the spring of 1876, Edison gave up the Newark factory and built a laboratory in rural Menlo Park, New Jersey, about twenty-five miles south of Newark. With financial support from Western Union, it was here that Edison and his assistants began research that would transform the world. The equipment at this secluded scientific village in Menlo Park had few rivals, even at leading universities. Edison intended this to be an all-purpose research laboratory and invention factory. German historian Werner Sombart commented that Edison was an example of a man who made a business of invention, as he promised to turn out a minor invention every ten days and a major one every six months. He operated this lab with an organized team of specialists whose tasks were allotted to them by their master—who was still in his twenties.

Menlo Park was the first industrial research laboratory, which would be imitated twenty years later by giant corporations in Europe and America. But there was an important difference. Those laboratories would provide an environment where creative minds could work and flourish. Edison's lab was created to serve only one mind—his. The staff at Menlo Park fluctuated between about two dozen and 220 by the end of 1879. Experimenters flocked to the lab just for the opportunity to work with Edison on his electric light-bulb. Some would have gladly worked for free just for the chance to work with the Wizard. But these men were always subordinate to Edison. Their scientific interests—if not relevant to Edison's problem or invention of the day—were ignored. This stifling of talent didn't seem to affect the invention factory in its heyday, but it would haunt Edison in later years when other companies with freer intellectual atmospheres began beating Edison to the punch.

LIGHTING UP THE WORLD

In 1878, Edison began important research on electric lighting. He was not alone; inventors worldwide also were investigating the process. In September, Edison saw a demonstration of a carbon arc light that produced an extremely bright light. He then began work on an incandescent lamp for use in homes. An incandescent lamp would produce a less intense light by passing electricity through a filament (wire) to make the filament glow. Because his past achievements commanded respect for such a sweeping goal, a syndicate of leading financiers, including Morgan and the Vanderbilts, advanced Edison $50,000 for research and development work on the incandescent electric light, which had been the despair of inventors for fifty years. These contracting parties even established the Edison Electric Light Company, one of the few times when capital has backed an unachieved invention. There followed an exhausting search for a suitable filament. Edison and his staff spent months searching for the filament material that would produce the best light. Physicist Nikola Tesla, who once worked for Edison, called this a needle-in-the-haystack method of experimentation. In October 1879, they successfully tested a carbon filament made from burned sewing thread, producing the first practical incandescent lightbulb.

On the evening of December 31, 1879, the tiny village of Menlo Park, New Jersey, became the site of a New Year's party unlike any the world had ever seen. People arrived by the trainload to gaze in awe at the latest wonder to emerge from the laboratory of the inventor Thomas Alva Edison. Visitors were greeted with a series of glowing glass bulbs mounted on posts along the street leading toward Edison's laboratory. Bulbs also burned in six nearby houses. Two lights shone above the gate at the entrance to the laboratory grounds; several more illuminated the yard surrounding the lab.

There were a few minor events that livened the evening. A woman got too close to one of the generators and discovered the power of its magnetic field when her hairpins suddenly flew off her head. A would-be saboteur, an employee of one of the gaslight companies—the industry that had the most to lose if Edison's invention proved a success—tried to use a concealed wire to short-circuit the lamps. When the safety fuses that had been installed in the system kept him from doing any real damage, Edison's men nabbed him and escorted him to the door. By the time the public exhibition was over, more than three thousand people had flowed through the doors of Edison's laboratory. They had traveled from New York City, Trenton, Philadelphia, and many points in between. They returned to their homes knowing they had witnessed something historic. What they had seen was only a hint of what was to come.

In 1880, they began using bamboo filaments, which increased the life of the bulbs. At first, the electric light was only a novelty because few homes and businesses had electricity. To make the invention practical for everyday use, electricity had to be readily available to customers. Edison began working to produce electricity in central power plants and to distribute it over wires to businesses and homes. His goal was to invent a safe, mild, and inexpensive electric light that would replace the gaslight in millions of homes, and he wanted to accomplish this by using an entirely different method of current distribution than that used for arc lights.

Renowned physicist Albert Einstein paid tribute to Edison when he said,

> You [Edison] have been equally successful as a pioneer, executive and organizer. Your construction of the electric lamp has to a great extent made the development of a great electrical industry possible. The great technical creators, of which you are one of the most successful, have produced in the course of a century an entirely new situation to which mankind has not yet adapted himself.[3]

MOVING ON

Edison considered himself to be a commercial inventor who could develop things to increase the convenience and pleasure of the multitude. Now in his thirties he was experiencing his finest hours. An astonishing number of new products bearing the mark of his originality were developed systematically from his growing reservoir of knowledge of various arts and industries.

Edison was one of many inventors who tinkered with the "speaking telegraph," as the telephone was then called. Alexander Graham Bell patented the telephone in 1876. In 1877, Edison designed a superior carbon-button telephone transmitter, which made a speaker's voice louder and clearer on the telephone. For the next century, most phones used transmitters based on Edison's improvement. Before his invention, people had difficulty hearing anything said over the telephone.

THE PHONOGRAPH

In 1876 and 1877, Edison worked on important experiments for recording and playing back messages sent over the telegraph and telephone. These experiments led to his invention of the cylinder phonograph. To record messages, Edison attached a needle to a diaphragm, a metal disk that vibrated in response to the sound waves of a voice. The needle rested against a rotating cylinder that was wrapped with tinfoil. When the disk vibrated, the needle made varying impressions in the foil. To reproduce the sound, another needle was attached to a diaphragm and funnel-like horn. This needle retraced the impressions or grooves in the foil and sound was reproduced. While developing the cylinder phonograph, Edison also made designs for recording sound on disks and tapes.

In December 1877, Edison exhibited his cylinder phonograph to the editors of the prominent magazine *Scientific American*. The next spring, he demonstrated it to scientific societies and at the White House for President Rutherford B. Hayes. The device seemed like magic—nothing similar had ever been invented. As a result, Edison continued his fame as the Wizard of Menlo Park.

However, the invention was so unusual that at first no one knew what to do with it. Edison envisioned the phonograph being used as a dictating machine. He also sought other uses. He designed toys that would use the device, including talking dolls and children's pianos. Later, other people introduced the idea of selling musical recordings for the phonograph, and soon Edison began making his own recordings.

POWER PLANTS AND ELECTRICAL MANUFACTURING

In 1881, Edison and his staff moved to New York City to promote the construction of electric power plants in cities. Edison built the Pearl Street Station, a steam electric power plant near Wall Street. The station opened in 1882 and soon provided electricity to many customers. By the 1890s, hundreds of communities throughout the world had Edison power stations.

To make the electric lighting system commercially successful, other equipment also had to be readily available, such as generators, power cables, electric lamps, and lighting fixtures. Edison and some of his associates invested in companies that manufactured these products.

One of the accidental discoveries Edison made in his lab in 1883 was almost beyond comprehension. In one of his vacuum bulbs, he observed a mysterious force that manifested itself by a flow of current between a hot and cold electrode. Later, this was shown to be due to the thermionic emission of electrons from the hot electrode. He patented the lightbulb, describing what became known as the "Edison Effect." Studied by other scientists a few years later, it became the basis of the electron tube and laid the foundation for the electronics industry.

TRANSITIONS

While Edison's reputation was riding high, his personal life took some dramatic turns. After several years of illness, Mary Edison passed away on August 9, 1884. Edison's grief so overcame him that he could hardly tell this dreadful news to his children. Edison buried himself in his work and spent more time with his children. Marian became a constant companion to him, and in the summer of 1885 Edison took a break from his laboratory for the entire summer and asked his longtime friends, Mr. and Mrs. Ezra Gilliland, to assist him in finding a suitable wife and mother to his three children. The Gillilands introduced Edison to Mina Miller, the well-educated daughter of Lewis Miller, the successful inventor of the Buckeye reaper. Edison was totally smitten by Mina, and they married on February 24, 1886. They purchased a large home in West Orange, New Jersey, and named it Glenmont. The following year Edison began construction on a new laboratory complex in West Orange that would be ten times the size of the Menlo Park lab. Over the next few years, Thomas and Mina had three children together: Madeleine, Charles, and Theodore. Charles Edison would later become secretary of the Navy and governor of New Jersey.

WEST ORANGE AND THE MOVIES

The new West Orange laboratory included a three-story office that contained thousands of journals and books. The lab also provided space for chemical, mechanical, and electrical experiments. Eventually, it included facilities for manufacturing the devices designed by Edison and his associates. For the remaining forty-four years of Edison's life, this lab was his true home and headquarters. It became the setting for many important inventions, including an improved phonograph using wax records, the mimeograph (which was purchased by A.B. Dick Company), the fluoroscope, an alkaline storage battery, a dictating machine, and motion picture cameras and projectors.

Edison helped found the motion picture industry. In early 1888, he met British-born photographer Eadweard Muybridge. One of many people experimenting with photography of motion, Muybridge inspired Edison to investigate the field. By fall, Edison envisioned a motion picture device that looked like the cylinder phonograph, "an instrument which does for the eye what the phonograph does for the ear."[4] Edison and his lab photographer, W.K.L. Dickson, began to record a series of images on celluloid film. Showing the images in rapid succession would make them look like continuous action. Over the next five years, Edison and his staff invented the peephole kinetoscope. The kinetoscope was the first practical motion picture device that used a roll of film. It consisted of a cabinet with a peephole or eyepiece on top. A customer who put a coin in the machine could watch a short motion picture through the hole. In 1893, Dickson built the Black Maria, Edison's film studio. The Black Maria was the first building designed for the purpose of making commercial motion pictures.

As exemplified by the kinetoscope, Edison used similar problem-solving strategies across many technologies. He reasoned by analogy with a distinctive repertoire of forms, models, and design solutions that he applied to invention after invention. As an example of Edison's logic, early drawings of the kinetoscope bear a striking resemblance to his wax-cylinder phonograph. Both inventions are made up of an axle that supports a cylinder that has information (either a sound recording or a sequence of still photos) wound along its length. Each device has a long, thin instrument (a stylus in the case of the phonograph and a viewing apparatus in the case of the kinetoscope) held perpendicular to the surface of the cylinder. Reese Jenkins, who assembled, and until 1994 headed, the Edison Papers Project staff, noted the similarity. Jenkins found evidence of a conceptual link between the two inventions in a patent caveat Edison drafted in 1888, and points out, "If we hadn't looked at his notebooks and draft caveats, we'd never know what the original impetus for the idea was."[5] The motion picture was not Edison's invention, but with his rare power of going straight to a practical end, he brought it to operational success when many others had failed.

From the mid-1890s to about 1915, Edison tried to control the motion picture industry in the United States. In 1896, his company introduced projectors designed by other inventors. It soon became a principle producer and distributor of motion pictures. In 1908, Edison and most other movie inventors pooled their patents. Together they formed the Motion Picture Patents Company that largely controlled the production, distribution, and exhibition of motion pictures. In 1917, the Supreme Court of the United States upheld a ruling that the company was an illegal monopoly. As a result, Edison and most other members of the Motion Picture Patents Company lost much of their influence in filmmaking. Many of them abandoned the industry that Edison had helped found. At the end of the nineteenth century, Thomas Edison, who had started life as the son of a modest businessman in the Midwest and had worked long hours at hard and often menial jobs, owned combined assets valued at more than $10 million and had single-handedly created the entertainment industry.

Ore Milling: A Great Idea That Fell Flat

As was his custom, Edison's attention was not only directed at motion pictures in the late 1800s. He was also at work designing gigantic equipment to process low-grade iron ore into high-grade ore for steel mills in the eastern United States. He established a processing plant in northern New Jersey in the early 1890s. At the plant, raw ore moved continuously on conveyor belts in a system like the assembly line later popularized by American automaker Henry Ford.

Edison invested millions of dollars in ore milling. His advanced technology was successful, but the project still ended in failure, largely because rich iron ore discovered in the Mesabi Range of northeastern Minnesota was less expensive to mine and process. The mass entertainment industry that he fathered yielded him rich profits that he badly needed, since he had overextended himself in developing the magnetic ore-separating process for low-grade iron deposits. After five years, when he decided to write off the ore-separating project, he had lost the entire fortune of $4 million earned by his electric light system. His reaction was typical: "Well, it's all gone, but we had a hell of a good time spending it!"[6]

The War of the Electrical Currents

Ore milling was not Edison's only defeat in the late 1800s. His mastery of the electric light did not carry over into the electrical systems needed to power them. Edison's limited knowledge of theoretical science weighed heavily against him in the battle of the electrical currents. In the late 1880s, more advanced electrical scientists were introducing alternating current (AC) at high voltages for long-distance transmission. Edison, having chosen direct current (DC), launched a press campaign to alarm the public about the alleged hazards of the high-voltage alternating current system and to persuade them that his choice was the best. But alternating current was clearly the best method of powering houses and industries. Edison was stubborn and refused to give in even when his clients opted for his competitors' systems. As a consequence, Edison not only lost the contract for the great Niagara Falls hydroelectric site to inventor and rival George Westinghouse, he also lost the battle between AC and DC and alternating current prevailed.

A STRING OF MINOR SUCCESSES

Undaunted by his poor judgments, Edison persevered at West Orange. During the 1880s and 1890s, Edison and his associates experimented with batteries. They worked on designing and producing lighter, more durable, and more powerful batteries. By the early 1900s, one of Edison's companies began to manufacture batteries. Railroads used them to power the signals and switches. Edison batteries were also used in electric automobiles and for electric starters in gasoline-powered cars.

Then in the early 1900s, one of Edison's companies began mass-producing portland cement, a gray powder used to make concrete. Edison had built one of the largest cement plants in the United States in western New Jersey. The plant used some equipment from his failed ore project. To help make the works profitable, Edison searched for new users of cement. He introduced poured concrete houses and sold cement for use in large factories and for building Yankee Stadium and other structures in New York City. He even designed concrete furniture. But like the storage battery, Edison's cement schemes yielded only moderate results and attached a fairly narrow market of interested businesses.

It was also at West Orange where Edison improved and sold his favorite invention—the phonograph. He and his staff investigated materials on which to make recordings. Then he produced chemicals to manufacture the recording materials. Cylinder phonographs, such as Edison's, were mechanically and acoustically better than disk phonographs. But disk records were easier to produce and store than cylinder recordings. Reluctantly, Edison switched to the disk format in 1913. He continued to develop and later sold the Ediphone, a dictating machine based on his cylinder phonograph.

EDISON'S PERSEVERANCE

During World War I (from 1914 to 1918), Edison headed the Naval Consulting Board of the United States, a group of inventors and businesspeople who aided the war effort. In large part as a result of his urging in 1920, Congress established the Naval Research Laboratory, the first institution for military research. After the war, Edison returned to his experiments at the laboratory, but turned over most of the administrative work to his son Charles.

Edison continued to pour himself into his work even though successes were coming much more slowly to him. Perseverance was always a cornerstone of Edison's strength. Some historians have pondered what it was that enabled him to push ahead in the face of numerous setbacks and to consider exactly how he learned from failure.

Edison could not conceive of any experiment as a flop. As historian Paul Israel puts it, "He saw every failure as a success, because it channeled his thinking in a more fruitful direction."[7] Israel thinks Edison may have learned this attitude from his enterprising father, Samuel, who was not afraid to take risks and never became undone when a business venture crumbled. Sam Edison would simply brush himself off and embark on a new moneymaking scheme, usually managing to shield the family from financial hardship. Israel feels this sent a very positive message to his son—that it is OK to fail—and may explain why he rarely got discouraged if an experiment did not work out. In addition to teaching Edison what would not work, failed experiments taught him the much more valuable lesson of what would work—although in a different context.

Few challenges failed to yield to Edison's intelligence, but one that did defeat him in one respect was the undersea telegraph. Edison designed a laboratory model of a transatlantic cable in which cheap powdered carbon was used to simulate the electrical resistance of thousands of miles of wires. Noise and vibration both in the lab and from outside was enough to change the pressure of the connecting wires on the carbon, causing change in its resistance. Since the accuracy depended on constant resistance in the carbon, Edison had to ultimately abandon this approach. However, later, when faced with the problem of how to improve the transmission of voices over the telephone, Edison used a funnel-shaped mouthpiece to focus sound waves on a carbon button. The pressure of those vibrations altered the resistance in the circuit in synchrony with the speaker's voice. In other words, what ruined Edison's underwater telegraphy experiments is exactly what made his telephone transmitter such a success. It made Alexander Graham Bell's telephone such a practical device that the transmitter was the industry standard for a century.

Just when it seemed that things were going well for Edison, the unthinkable happened. In 1914, a fire destroyed a large portion of the West Orange laboratory complex. Amid the charred rubble, Edison bent down to pick up a stained photograph of himself. Looking at the cracked glass he said, "Never touched me," and then added, "Well, lads, this is a good omen. It takes more than a big fire to get us down. Let's go around and survey the damage. Tomorrow we shall start bigger and better buildings to replace the ones we've lost!"[8] And two weeks after the fire, the first of the new buildings was already in operation.

ENDLESS SEARCHING

In the late 1920s, Edison sought a substitute for rubber plants as a source of latex. He examined thousands of plant specimens and finally selected a variety of goldenrod. American tire manufacturer Harvey S. Firestone presented Edison with four automobile tires made of the new rubber. However, Edison's rubber proved to be less profitable than desired and the project was ultimately abandoned.

Always the inventor and innovator, Edison continued to pursue the problem of the country's rubber supply, fearing a national shortage if America were to participate in another war. Friends and automotive icons Henry Ford and Harvey Firestone had made him aware that Britain held a monopoly on rubber with its large Malayan rubber forests, and they encouraged Edison to find a solution to overcome America's dependence on British rubber. Edison continued to work and experiment while suffering from several illnesses that struck him in his later years. Worried more about the rubber problem than his health, Edison was still searching for an answer when he died in bed at his home in West Orange, New Jersey, on October 18, 1931.

LEGEND AND LEGACY

Given that Edison was almost always available for interviews and the fact that his major inventions were so well publicized (and his flops glossed over), his fame was assured. During the years that followed World War I, Edison would become the most famous of all Americans. He was so well regarded that interviewers often asked him for his opinion on a host of topics. In his later years he was quite willing to ignore his business ventures and dispense sage wisdom. As Ronald Clark notes,

> Once anxious to elaborate on the future of his latest invention, he was now prepared to tackle the troubles of the world and humanity, and usually just as ready with a solution. He still saw into the future with considerable skill, foreseeing the problem of traffic in great cities, the shorter working day and the leisure problem that it would create. . . . He still had an inquiring interest in everything and astonished one reporter by telling him that [at the age of seventy-four] he had started a major investigation of the ether.[9]

Edison's contributions to the nation's welfare were recognized when, in 1928, he received a special congressional gold medal. He was also the first civilian to receive the navy's Distinguished Service medal, granted for his service as chairman of the Naval Consulting Board during World War I.

As do many aging men, he regretted a few things—particularly the first commercial "talkies": "They have spoiled everything for me. There isn't any more good acting on the screen. My, my, how I would like to see Mary Pickford or Clara Bow in one of those good old fashioned silent pictures. They concentrate on the voice now; they've forgotten how to act. I can sense it more than you because I am deaf. It's astounding how much more a deaf person can see."[10]

The countless contributions of Edison and his associates—the quadruplex telegraph, the phonograph, the practical incandescent light and the distribution systems for it, crucial improvements in the telephone and electrical generators, the motion picture camera—made him a living legend. Just as worthy as these inventions were Edison's pioneering efforts in creating an industrial research laboratory—first at Menlo Park and then at West Orange. His research and manufacturing complex was the first of its kind in the world, and these labs became the models for many other companies.

Edison was the transitional figure who bridged the gap between the crude workshops of the nineteenth century and the facilities that make up research and development departments in modern corporations today.

Having a special creative spark and an ability to conceive of things in ways no one else had thought of, Thomas Edison was an exceptional technical thinker, a shrewd if not always successful strategist, and a man with unfailing enthusiasm, persistence, and confidence that kept him moving forward in the face of awesome setbacks and fierce competition from rivals. Edison was a survivor and for most of the world remains larger than life—larger than the pages any book can encompass.

NOTES

1. Quoted in Robert Silverberg, *Light for the World: Edison and the Power Industry.* Princeton, NJ: D. Van Nostrand, 1967, p. 31.

2. Quoted in Gene Adair, *Thomas Alva Edison: Inventing the Electric Age.* New York: Oxford University Press, 1996, p. 37.

3. Quoted in Lawrence A. Frost, *The Edison Album: A Pictorial Biography of Thomas Alva Edison.* Seattle: Superior, 1969, p. 160.

4. Quoted in Frost, *The Edison Album*, p. 115.

5. Quoted in Reese V. Jenkins, ed., *The Papers of Thomas A. Edison. Vol. 1: The Making of an Inventor*, et al. Baltimore: Johns Hopkins University Press, 1989, p. xxxi.

6. Quoted in Adair, *Thomas Alva Edison*, p. 56.

7. Quoted in Paul Israel, *Edison: A Life of Invention.* New York: John Wiley & Sons, 1998, p. 237.

8. Quoted in H. Gordon Garbedian, *Thomas Alva Edison: Builder of Civilization.* New York: Julian Messner, 1947, p. 206.

9. Quoted in Ronald W. Clark, *Edison: The Man Who Made the Future.* New York: Putnam, 1977, p. 233.

10. Quoted in Clark, *Edison*, p. 237.

CHAPTER 1

Thirsty for Knowledge

PEOPLE
WHO MADE
HISTORY

THOMAS EDISON

A Teenaged Businessman

Gene Adair

As a hard-working lad with an imagination for enterprise, Thomas Edison started his own train
"butcher" business, selling snacks and newspapers
to train passengers. Biographer Gene Adair, involved
in publishing since 1981 and currently marketing
manager at University of Tennessee Press, gives a
glimpse of Thomas Edison as an eager young boy.
Working on trains gave Edison the opportunity to see
industries in neighboring cities, feeding his interest
in machines. But young Edison was also taken with
science and he even obtained permission to move
his home laboratory to a baggage car on the train.
Also while working aboard the train, Edison tried his
hand at publishing a weekly paper for passengers.
Eventually, he turned to selling other people's newspapers and discovered that by having telegraph operators send important news to stations down the line,
he could ensure that all the timely newspapers he
carried would sell out when he reached those stops.
This sparked an interest in the workings and potential uses of the telegraph that heralded Edison's fascination with invention.

Thomas Alva Edison was born in Milan, Ohio, on February
11, 1847. He was named Thomas after one of his uncles; his
middle name came from that of a close family friend.
Growing up, he was never called Tom—it was always Alva
or Al. . . .

Alva attended school for the first time in Port Huron, starting when he was about eight. His parents first enrolled him
in a private school run by the Reverend George B. Engle, and
later he attended the Port Huron public school. The kind of

Excerpted from Gene Adair, *Thomas Alva Edison: Inventing the Electric Age.* Copyright
© 1996 Gene Adair. Reprinted with permission from Oxford University Press, Inc.

education these schools offered, in which students were expected to learn their lessons by memorizing them, had little appeal for an inquisitive dreamer like Alva Edison. His teachers failed to understand him, and his talent for mischief just made matters worse. . . .

In all, Alva probably attended school for no more than a few months. As he recalled years later, he one day overheard a teacher declare that he was "addled." Upset, he ran home and told his mother, who indignantly withdrew him from the school and vowed to teach him on her own. Although Nancy Edison was probably as strict a disciplinarian as any of Alva's other teachers, she gave him lessons that were far more stimulating. She read to him from Dickens's novels and Shakespeare's plays, from Edward Gibbon's *Decline and Fall of the Roman Empire* and David Hume's *History of England*. She also encouraged him to read on his own. He became entranced with one work in particular: *A School Compendium of Natural and Experimental Philosophy*, an elementary science text by Richard Green Parker. The book described simple experiments that Alva could perform himself, and before long he was trying them all.

Science and reading appealed to the young Edison much more than the household chores he was expected to perform, such as tending his father's vegetable garden and selling its produce. His allowance went for chemicals he purchased from a local druggist. At first he performed his experiments in his bedroom, but his chemicals made such a mess that his parents insisted he move them to the cellar. There he labeled all his bottles "poison" to keep them out of others' hands.

A TEENAGED BUSINESSMAN

By the time he was 12, Alva felt the need to strike out in a new direction. Over his mother's objections, he insisted on going to work. Whatever resistance Nancy may have offered, however, was offset by a sad necessity: the Edisons could use the money. No longer the prosperous businessman he had been in Milan, Sam was now constantly in debt. So, in 1859, Alva became the family's most reliable breadwinner.

The railroad provided the future inventor with his first employment. The Grand Trunk company had just opened a line into Port Huron from Detroit, 63 miles to the south. Sam arranged for Alva to work as a candy butcher, a vendor who sold snacks and newspapers to the passengers. In later years, Edison would remember his job on the Grand Trunk Railroad as "the happiest time of my life."

Rising at six every morning, Alva drove a horse and cart to the station and boarded the train in time for its 7:15 departure. As the train puffed toward Detroit, stopping at several towns along the way, Alva walked through the three passenger coaches carrying a basket filled with his wares. "Newspapers! Apples! Sandwiches!" he shouted to the passengers huddled on wooden benches. "Molasses! Peanuts!"

Four hours after leaving Port Huron, the train arrived in Detroit. The returning train did not depart until the late afternoon, when Alva repeated his routine. It was usually 11 o'clock before the boy was in bed.

Alva's long daily layovers in Detroit expanded his sense of the world. With nearly 50,000 people, Detroit was a major shipping and industrial center buzzing with activity. Alva enjoyed visiting the city's machine shops and watch-

Nancy Edison

ing the trains being switched in the rail yard. One of his favorite haunts was the train station's telegraph office, where he gazed in fascination as the operators signaled train movements to other stations.

A MOBILE LABORATORY

Detroit also nurtured his love of chemistry. One of its main industries was the production of chemicals and pharmaceuticals, so Alva had no trouble restocking the collection of bottles he kept at home. After a while, he decided to move his laboratory onto the train. With the permission of the conductor, Alexander Stevenson, he set up his chemicals in an unused corner of the baggage car and devoted his free hours to experiments.

Unfortunately, his mobile lab came to an abrupt end when

some phosphorus sticks, accidentally exposed to the air, ignited and started a fire on the baggage-car floor. Helping to smother the blaze, Stevenson burned his fingers badly. At that point, he banned Alva's little laboratory from the train.

The incident became the source of a popular Edison legend. According to this story, Stevenson boxed Alva's ears to punish him for the accident, thus causing the partial deafness that plagued him throughout his life. Edison himself discounted this version, claiming that his deafness had started earlier with another incident on the train. One day, while some newspaper customers delayed him on the platform, the train began to leave the station. Dashing after it, he was spotted by Stevenson, who grabbed him by the ears and pulled him aboard. At that moment, Edison recalled, "I felt something in my ears crack and right after that I began to get deaf."

In all likelihood, however, the real culprit for Edison's deafness was not a rough encounter with a train conductor. His long history of ear infections and a possible bout of scarlet fever were probably the true causes of his hearing loss. In any case, the deafness does appear to have set in around the time he began working on the Grand Trunk Railroad. "I have not heard a bird sing since I was twelve years old," he lamented in his diary years later.

AN INDEPENDENT THINKER

These hearing problems pushed Alva deeper into the world of books. Victor Hugo's novel *Les Misérables* became one of his favorite works. This sprawling tale, which tells of an ex-convict named Jean Valjean and his struggles against a pitiless society, no doubt appealed to a romantic streak in the young Edison. Thomas Paine's *The Age of Reason* had an even more pronounced effect on him. Recommended to him by his free-thinking father, Paine's book advanced some radical notions that fascinated Alva. Although Paine asserted the existence of God, he criticized traditional religious beliefs and teachings. Paine argued that churches were merely "human inventions set up to terrify and enslave mankind" and declared, "The world is my country; to do good my religion."

Paine's words made sense to young Edison and bolstered his growing skepticism about organized religion. His devout mother was unhappy when he stopped accompanying her to church, but there was little she could do to counter the boy's increasingly independent ways.

At 15, Alva joined the Young Men's Society of Detroit and used its library and reading room. Although he later boasted that he had read the entire library, he was stretching the truth. As he admitted to a friend in 1905, "reading the library" may have been his goal, but he gave it up after plowing through "about ten books that were pretty dry reading."

Among the volumes he claimed to have struggled with—and disliked—was Sir Isaac Newton's great theoretical opus *Philosophiae Naturalis Principia Mathematica* (Mathematical Principles of Natural Philosophy), the work that lay the foundations for modern science. Unfortunately, the only thing Edison took from it was "a distaste for mathematics from which I have never recovered."

EARLY INFLUENCES

More to his liking was Andrew Ure's *Arts, Manufactures, and Mines,* which disdained scientific theory in favor of practical knowledge. Ure ridiculed the "speculative scientists" and praised artisans and mechanics as the real bringers of progress. Ure's arguments were not lost on the young Edison, whose practical bent—the desire to make something useful—would be the hallmark of his later inventions.

While Alva's spare-time habits of reading and performing experiments sharpened his mind, his job on the train sharpened his business savvy. He proved such a successful salesman of newspapers, candies, and fruits that he expanded his business with the help of friends and of produce from his father's vegetable garden. "After being on the train for several months," Edison remembered, "I started two stores in Port Huron—one for periodicals, and the other for vegetables, butter, and berries in the season. They were attended by two boys who shared in the profits."

A YOUNG PUBLISHER

His entrepreneurial spirit showed itself in other ways. After the fire that sealed the fate of his mobile laboratory, he put the space in the baggage car to a different use. After acquiring a little printing press and some old type, he began to publish the weekly *Grand Trunk Herald,* which reported on small events along the Detroit-Port Huron line and sold for three cents a copy. Setting the type by hand exhausted him, however, and publication of the *Herald* ceased after only a few issues.

Still, Alva was not ready to quit publishing altogether. He turned for help to an acquaintance named Will Wright, who worked at the *Port Huron Commercial.* Alva had an idea for a new publication, and he persuaded Wright to print it. This arrangement freed Alva to concentrate on writing and editing the new paper, which he called *Paul Pry.* Filled with gossip and society news, *Paul Pry* contained one story that so enraged a Port Huron doctor that he threatened to toss Alva into the Saint Clair River. Thus, the young Edison decided that journalism was not such an attractive career after all.

Although his own publishing ventures were short-lived, Alva continued to prosper by hawking other people's newspapers. In the spring of 1862, he enjoyed his biggest success as a teenaged businessman. By that time, the Civil War had been raging for a year, and news of the terrible conflict filled the daily columns. On April 6, when he arrived at the offices of the *Detroit Free Press* to pick up his papers, he encountered a large and anxious crowd seeking word about a major engagement then underway in Tennessee. It was the battle of Shiloh, and the early reports spoke of tens of thousands of casualties.

An idea hit him. Knowing that the battle would be big news that day, he ran back to the train station and struck a deal with the telegraph operator. In exchange for a promise of free papers and magazines, the telegrapher agreed to wire a bulletin about Shiloh to all the stops along the line to Port Huron. According to the instructions Alva set forth, each stationmaster, in turn, was to then write the reports on the blackboards ordinarily used to announce train schedules.

Returning to the *Free Press* offices, he convinced the editor, Wilbur F. Storey, to let him have a thousand papers on credit. That evening, as the train rolled into each station, Alva found a huge crowd waiting to buy his papers. At the first stop, Alva was able to sell the papers for five cents each. By the time the train reached Port Huron, they were going for a quarter. Alva managed to sell every copy.

Not only had his idea worked, it had impressed him more than ever with the power of the telegraph. This marvelous device, developed in the late 1830s by Samuel F.B. Morse, had revolutionized the communications of the era. Through the mysterious force of electrical current, messages could be sent instantaneously over a distance of up to 200 miles. The technology intrigued Alva to no end, and he began to think seriously about becoming a telegrapher.

Even before taking the job on the Grand Trunk Railroad, Alva had tinkered a bit with some wet-cell batteries and a crude telegraph set he had built himself. Daily exposure to the telegraph operators who worked along the train line had intensified his interest. But he needed someone to teach him the craft.

A Vagabond Telegrapher

Neil Baldwin

Noted author of the acclaimed biographies of poet William Carlos Williams and painter Man Ray, Neil Baldwin examines Thomas Alva Edison as man and myth. In this excerpt from his book *Edison, Inventing the Century,* Baldwin offers a revealing portrait of Edison, assessing a few of the significant influences on him and exploring some of his character traits. As a young entrepreneur, Tom subcontracted his train "butchering" business to friends, stopped publication of his newspaper, and spent his time with the station master listening to telegraph transmissions. The telegraph was the newest news media that moved information electrically and Tom was fascinated by it. A quirky incident gave Tom the opportunity to learn telegraphy and provided the means that would lead him throughout the eastern states on a journey to becoming an inventor.

At fifteen, he preferred to be called Tom. His coming of age was governed by the railroad, his lifeline, a gateway to the ever wider world of commerce and communication. And as the railroad spread in extent and influence, so did the telegraph in its wake. Both brought the frontier within reach. Understanding this symbiotic technological relationship helps us appreciate Tom's personal media shift, breaking away from static newspaper type and into "writing with lightning." No new technology up to that time ever had a more accelerated growth. By the time Edison was fifteen, telegraph wires reached all across America, from Washington, D.C., to San Francisco.

Excerpted from Neil Baldwin, *Edison: Inventing the Century.* Copyright © 1995 Neil Baldwin. Reprinted with permission from Hyperion.

ATTRACTION OF THE TELEGRAPH

The telegraph was born a mere ten years before Thomas Edison. Invented by Samuel F.B. Morse in 1837, the first telegraph instrument resembled an electric switch, allowing current to pass for a limited time before being shut off with the touch of a finger. Messages were transmitted by such electric pulses passing over a single wire. Marks—dots and dashes—were made on a paper tape moving around a cylinder, varying in relation to the duration of the pulse.

The earliest telegraphic signals could only be transmitted about twenty miles, beyond which they were too weak to be recorded. Morse developed a relay—essentially an additional surge of current on the line—to repeat the original signal and send it further.

In 1833, Alexis de Tocqueville had been struck by the American outright affection for freedom of the press, aptly linking this obsession with the equally indigenous quality of self-reliance which "the inhabitant of the United States learns from birth." This "tumultuous agitation" of the spirit made the exemplary American restless, enterprising, enraptured by speed, and, above all else, an innovator.

The young Edison was a perfect exemplar of Ralph Waldo Emerson's "Representative Man," for apart from simply needing to make a living, he soon came to recognize the imperatives of commercial necessity even as he responded to a more profound creative impulse. His first patented invention was now a mere half-dozen years away, and his most important communications-related inventions in the future would consistently be refinements of telegraphic principles, structured to accelerate the transfer of information. The telegraph, derived from that special brand of American speed—the first message to outrun the messenger, as [historian and social critic] Marshall McLuhan observed—thus came into being as an expedient outgrowth of the newspaper. . . .

It cannot be emphasized too strongly that before the telegraph, communication was linked to established transportation means—infrastructure systems, roads, canals—and likewise to fixed conveyance on the page—newspapers, books, and personal correspondence—that was only as quick as the means by which the mail bag was carried. The telegraph transcended these limits, moving information electrically. The telegraph as a pivot-point marked the beginning of the end of nineteenth-century small worlds.

Short and long bursts of current seduced an ambitious, hard-of-hearing boy into a clattering embrace of dots and dashes he could understand: "When in a telegraph office," Edison recalled of those first enraptured encounters, "I could hear only the instrument directly on the table at which I sat, and unlike the other operators I was not bothered by the other instruments." Edison's pattern of downplaying his deafness began during this initiation time. What to others seemed a poignant tragedy—that after the age of twelve he "could not hear a bird sing"—was to the inventor, the fabricator, a fortuitous break. Ambient noise was immaterial: "Broadway is as quiet to me as a country village is to a person with normal hearing," he waxed poetically.

DEAFNESS IS AN ASSET

A canny analogy: Edison's idealized pastoral roots would stay with him forever, fixed in time like a sepia photograph. But his deafness evolved into more than a nostalgic echo simply because its onset coincided with his boyhood in a simpler era. Edison would always insist that being deaf set him apart from the masses of men, gave him an excuse to turn away from tiresome social involvements, making him a far more productive thinker. When he became a household name, Edison the capitalist, the "Wizard," would receive hundreds of letters from hearing-impaired people all over the world pleading with him to harness his formidable imagination to find a remedy for deafness or to invent an apparatus that would become the ultimate hearing aid, the miracle solution, the cure-all. These solicitations were routinely ignored, marked in blunt pencil "No ans." and passed along to his secretary. Edison refused to surrender what was essentially his passport to the inner world.

A NEAR MISS SETS HIS COURSE

By the fall of 1862, in his words, Tom "commenced to neglect [his] regular business," subcontracting his "butchering" responsibilities to friends Jim Clancy and Tommy Southerland; he ceased publication of the Grand Trunk *Herald,* much preferring to spend his day loitering about the Mount Clemens depot on the Port Huron to Detroit line, where the stationmaster, J.U. MacKenzie, allowed him to listen in on the flow of telegraph transmissions. There was considerable commercial traffic through Mount Clemens, a constant shunting of freight cars to be attached to the daily mixed train.

MacKenzie's three-year-old son Jimmie was playing on the platform one morning as Tom and the stationmaster were talking shop. The story goes, according to Edison—and immortalized in the fabulously dramatic etching in *Scribner's* magazine, "Saving the Child"—that the toddler wandered blithely onto the tracks as a freight car came rolling toward him. The brakeman, braced on the roof of the car, alarmed, called out, unable to turn the brake wheel quickly enough, and quick-eyed Tom darted into the path of the oncoming car, dove onto the tracks, and grabbed the child on the fly, shoving him to safety, neither of them badly hurt beyond gravel cuts and bruises. The hysterical mother presses her hands to her brow, the brakeman atop the freight strains at his "stemwinder"; and Tom, on the run, impelled forward, holds the child by his arms and lifts him into the air, as the steel wheels make their inexorable way.

In gratitude, MacKenzie offered to teach Tom telegraphy, since the lad had the interest and the aptitude, and had already taught himself the Morse code and built a rudimentary telegraph key. Speed was Tom's primary goal. In three months of intensive lessons he mastered the skill, and landed a job at Micah Walker's loosely named "jewelry" store in downtown Port Huron, site of the Western Union telegraph office. It was an eclectic kind of place. Walker sold clocks, watches, old spoons and forks, and did gold and silver electroplating. He sold rifles, organs, dominoes, and chinaware. He sold schoolbooks, stationery, and all manner of writing implements, day books, blotters, and sheet music, as well as technical manuals and scientific magazines, which Tom had the liberty to peruse during his downtime. As Tom read, he forced himself into the habit of grouping several words at once, always aiming toward greater efficiency. In the evening, after supper, he returned to the shop to practice receiving press reports in solitude, to satisfy his hunger for information as well as to gain additional facility with longer, more complex journalistic dispatches from the [civil war battlefront]. . . .

AN UNBROKEN CHAIN OF TASKS

The language of Edison's original, spontaneous, handwritten reminiscences about this apprenticeship phase of his life is noteworthy in its portrayal of a relentlessly driven, self-starting, and solitary being, with singular disregard for the constraints of a typical day: "I was small and industrious," he scrawls with matter-of-fact pride in himself as a boy. "I could fill the position all right. . . . Night jobs suited me as I could have the whole day to myself. . . . After working all day, I worked in the office nights as well. . . . I seldom reached home before 11:30 at night." To Edison in retrospect (he was sixty-one when he wrote these words), his adolescent life seems to have been an unbroken chain of tasks with the one purpose of self-betterment, far more competitive with himself than with the other guy. . . .

Tom outgrew Walker's shop, and took the 7:00 P.M. to 7:00 A.M. railway telegrapher's shift at Stratford Junction, Ontario, on the Grand Trunk Line, seventy-five miles north of Port Huron toward Toronto, his first job away from home—again despite [his mother] Nancy's fears—as a "Knight of the Key." He had cultivated the talent of sleeping a minute or two here and there—sitting in his chair, lying on top of or under tables with the crook of his elbow for a pillow—for which he eventually became much renowned. To catch his forty (or twenty) winks, Tom made an arrangement with the night yardman to awaken him when his signal came over the wire. This deal failed when a freight train rushed through on Tom's watch and he was not able to detain it, and a collision with another train coming from the opposite direction was narrowly avoided. Summoned for a dressing-down before the district superintendent in Toronto, the stationmaster was "hauled over the coals" for permitting such a high degree of responsibility to such a young man.

Six months later, while Tom was back in Port Huron licking his wounds in the wake of this precipitous failure, his beloved sister Tannie died in childbirth at the age of thirty. In despair, he picked up his itinerant lifestyle again, and was off to Lenawee Junction, near Adrian, Michigan, fifty miles southwest of Detroit, again working as a night telegraph operator, this time for the Lake Shore and Michigan Southern Railroad.

He preferred the less favored night jobs because they provided him with "leisure" during the daylight hours and gave him readier opportunities for employment. Yet even following orders, Tom landed in difficulty. He was handed an urgent dispatch by his supervisor and advised that, if necessary, he should break in to whatever transmission was currently on the wire. Tom spent ten minutes struggling with the operator further down the line for transmission time. Unbeknownst to him, this anonymous agent happened to be the district superintendent, who appeared at the Adrian office infuriated. Tom defended himself, saying that he had been told to interrupt the current transmission, appealing to his boss for support, but the man summarily denied giving any such command. Tom was the scapegoat. "Their families were socially close & I became a wanderer," Edison wrote of the affair. "My faith in human nature got a slight jar."

MOVING FROM JOB TO JOB

In the early winter months of 1864, it was on to Fort Wayne, Indiana, for another half-year stint, a day job on the Pittsburgh, Fort Wayne and Chicago Railroad; and then to Indianapolis, working for Western Union. Tom found a room at a boardinghouse just four blocks away from the Union depot. Although still not hired for the coveted press wire job, Edison, living nearby, could come back after hours and sit next to the press operator, copying dispatches on his own time, until the early morning hours.

Finding it difficult to keep up with the more complicated press messages using conventional handwriting, Edison came up with an ingenious solution. He rigged up two Morse registers, the first of which recorded the dots and dashes of the incoming message in the form of indentations on a continuous strip of paper. He then ran this encoded strip through the second register, activating its sounder, but at a pace moderated to a frequency considerably slower than the original forty words per minute. With the help of a co-worker controlling the second machine, Edison was able to make virtually flawless copy. He had succeeded in adapting the machinery in tune with his particular sensory requirements.

It was next on to the big city of the Ohio River Valley, the state's preeminent metropolis, Cincinnati, proud home of Procter and Gamble, less proud of its image as the pork-producing capital of the midwest. Tom was still paying his dues in the telegraphers' caste system as a "plug," or second-class, night shift operator at the main Western Union office, on Third Street. He worked the wire that ran to Portsmouth, Ohio, and still kept up his practice by offering to substitute for any press wire operators who wanted some time off. His goal was "to become proficient in the very shortest time.". . .

Edison was becoming more collegial. While in Cincinnati, he joined with his co-workers to form the local chapter of the

National Telegraphic Union, founded the year before as an attempt to consolidate this rather makeshift, exponentially growing, unruly profession of drifting young men, and give them a united arbitration voice. The Union also published and distributed its own journal, *The Telegrapher.* The prophetic motto on its masthead loftily, if rhetorically, asked, "Is it not a feat sublime?/Intellect hath conquered time." Thomas Edison became a persistent editorial voice in its pages.

Promoted finally to first-class operator, with a commensurate big salary boost to $125 a month, Tom felt footloose again in the face of actual stability. A friend in Memphis wired him with news of the possibilities there, "and as [he] wanted to see the country [he] accepted it." His brief stay on the Mississippi was occupied by deeper voyages into literature. Consistent with his admiration for the founding fathers and in true democratic spirit, Tom read a biography of Thomas Jefferson. He claimed that in November 1865 he manufactured a repeater that for the first time since the end of the Civil War brought New York City and Memphis back into telegraphic contact. For ambiguous reasons, Tom was once again dismissed.

His southern sojourn continued at the Associated Press Bureau in Louisville, Kentucky, a debris-strewn, ramshackle office crowded with minuscule desks, the plaster flaking from the ceiling, and a dysfunctional soot-jammed wood-burning stove. The switchboard was woefully cramped and inadequate, its connections blackened and crystallized with age, and the planked floor of the battery room was corroded with nitric acid. It was a tumultuous place, operators barging in half-drunk at all hours of the day and night. . . .

Edison's year on the Louisville Western Union press wire was a valuable one. Transcribing dispatches with increasing facility, to compensate for his admitted deficiencies in sending messages, he perfected the speedy, copperplate handwriting with abbreviations that would become his lifelong trademark. . . .

Fired for spilling sulfuric acid in the bureau's battery room, which ate through the floor and wreaked havoc in the manager's office below, Tom retraced another earlier trail and returned to Western Union's Cincinnati bureau, which had now moved from Fourth and Walnut to newer, larger quarters on Third Street. Friend Ezra Gilliland and other former colleagues of Edison's recalled with amusement the many times Tom would manage to get himself excused from work, pleading illness, and invariably "strike a bee line" for the Mechanic's Library on Sixth and Vine, or the Cincinnati Free Library. Edison's few surviving pocket notebooks bear witness to his assiduous research and to the wide spectrum of his interests: tables of conductivity, comparing the relative merits of copper and silver; sketches for self-adjusting relays that through the use of more sensitized springs would help make the process of receiving transmissions more efficient; and enhanced repeaters, to allow for longer-distance transmissions without having to transcribe and retransmit messages.

In the library stacks, Tom tracked down Dionysius Lardner's classic work on the *Electric Telegraph,* as well as his *Handbook of Electricity, Magnetism and Acoustics.* He read Richard Culley's *Handbook of Practical Telegraphy,* Charles Walker's *Electric Telegraph Manipulation,* and Robert Sabine's *History and Practice of the Electric Telegraph.*

But heading Thomas Edison's neatly jotted list of research needs was the first volume of *Experimental Researches in Electricity and Magnetism* by Michael Faraday, a pervasive influence who, like Thomas Paine, was a definitive role model for Edison as his working methodology coalesced. . . .

Faraday discovered the principle of electromagnetic induction, demonstrating that an electric current could be produced by thrusting a magnet into a coil of wire and withdrawing it, thus giving birth to the dynamo and the transformer. In so doing, he broadened the domain and identity of electricity, envisioning not only an abstract power, but a commodity, and laid the foundations for the modern electrical industry. He showed that within the confines of his basement research laboratory, where he ostensibly focused upon the pursuit of knowledge for its own sake, theories could be formulated with commercial applications; research indeed led to development. Thomas Edison would soon make the identical transition from the workshop to the world at large. . . .

On to Boston

By the time he turned twenty, Tom was back in Port Huron. All was not well at home. The family had been evicted by the army from the big house near Fort Gratiot; after being commandeered, it burned down. The Edisons were now on

Cherry Street in more modest quarters, taking on boarders to help make ends meet. Nancy Edison was suffering, as she did more and more often in these years, from vaguely defined but chronic "nervous trouble." Sam's ongoing land speculation and contracting activities were failing. Tom, the tired and hungry prodigal son, became ill and was forced to spend the winter of 1867 in bed.

Then a letter arrived from Milton Adams, Tom's friend from Cincinnati, now working in Boston for the Franklin Telegraph Company. There were openings at the Western Union Boston bureau, and Milt could get Tom a job—if he came quickly.

The Young Entrepreneur

Joseph and Frances Gies

With a burgeoning interest in electricity, twenty-year-old Edison developed his first patentable invention—an electronic voting machine. Soon after, his knowledge of electrical mechanics combined with fortuitous events led him to repair and then improve upon a stock ticker for an established company. Paid the astonishing amount of $40,000 for his new device, Edison now had the means to devote his time exclusively to inventing. Joseph and Frances Gies, acclaimed husband and wife writing team, recount the elements of genius and chance that propelled Edison into young entrepreneurship.

At twenty-one, after visiting Port Huron, Edison boarded a Grand Trunk train for Boston, with the promise of a Western Union job with his Memphis friend, Milton Adams. He arrived looking his seediest, in ill-fitting and none-too-clean clothes, a battered broad-brimmed hat, down-at-heels shoes. He was well aware of the eccentricity of his own dress: "My peculiar appearance caused much mirth," he candidly recorded. The other operators planned a hazing, arranging to have his first message sent by one of the fastest men on the New York line. The New York man began slowly, gradually increasing to top speed; Edison effortlessly kept pace, and finally opened the key to advise the operator, "Young man, change off and send with your other foot."

FARADAY'S BOOK INSPIRES EXPERIMENTS AND INVENTION

In Boston, Edison browsed through the secondhand bookshops along Cornhill Street. His prize find was a two-volume edition of Faraday's *Experimental Researches in Electricity,* which opened a new world. "His explanations were simple,"

Excerpted from Joseph and Frances Gies, *The Ingenious Yankees.* Copyright © 1976 Joseph and Frances Gies. Reprinted with permission from HarperCollins Publishers, Inc.

Edison wrote later. "He used no mathematics. He was the master experimenter." On quitting the night shift at 4 A.M. he began reading Faraday and read until it was time to go back to work. He tried Faraday's experiments, and told Milt Adams, "I am now twenty-one. I may live to be fifty. Can I get as much done as he did? I have got so much to do and life is so short, I am going to hustle."

With the discovery of Faraday, experimentation began to crowd everything else out of Edison's life. Bored with his favorite task of "taking press," he amused himself by crowding hundreds of words on one page, in a hand so minute that it had to be recopied before the newspaper compositors could use it; rebuked, he countered by centering a single word on each sheet of paper. He was asked to resign, which suited him.

He had already discovered Charles Williams's electrical shop on Court Street where Thomas Watson went to work a few years later, and where Bell had his instruments made. Advertising in a trade journal that "T.A. Edison has resigned his situation in the Western Union office, Boston, and will hereafter devote his full time to bringing out his inventions," Edison set up his workshop in a corner of the Williams establishment, where he produced his first patentable invention, a voting machine for legislatures, which registered "ayes" and "nays" on a roll of chemically-treated paper. Borrowing money for the trip to Washington, he demonstrated the device before a congressional committee. It worked perfectly, but the congressmen pronounced it "the last thing on earth that we want here. Filibustering and delay in the counting of the votes are often the only means we have for defeating bad legislation. . . . Take the thing away." Edison returned to Boston swearing never to invent anything "which was not wanted, or which was not necessary to the community at large."

His next venture was an improved stock ticker; again the device worked well, but this time he neglected to safeguard his patent rights and saw his unguarded intellectual property picked off by the privateers of free enterprise. Another effort, an improved duplex telegraph, was a technical failure, and he suddenly found himself in debt. Boston had proved unlucky, and leaving behind his instruments, books, and personal belongings, he borrowed the fare for a night steamboat trip to New York.

Edison made the rounds of the New York telegraph offices,

borrowing from an operator a dollar that, beginning with a supper of apple dumplings and coffee, fed him for three days. Calling at the office of the Gold Indicator Company, central bureau of the stock ticker that relayed price changes from the floor of the Gold Exchange to brokerage houses, he obtained permission to sleep on a cot in the battery room.

Three days later, in the midst of a market crisis, the central stock ticker broke down. The financial district was in pandemonium, with hundreds of messengers storming the Gold Indicator Company. Just as the president of the company, S.S. Laws, arrived, Edison succeeded in diagnosing the problem: a contact spring had broken off and fallen between two gear wheels. Laws importuned, "Fix it! Fix it! Be quick, for God's sake." Edison replaced the spring and reset the indicator dial, while clerks hastened off to restart the receivers in the brokerage houses.

Next day Laws sent for Edison and hired him as assistant to the company's chief electrical engineer, Franklin Pope. A month later Pope left to start his own firm, and Edison inherited his job, at $300 a month. He was in charge of the indicator on September 24, 1869, "Black Friday," when financial manipulators Jay Gould and Jim Fiske attempted to corner the gold market. As prices first rocketed upward and then, on President Grant's order to the Treasury to sell gold, plummeted, Edison and his crew struggled to keep the indicator in touch with fluctuations. "I sat on top of the Western Union telegraph booth to watch the surging, crazy crowd," he wrote later. ". . . Amid great excitement, Speyer, the banker, went crazy and it took five men to hold him; and everybody lost their head. . . . The Western Union operator came to me and said, 'Shake, Edison, we are O.K. We haven't a cent.' I felt happy because we were poor."

BIG MONEY, BIG BUSINESS

A week later Laws sold out to Western Union. Edison left the company to form a partnership with Franklin Pope to develop another improvement on the stock ticker, a device every day more revered in Wall Street. They also took in a silent partner, J.W. Ashley, editor of *The Telegrapher*, who contributed advertising space to the partnership. When Western Union bought their improvement for $15,000, Edison, who had done all the work, got only $5,000. After a few similar transactions, he terminated the partnership.

Shortly after, Marshall Lefferts, president of Western Union, engaged him to add further refinements to the stock ticker. Three weeks later Edison brought a model to Lefferts's office for a demonstration. According to one of his favorite stories of later years, when Lefferts asked him to put a price on his rights, and on certain other work he had done for Western Union, Edison demurred, afraid to ask for the $5,000 that he thought would be "about right," and ready to settle for $3,000. "General, suppose you make me an offer." Lefferts stunned him with an offer of $40,000. The check—the first he had ever handled—made another good story: When the bank teller handed it back to him for endorsement, Edison ran to Lefferts's office with it thinking he had been cheated. Lefferts sent his secretary to help cash the check, but that only created another problem. The teller counted out $10 and $20 bills in a cubic-foot stack which the inventor sat up all night to guard. Next day he found out about bank accounts.

All his life Edison had spent every dollar, or nickel, he could spare on books and apparatus for his research. Now he suddenly had $40,000 and a commission from Lefferts to manufacture the new improved stock ticker. With some of his capital he set up in a loft in Newark (4–6 Ward Street) and as his work force grew to fifty and then 250 hands, he

Edison's staff stands in front of his first factory in Newark, New Jersey. At this factory Edison continually launched new projects and averaged a patent a month.

wrote his parents in Port Huron, "I am now what you Democrats call a 'Bloated Eastern Manufacturer'!"

He was indeed a manufacturer, but the role was too constricting for his bursting intellectual energy. Ideas were tumbling out of his head every day, and in the crowded Newark loft he launched one new research project after another until he had forty-five going simultaneously. He averaged a patent a month.

As his chief assistants he hired a nucleus of outstanding men, each of whom had his own specialty to contribute to the team: John Ott, a mechanic who became his chief draftsman; a Swiss clockmaker named John Kruesi, who superintended the laboratory; an Englishman, Charles Batchelor, who transformed Ott's drawings into working models; Will Carman, who kept the accounts and managed the machine shop.

In 1871 Edison took time out to fall in love with and marry sixteen-year-old Mary Stilwell, an employee of his Newark shop. Time out, but not much; an hour after the ceremony he remembered a production problem and was back in the shop in his shirtsleeves. A family tradition had it that at midnight someone reminded him of the time and he exclaimed, "Midnight! By George, I must go home then! I was married today!"

In 1873 his headlong work schedule was interrupted by another kind of adventure. His first experience with big business, the $40,000 deal with Marshall Lefferts, had been a pleasure. Now he discovered another side to Wall Street. A rather mysterious firm called the Automatic Telegraph Company commissioned him to produce an automatic printing telegraph, a marriage of telegraph and stock ticker, which would both receive and type out messages. After four months of intensive research and systematic testing whose results he graded in his daybook in his own code as "N.G." (no good), "D.B." (damned bad), "N.B." (no better), "L.B." (little better), "E." (encouraging), and "V.E." (very encouraging), he produced a successful working model. At the same time Edison was also working on a revolutionary development for Western Union, a quadruplex that could carry four messages simultaneously, two in either direction. In April 1873 Edison sailed for England to demonstrate his quadruplex, and returned home to find New York in the grip of a financial panic. His own business was threatened by the failure of Western Union to meet payments due for his work—to avoid paying him, president William Orton, Lefferts's successor, had simply decamped for an "extended tour."

The slippery financier Jay Gould now revealed himself as the power behind the Automatic Telegraph Company, and offered to buy the inventions Edison was working on for Western Union. Edison agreed, and was promptly double-crossed. Gould used his anticipated control of the patents to force mergers with the Atlantic and Pacific Telegraph Company and Western Union, then turned around and discarded the patents without ever paying Edison anything. Having achieved his object of winning a telegraph monopoly, Gould had no interest in improved technology, as Edison perceived at once: "I knew no further progress in telegraphy was possible, and I went into other lines."

In the fall of 1875 he made an accidental discovery in pure science that put his name permanently into the science vocabulary. The "Edison effect"—bright sparks pro-

---

THE HUMAN SIDE OF EDISON

In this biography that was endorsed by Thomas Alva Edison himself, William Meadowcroft gives an upclose and personal profile of this amazing inventor.

Let us turn from what Edison has done to what Edison is. It is worth while to know "the man behind the guns." Who and what is the personal Edison? . . .

A . . . very marked characteristic of Edison's personality is an intense and courageous hopefulness and self-confidence, into which no thought of failure can enter. The doubts and fears of others have absolutely no weight with him. Discouragements and disappointments find no abiding place in his mind. . . .

Difficulties seem to have a fascination for him. To advance along smooth paths, meeting no obstacles or hardships, has no charm for Edison. To wrestle with difficulties, to meet obstructions, to attempt the impossible—these are the things that appear to give him a high form of intellectual pleasure. He meets them with the keen delight of a strong man battling with the waves and opposing them in sheer enjoyment.

Another marked characteristic of Edison is the fact that his happiness is not bound up in the making of money. While he appreciates a good balance at his banker's, the keenness of his pleasure is in overcoming difficulties rather than the mere piling up of a bank account. Had his nature been otherwise, it is doubtful if his life would have been filled with the great

duced by a vibrator magnet—indicated the passage of energy through space, suggesting the possibility of communication without wires. Similar sparks had been observed by Joseph Henry and Faraday, and James Clerk Maxwell had theorized about the electromagnetic waves that caused them. Edison's report aroused great interest among scientists, but the world was not quite ready, and for the time being the "Edison effect," with its near uncovering of electronics, remained a tantalizing mystery.

That same fall Edison reached a momentous decision. It amounted in a way to no more than a logical extension of his already established working arrangements. Though the basic idea of the Newark company was manufacturing, and invention theoretically a sideline, Edison in his own mind had from the beginning reversed the priorities, regarding the manufacturing operation as a more or less distracting bore. The Panic of '73 even showed it to be an unprofitable bore,

achievements that it has been our pleasure to record.

In a life filled with tremendous purpose and brilliant achievement there must be expected more or less of troubles and loss. Edison's life has been no exception, but, with the true philosophy that might be expected of such a nature, he remarked recently: "Spilled milk doesn't interest me. I have spilled lots of it, and, while I have always felt it for a few days, it is quickly forgotten, and I turn again to the future.". . .

In a recent conversation a friend expressed surprise that he could stand the constant strain, to which Edison replied that he stood it easily, because he was interested in everything. He further said: "I don't live with the past; I am living for to-day and to-morrow. I am interested in every department of science, art, and manufacture. I read all the time on astronomy, chemistry, biology, physics, music, metaphysics, mechanics, and other branches—political economy, electricity, and, in fact, all things that are making for progress in the world. I get all the proceedings of the scientific societies, the principal scientific and trade journals, and read them. I also read some theatrical and sporting papers and a lot of similar publications, for I like to know what is going on. In this way I keep up to date, and live in a great, moving world of my own, and, what's more, I enjoy every minute of it."

William H. Meadowcroft, *The Boys' Life of Edison.* New York and London: Harper & Brothers, 1911, pp. 233–38.

at least part of the time, and he now resolved to drop it completely and concentrate on invention.

Consequently the Newark loft no longer served his purpose, and he looked around the neighboring countryside for a place where he could build the kind of plant he needed. On the Pennsylvania Railroad between Elizabeth and Metuchen, rural and secluded and yet only twenty-five miles from New York, he found a whistle stop that he thought would do. The name of the place was Menlo Park.

CHAPTER 2

The Wizard of Menlo Park and His Amazing Invention Factory

PEOPLE
WHO MADE
HISTORY

THOMAS EDISON

Committing to Inventing: Menlo Park and Pearl Street Station

Thomas P. Hughes

In the late 1860s while working for Western Union, Edison committed himself to invention by becoming an independent inventor—choosing his own problems to solve, making his own inventions, and forming new companies only to sell them for profit. After setting up a telegraph manufacturing shop and laboratory in Newark, New Jersey, he later left this to establish his invention factory at Menlo Park. Acclaimed writer and Mellon professor of the History and Sociology of Science at the University of Pennsylvania, Thomas P. Hughes relates that it was here that Edison focused on inventing a system of electric lighting. By 1882, the system was patented and tested with the equipment being manufactured by various Edison companies. Pearl Street Station, the first station that generated a public supply of electricity, was put into operation. Even though it initially ran at a deficit, the first demonstration plant was used to interest leaders and financiers in buying licenses to operate exclusive electric system franchises globally. Within eight short years, Edison stations had been established throughout the world. Edison's decade at Menlo Park, from 1876 to 1886, proved to be his most brilliant and productive.

At the same time that Thomas Alva Edison flourished, the United States emerged upon the world scene as the great technological nation. This simultaneity was not altogether accidental, for Edison drew upon the sustaining environment and, at the same time, helped create it. His most fruitful years were those spent at Menlo Park, New Jersey, from

Excerpted from Thomas P. Hughes, "Thomas Alva Edison and the Rise of Electricity," in *Technology in America: A History of Individuals and Ideas*, edited by Carroll W. Persell Jr. Copyright © 1981, 1990 The Massachusetts Institute of Technology. Reprinted with permission from the MIT Press.

1876 to 1886, which was about the time America rose to pre-eminence in invention and industry. By 1890 the United States led the world in the number of patents granted and in its iron and steel production. Furthermore, its production of coal—the basic fuel and an important chemical—ranked second to none. Of the many inventive Americans in this productive era, Edison was the most prolific with no less than 500 patents by 1885 and with hundreds more to follow. Not only did he have the largest number of patents, but the devices and processes they covered were financially rewarding and technologically impressive. . . .

EDISON COMMITS TO INVENTING

By 1868 he was working for Western Union in Boston, and there he committed himself to invention. At first his inventing could only be during off hours, but he found time to build and patent an automatic vote recorder for which he could find no market. (He later said that it was then he decided to identify a market always before he invented—an obvious strategy employed by most professional inventors, then and now.) No amateur, and determined to live by his new profession, Edison journeyed to New York in 1869. With him he carried ideas for improvements in telegraph systems and a sharp eye and a clear head for opportunity. Opportunities opened to him shortly when chance allowed him to repair a Wall Street printing telegraph at a time when its price quotations were badly needed. Subsequent support from the grateful owner, who was well connected in the telegraph business, gave Edison an entree. Less familiar are accounts of the intricate business and technological activities in which he became involved as he invented telegraph improvements, including a quadruplex design, for several, even competing, telegraph companies. When Western Union fell into the hands of Jay Gould, the notorious financier and waterer of stock, Edison said his kind of inventiveness was no longer needed there, so he became an independent inventor, choosing his own problems, making his own inventions, and forming new companies to market them. In 1870 he had set up a telegraph manufacturing shop and laboratory in Newark, New Jersey; in 1876 when he decided to become an independent inventor, he drew upon his capital and his growing reputation to fulfill a vision—the establishment of an invention enterprise or, as some said, an invention factory.

He chose Menlo Park, a lonely site on the Pennsylvania Railroad between New York City and Philadelphia, which as bases of supply and ready markets were only an hour or so away by train. But at Menlo Park, unlike the cities, there was a freedom from worldly distraction and an invitation to concentration. Edison realized this as he moved old experienced aides such as John Kreusi, the machinist and ingenious model maker, from the Newark shop and brought in new ones who would have to learn the Edison style and absorb the deep commitment to inventing a method of invention.

INVENTION FACTORY IS A REALITY

The compound at Menlo Park was both cozy and workmanlike. The buildings provided the resources needed by a professional inventor, and Edison soon became known as the Wizard of Menlo Park. Within a few years of settling at the new site, Edison had a building for an office and a technical and scientific library (long series of the world's leading journals were housed there for the seekers of ideas about the state of the art), as well as another large building that housed on its two floors a remarkably well-provided chemical laboratory, an electrical testing facility, and, initially, a machine shop. (Later, the machine shop—the producer of electrical and mechanical models, small and full-scale—was separately housed.) After Edison concentrated upon the invention of a system of electric light, small buildings for blowing the glass bulbs and for obtaining the filament carbon were added. A carpentry shop rounded out the facilities. When the invention factory was built and full of life, a number of watercolors and drawings captured the public imagination by portraying it snow-covered, suggestive of a bountiful Santa Claus and his busy elves. In fact, the place worked more like a center for advanced invention.

The sociology of the Menlo Park group deserves more study. It was far more complex in its interactions than the popular impression of the inventive genius delegating work to eager, pliable assistants. Thousands of laboratory notebooks from Menlo Park suggest that Edison, sensitive to innumerable factors, decided upon the ultimate objectives, but that a handful of men immediately around him engaged in team research and development, coordinated and monitored by him. The historical record also reveals that the members of the inner circle occasionally changed, as did the equipment at Menlo Park, in accord with the nature of the project. . . .

PICK A PROBLEM, FIND A SOLUTION

Edison was the leader of an invention and development group (today it would be labelled research and development), but he was also something more—an inventor-entrepreneur. Only a few men today attempt to carry such a broad range of responsibilities as designated by the term inventor-entrepreneur. Edison not only presided over invention and development, but he also took part in financing, publicizing, and marketing for the project. His most famous project, the electric light system, serves well to illustrate the point.

To choose a problem or a project is a critical decision for an independent inventor; an inventor hired by a corporation usually has guidelines explicitly defined or implicitly revealed by the vested interests of the corporation or agency for which he works. Edison decided, for complex reasons, to expend his resources upon the electric light project in 1878. Friends in science and engineering told him that the state of the art in incandescent lighting suggested that practical achievement might be near. Technical periodicals and patents also signalled activity in incandescent lighting. Such information alerted Edison to the possibility that he might solve the remaining critical problems—such as a durable filament—that would make the difference between ingenious tinkering and commercial success. He had confidence in his ability to solve electric lighting problems because, like so many professional inventors, he knew his characteristics and drew upon the experiences that had helped shape them. In short, he was, after years of work on the telegraph, an expert on electrical matters. The electromagnetic phenomena of the telegraph, the electrochemistry of the battery, the fine mechanics of the relay, and the laws of circuitry, all had relevance to the new endeavor, if one could transfer, adapt, and invent by analogy.

Another reason for working on electric light was the nature of Menlo Park itself, both its physical and personnel resources. For its day Menlo Park represented a considerable investment of resources and, as a result, it had substantial momentum. It had mass, movement, and direction. Therefore, certain problems could be solved best at

One of Edison's first inventions was the "Jumbo" generator created with the ability to power 1,200 16-candlepower lamps and first used to serve New York's Wall Street district with electricity.

Menlo Park, and others better elsewhere. Edison and his advisers realized that the problem of inventing and developing an electric lighting system suited Menlo Park, for a system involved electromagnetic machines (generators), delicate apparatus (switches, fixtures, controls, incandescent lamps, and so on), and complex circuitry. Because of the diversity of problems posed by the varied components, the complex of facilities and people at Menlo Park could be advantageously employed. The system required the repeated testing and experimentation for which Menlo Park and its men were also well suited. Most important, a system of electric lighting needed vision, planning, and coordination for which Edison had a genius and for which Menlo Park was designed. . . .

The project needed a business and financial structure as well as the technological one provided by Menlo Park. So with the advice of Grosvenor P. Lowrey, whose strong characteristics as an experienced business and financial entrepreneur nicely rounded out his own, Edison established in the fall of 1878 the Edison Electric Light Company. Its purpose was to fund the inventive enterprise of Edison insofar as it pertained to electric light and power, and to promote throughout the world the adoption of the patented inventions. . . .

By September 1882 the system had been conceived, designed, patented, and tested on a small scale at Menlo Park. The equipment had been manufactured by the various Edison companies. The first Edison central station for public supply was then placed into operation, serving, as planned, New York's Wall Street district with about a one-mile radius. The Pearl Street Station had six steam engines, driving six Edison Jumbo generators, each capable of supplying 1,200 16-candlepower lamps. Within a year, about 8,000 Edison lamps were being supplied from a 110-volt distribution system. The world celebrated its first central station's technical success.

Financial reports show, however, that for the first few years the Pearl Street Station sold electricity at a loss. This was sustained for several reasons. Foremost was the consideration that Pearl Street served as a demonstration plant to interest local civic leaders and financiers throughout the country and abroad in buying the licenses to operate an exclusive franchise and the equipment of a central station similar to Pearl Street. Another reason was the valid assumption that as service was improved, customers were added, unit fixed-costs were lowered, and various economies were achieved through rationalization, the operation would then become profitable. It did, before fire destroyed the historic station in January 1890. By then, there were Edison stations in large cities and small towns throughout the world. The era of the Edison direct-current station had been established; this era in the 1890s gave way to that of the alternating or polyphase station serving a larger area with both power and light over high-voltage systems. Thomas Edison did not demonstrate the flexibility to make the transition.

INVENTIVE POWERS DIM

Edison's period of brilliance passed with the triumph at Pearl Street. He lived and worked on until 1931, adding to this long list of inventions and patents, and making substantial innovations, but his later contributions to the technology of motion pictures, magnetic ore separation, portland cement manufacture, the storage battery, and the derivation of rubber from indigenous American plants lacked the incisive insight and the dramatic rendition of his work on quadruplex telegraph, the telephone transmitter, and the early phonograph, all of which—like the lighting system—came before 1882. Perhaps a key to the apparent diminution of the inventive powers can be seen in the considerable and unsuccessful effort he made to introduce a process of magnetic ore separation.

After success at Pearl Street, other events in Edison's life added up to a watershed—the gradual turn downward after the peaks of achievement. In 1884 his first wife died of scarlet fever, and some of his friends believed that Edison, deeply grieved, then lost his taste for Menlo Park. In 1886 he moved into a new laboratory of his own design at West Orange, New Jersey. It was much larger and more complex than the rural compound so easily pervaded by his personality. Also in 1886 he married Mina Miller, an attractive young socialite from Akron, Ohio, for whom he purchased an estate, Glenmount, in the hills above his new laboratory. (His first wife, Mary, had worked in his Newark shop, and they had lived in a relatively simple house in Menlo Park.) Between 1882 and 1892 he was also losing influence in his electrical manufacturing companies, and at about the time he embarked upon the ore project, he finally sold out his stock in the enter-

THE MENLO PARK MYSTIQUE

In this Edison biography, Robert Friedel and Paul Israel depict the uniqueness of the Menlo Park laboratory, noting that the ten extraordinary years there would never be replicated at the West Orange lab.

Although Menlo Park has, with considerable justification, been called the world's first industrial research laboratory, it was not—in its essential organization—a prototype for those to follow. Later laboratories would provide an environment within which separate creative minds could work, stimulating each other and making common use of the facilities. For Edison, the laboratory was structured to serve only one creative mind, his own. As he said, "I am not in the habit of asking my assistants for ideas. I generally have all the ideas I want. The difficulty lies in judging which is the best idea to carry out." This is not to say that others were completely stifled, but the rule in the lab was to carry out Edison's specific instructions first, pursuing other work if there was time. And without the master to provide direction, as happened from time to time, the pace of action dropped precipitously. . . .

The glue that held all of this together was clearly Edison himself. A loner who was uncomfortable in normal circumstances, he had developed during his years as an itinerant telegrapher a talent for easy rapport with workingmen. Motivation for the men came from several sources. There was reprises and saw them consolidated in 1892 not as Edison General Electric, but as simply General Electric. . . .

RIDING THE CREST OF PUBLIC ACCLAIM

Despite the outcome of the ore separation project and despite the lack of brilliance surrounding later projects such as the storage battery, Edison rode the crest of public acclaim until, by the time of his death, he approached the status of a secular saint, a representative to masses of Americans of the best in the American character. They saw him as a plain-spoken, self-educated, practical-minded, eminently successful, native genius. They believed him an inspired empiricist, both an experimenter and tinkerer. He was an American success story—that of a hard-working, hard-nosed, down-to-earth man who provided material in abundance for an upwardly mobile society. The public wanted more of him than inventions; his pronouncements about education, religion, and

spect; Edison worked harder, longer, and more effectively than the rest. At the same time he was a peer. When John Ott first saw Edison, he "was as dirty as any of the other workmen, and not much better dressed than a tramp. But I immediately felt there was a great deal to him."

Also, the operation was structured so that he worked with the others. Because everything flowed from his inventiveness, he was naturally interested in everything that was being done and pursued all activities with a watchful eye and pertinent suggestions. He knew when to take a break. Often this was at midnight, with coffee, pie, a cigar, loud music on the organ, and a round of jokes. Edison once said, I was very fond of stories and had a choice lot . . . with which I could usually throw a man into convulsions." He was also an impossible prankster, able to liven up proceedings when necessary, and encouraged others to do likewise. . . .

One can only speculate how long the spirit of Menlo Park could have survived, or how many people it could tolerate. The numbers during the lamp days were apparently still tolerable. But when Edison recreated the laboratory on a much larger scale in a more urban area, at West Orange, the essential character was no longer present.

Robert Friedel and Paul Israel with Bernard S. Finn, *Edison's Electric Light, Biography of an Invention.* New Brunswick, NJ: Rutgers University Press, 1986, pp. 146–48.

other general questions commanded front-page newspaper space and became oracular statements for countless admirers.

In fact, Edison was more complex. He spoke plainly when raising money from Wall Street financiers who distrusted long-haired scientists; he was self-educated, but his reading included the classics of Western literature and the notebooks of Michael Faraday; he was eminently successful, but not simply because he had inventive genius; and, truly, he practiced the art of the experimenter with consummate skill, but he also knew the science of his day and used it to formulate hypotheses and organize experimental data. In the laboratory with his associates, he could be described as "the wizard that spat on the floor," but it is unlikely that the floors were so stained at Glenmount. Long before professional public relations perfected image-making, Edison presented to the world an inventor whom it would support and a hero whom it needed.

During his lifetime the center of industrial research moved from Menlo Park and West Orange into the General Electric, Bell Telephone, and DuPont Laboratories. Men with advanced degrees in science working in the laboratories did not simply use the available science to solve their technological problems; they generated the science as needed. Americans, by the time of Edison's death, began to look to men in white coats bending over microscopes as images of the new research and development bringing "better things for better living."

Despite his limitations, however, Edison was nonetheless a representative American and a key to understanding its late 19th-century character, when it became the world's leading technological and industrial power. America, then, had moved beyond steamboats, railroads, and textile mills; it had not yet reached the stage of automatic controls, missiles, and computers. Edison possessed just the touch to provide the lights and sounds that brought a sense of well-being, even affluence, to hard-working people still laboring on the construction site that was young America.

The Decline of the Invention Factory and the Rise of Research and Development

Paul Israel

Telegraphy was influenced by the new scientific knowledge of electricity, and by the end of the 1890s this source of knowledge about electricity was shifting from practical experience and self-education gained in machine shops to formal engineering programs in colleges and universities. This trend ultimately gave rise to industrial research labs where the theoretical process of invention was removed from the practical manufacturing division of corporations. Paul Israel, assistant editor of the Thomas A. Edison Papers at Rutgers University, shows the shift in the pattern of American invention and states that Edison's Menlo Park lab was one of the first organizations to adapt the machine shop solely to inventive work. Although Edison's machine shop increased the rate at which inventions were developed at Menlo Park, other companies found that their machine shops were already taxed making improvements to existing technologies. Therefore, despite Edison's success, his model of the invention factory was made obsolete as industries saw wisdom in segregating their businesses into manufacturing and research and development.

The growing importance of engineering solutions in the 1880s and 1890s should not overshadow the continuing similarity between inventors and engineers in telegraphy. Telegraph engineers derived technical knowledge from the same sources that the industry's inventors relied upon—practical

Excerpted from Paul Israel, *From the Machine Shop to Industrial Laboratory: Telegraphy and the Changing Context of American Invention, 1830–1920*, pp. 153–54, 156–57, 175–76, 177–83. Copyright © 1992 The Johns Hopkins University Press. Reprinted with permission from The Johns Hopkins University Press.

experience at the operator's key or mechanic's bench and independent study in technical journals and books. Indeed, the engineering corps was largely made up of inventor-engineers, who replaced inventor-entrepreneurs as the principal developers of telegraph technology. Both emerged from telegraph shop culture with its origins in the tradition of American mechanical invention.

IN-HOUSE INVENTORS

In some respects the growing emphasis on engineering resembled an earlier period of system engineering in the late 1850s and 1860s, when the growth of large telegraph systems first produced a need for improved components such as repeaters and insulators to increase operating efficiency. In that era, however, telegraph companies relied on the individual initiative of operators, managers, or manufacturers to produce technical improvements as independent inventors. By the 1880s, telegraph companies had established engineering and patents departments for supervising ongoing technical development. The men employed in these departments not only reviewed the work of outside inventors but undertook inventive work themselves. They were primarily engaged in solving engineering problems and developing standardized procedures for the technical operations of their companies.

Standardization of practice was only one element of engineering activity. Creative design was a key characteristic of the professional engineer, and in telegraphy such design often evolved from inventive activity. The men who staffed engineering positions in the industry produced minor but important inventions designed to increase the efficiency and economy of the systems under their charge. With the expansion of staff technical positions in the 1870s and the employment of competent men to fill them, companies began turning to their electricians when faced with technical challenges from competitors.

Like earlier inventors, most technical personnel began their careers in the operating corps and were self-educated in electricity. Many engaged in invention before they assumed more responsible engineering positions and used their creativity to demonstrate their technical skills. Although Francis Jones, the chief electrician of Postal Telegraph, advanced farther than most, his career was in many ways typical of those who became members of corporate engineering staffs. Jones began his career in 1867 as an operator in St. John, New Brunswick. After moving to Western Union's Chicago office in 1873, he continued his study of electricity and began experimenting with duplex and quadruplex telegraphs, devising improvements that were adopted by the company. Jones also became secretary of the recently founded American Electrical Society in 1875 and was rewarded for his demonstrated technical abilities with the newly created position of general circuit manager. Illness forced Jones to resign from Western Union, but he later worked as electrician for the rival Bankers and Merchants Telegraph Company. In that position he continued to invent, devising the only duplex telegraph that worked adequately on long lines and did not use Stearns's condenser design. After Bankers and Merchants failed, Jones became chief electrician of the Postal Telegraph Company. There he invented a system to run quadruplex telegraphs by dynamos which did not infringe Stephen Field's system used by Western Union. . . .

MONOPOLIZING AN INVENTOR'S TALENTS

Telegraph companies were willing to invest in engineering inventions that increased the efficiency or improved the economy of their existing systems, but they were little interested in alternative telegraph systems. Independent inventors . . . might produce engineering inventions, but they seldom moved into the corporation as engineers. Inventor-entrepreneurs who did become salaried employees for a company often found that their desire for independence conflicted with the goals of management, as occurred when Edison became electrician for Atlantic and Pacific. Jay Gould's decision to make Edison company electrician probably stemmed more from his desire to monopolize Edison's talents as an inventor, thus denying them to Western Union, than it did from his interest in Edison's services as an engineer. During the first six months of 1875, Edison did act in an engineering capacity in order to establish his automatic system on the A&P lines. He also offered suggestions for improving the company's operations. However, Edison's primary interest was in continuing to invent. Although he retained the title of company electrician for Atlantic and Pacific, Edison gave up active participation in its daily affairs because company president Thomas Eckert took a different view of the relative importance of Edison's two roles. Edison was unwilling to act as engineer for the company if this meant that his inventive work would be circumscribed by corporate goals. Although Edison was forced to turn again to Western Union to support his laboratory independently of manufacturing, he did so on terms that provided relative freedom for his experimental work. Edison used his successful inventive work for Western Union to achieve a large degree of independence. By the end of the decade, as opportunities for significant inventive work in telegraphy declined, he used that independence to turn his attention to developing inventions for other electrical technologies.

Edison was among a small group of men who sustained careers as independent electrical inventor-entrepreneurs in the era of the large corporation. They did so by . . . turning their attention to problems in newer electrical fields such as electric light and power. Stephen Field, for example, moved from telegraph invention to work on developing electric railroad technology. Independent inventors . . . who continued working on telegraphy found that independent investors, European governments, and cable telegraph officials were more interested in their work than the managers of American telegraph companies. . . .

PRACTICAL EXPERIENCE LOSES APPEAL

By the turn of the century, engineering theory rather than practical knowledge was considered the best guide to the design of new technologies. The changing character of technical knowledge was evident in the careers of two of the more famous inventors of the new century. Lee De Forest invented the radio audion tube, and Charles Kettering made significant inventions in a number of fields, most notably those developed for General Motors. Intent on a career as an inventor, De Forest attended the Sheffield Scientific School at Yale. Kettering graduated from the Ohio State University department of engineering. Their practical inclinations and interest in experimentation were not unlike those exhibited by Edison, yet both men possessed a more theoretical and mathematical bent and considered a university education necessary to develop the faculties essential to pursue invention. This was a far cry from the traditional course of practical experience and self-education that had characterized inventive careers in the nineteenth century.

LABOR PROBLEMS CAUSE EDISON TO OUST THE UNIONS
This brief excerpt from Lawrence Frost's biography of Edison shows a cunning side to Edison and how he protected himself against union workers who went on strike.

Edison was having labor trouble. Where he [previously] had dozens of workers he now had hundreds. By 1888 he would employ almost 3,000. When his shops were small his men were expected to work 18 hours a day but were paid a bonus for additional effort. Since they liked him and found the work interesting and even exciting, they did not complain.

When the lamp manufacturing started it became necessary to train additional men several months in the art of sealing in the filament. When these employees numbered 80, they formed a union and made evident their independence.

Secretly, Edison developed and manufactured 30 machines that would do the operation. When the labor agitator was fired, the union promptly went on a strike. While they were out, Edison installed his new filament sealing machines. The union never was invited back. An additional benefit was the lowering of the manufacturing costs of his lamps.

The inventor had raised the pay of his workmen at the Edison Machine Works in New York 25 cents a day. There were some who thought they could obtain more by striking. While the men were out, Edison purchased two brick buildings in Schenectady from the McQueen Locomotive Works, moving all his machinery there. Later his men said they would like to come back to work, so he told them they could. When they showed up at the Goerck Street shops they found them empty.

Lawrence A. Frost, *The Edison Album, a Pictorial Biography of Thomas Alva Edison.* Seattle: Superior Publishing, 1969, p. 105.

Though De Forest possessed a doctorate from Yale, he exhibited the same drive for independence and entrepreneurial characteristics typical of the nineteenth-century inventor; the type had not disappeared but their backgrounds were shaped by new institutions. Kettering, too, exhibited entrepreneurial characteristics, but was more typical of the engineers and Ph.D.–bearing physicists and chemists who entered industry in the twentieth century, and worked within the bureaucratic structure of the emerging corporate industrial research establishment.

The changing nature of technical knowledge and education, which helped promote a growing appreciation for the usefulness of basic scientific research, also contributed to the explosive growth of industrial research institutions in the first two decades of the twentieth century. Changing competitive conditions in American industry further fueled this growth. Antitrust legislation threatened to restrain large corporations such as Western Union in driving rivals from their markets. Western Union reacted by tolerating limited competition which did not threaten the company's dominance. Firms in other industries found that control of technology could serve as a barrier not affected by antitrust law. They also recognized that rivals controlling key technologies could also gain advantage over them. They responded defensively, by adopting research programs that took advantage of those changes in technical knowledge which placed greater reliance on scientific information and techniques in the development of new technology.

These changing conditions initially had a limited impact on telegraphy. Industry leaders were steeped in the mechanical-shop tradition of mid-century technology. But the rise of competition from the Bell system's long-distance telephone lines forced a reevaluation of telegraph technology. The technical challenges created by this competition also challenged the resources of shop-trained engineers and inventors. The decline of traditional shop invention became evident when the American Telephone and Telegraph Company (AT&T) succeeded in gaining control of Western Union. It was Western Electric engineers working for AT&T who invented the new high-speed printing telegraph systems that were adopted by Western Union. The telephone company also influenced Western Union to develop a new industrial research program. . . .

THE LAB AS A TRUE INVENTION FACTORY

As early as 1887, one year after completing its first long-distance line between New York and Philadelphia, the Bell Telephone Company leased a private-line telegraph for use by brokers. The growth of privately leased telegraph lines in the Bell system contributed to the company's decision in 1910 to acquire Western Union. The year before, the company had begun a research program at Western Electric to develop its own page-printing telegraph, and Western Union's experience with printing telegraphy was an important consideration. Between 1910 and 1912, Western Electric engineers worked with Western Union engineers to develop what became known as the multiplex printing telegraph, designed to serve Western Union needs in handling messages on its main lines. This system used a punched tape transmitter with a five-unit code based on that of the French Baudot printing telegraph. It printed on a page form, could be quadruplexed, and allowed correction of the taped message, an important consideration for the telegraph company.

The development of the multiplex printing telegraph also marked an important period of transition in the development of new inventions at Western Union. During the nineteenth century, most major telegraph inventions were conceived by individuals working as independent inventors or as contract inventors. A few were the product of company employees. For only a brief period, under the direction of William Orton, the company sought to control the direction of such inventions and to regularize research and development. In particular, Orton's support for Edison's invention factory at Menlo Park marked a faltering step toward an early form of organized industrial research.

But Orton was an unusual executive officer for a large American corporation in the nineteenth century. His close relationships to a number of inventors, and his willingness to understand not only the technical needs of the company but the technology itself gave him a much greater appreciation for the inventive process than most managers. Following Orton's death, telegraph invention at Western Union largely depended upon the "enthusiastic but undirected efforts of a few employees who were responsible from time to time for the development of new ideas." Although Orton did not entirely escape from nineteenth-century beliefs in the unpredictability of inventive genius, he nonetheless recognized that Edison himself was attempting to make invention an industrial process at his Menlo Park laboratory.

At Menlo Park, Edison used money from his contract with Western Union to support his mechanical department, the precision machine shop he had adapted from his telegraph manufactories. By adapting the machine shop solely to inventive work, Edison and his assistants could rapidly construct, test, and alter experimental devices, thus increasing the rate at which inventions were developed. In this way the laboratory became a true invention factory. The best description of the machine shop at this time is found in Edison's letter to Orton asking for financial support for it.

> I have in the Laboratory a machine shop run by a 5 horse power engine, the machinery is of the finest description. I employ three workmen, two of whom have been in my employ for five years and have much experience. I have also two assistants who have been with me 5 and 7 years respectively both of which are very expert.

A later photograph shows the shop filled with precision metalworking machines similar to those he employed as a telegraph manufacturer. Much of the machinery, as well as the men to run them, came from Edison's Newark shops. Edison also drew on his telegraph background in defining problems and seeking their solutions during his inventive work at Menlo Park.

In addition to serving as the principal influence on the design and operation of Edison's Menlo Park laboratory, the telegraph-shop tradition also influenced other attempts to develop forms of organized invention. Edison was not the only telegraph inventor to build a private laboratory. Patrick Delany, for example, built a laboratory in South Orange, New Jersey, not far from Edison's more famous West Orange laboratory, while Stephen Field and Franklin Pope had private laboratories at their homes. Some telegraph manufacturing shops included small laboratories for experimental work on their premises, but Edison's laboratory was a very visible model for other inventors.

FROM MACHINE SHOPS TO R&D LABS

The influence of the telegraph-shop tradition, and of Edison's laboratory, was evident in the early telephone industry. Many of the important early improvements on telephone technology were made in the manufacturing shops, most of which initially manufactured telegraph equipment. After Bell bought Western Electric from Western Union, that shop became the principal source of both telephones and telephone improvements. To coordinate its acquisition and adoption of new inventions, the company also established an electrical and patent department in 1880, placing it under the direction of Thomas Watson, the former machinist who had become [Alexander Graham] Bell's principal experimental assistant. When American Bell established an experimental shop in 1883, company officials placed it under the direction of Ezra Gilliland. A former telegraph operator, manufacturer, and in-

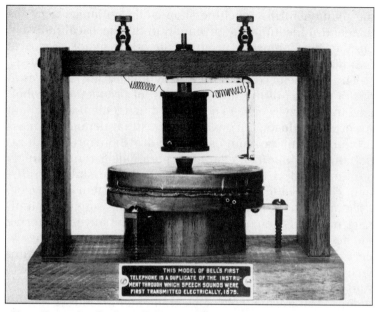

After Alexander Graham Bell introduced his first telephone, employees worked on ways to improve the invention. In 1883 Edison was hired as a consulting inventor for the American Bell company.

ventor, Gilliland was also a long-time Edison associate and helped convince the company to hire Edison as a consulting inventor with the handsome retainer of $6,000 per year. The influence of this telegraph-shop tradition waned by the end of the century, as the Bell company turned to scientifically trained engineers in order to develop long-distance telephone service. American Bell was unusual in its establishment of formal research departments to develop new inventions.

In telegraphy and other industries, neither operating engineers nor manufacturing shops could be relied on to produce inventions. One of the leading telegraph engineers expressed this concern when he argued that

> in the majority of cases the active engineers in an art are fully occupied with the successful operation of existing apparatus or with problems connected therewith, and are given neither the time nor the financial aid necessary to undertake original research for the advancement of the art with which they may be associated.

The development of specialized research departments such as that at Western Electric was an implicit recognition that the manufacturing machine shop could no longer serve as the central institution of invention in the electrical industry. Similar developments occurred at other major electrical manufacturers such as General Electric and Westinghouse.

The decline of research in the manufacturing shop was in part a product of the rationalization of production symbolized by the emergence of scientific management throughout American industry. Growing markets that demanded mass production and economies of scale drove this process of rationalization among the large corporations that increasingly dominated electrical manufacturing. While skilled craftsmen continued to make up a significant portion of the electrical manufacturing workforce, companies sought to eliminate much of their independence and initiative, furthering the decline of shop culture as a source of invention. The expert experimental machinist of the small electrical manufacturing shop of the nineteenth century was more likely to find employment with new research institutions.

Furthermore, the scale of telegraph manufacturing relative to other electrical industries was very small. The spread of telephones and electric light and power dwarfed the limited market for telegraph equipment by the end of the century, and caused many electrical manufacturers to commit the bulk of their resources to the new and growing electrical technologies. Manufacture of standard telegraph instruments other than those produced by the shops of the two operating companies accounted for less than half a million dollars by 1900, while specialized urban telegraph services such as fire alarms and district call boxes reflected a modest mass market with a manufacturing value of $1.2 million. One of the few remaining manufacturers to continue producing general telegraph equipment and to remain a source of telegraph innovation was J.H. Bunnell and Company in New York, although Bunnell's death in 1899 marked a turning point for this firm as well. More commonly, telegraph equipment was either a sideline for manufacturers of other electrical equipment or produced by in-house shops such as those of Gamewell Fire-Alarm Telegraph Company or the Page Machine Company, which provided printing telegraphs for Dow Jones & Company's business news service. Such in-house shops often served as research branches for these firms in much the same way that Western Electric did for the Bell system.

At Western Union the company's repair shop became the

basis for an electrician's workshop in 1901. Although "to all intents and purposes it was a laboratory . . . [with] the best machines and apparatus then available for experimental working in telegraph equipment," the shop was more a testing laboratory than a research facility. Firms in other industries had also begun establishing similar facilities as they slowly responded to new technical challenges. Many of these laboratories, like the one at Western Union, were intended to test materials and standardize existing apparatus rather than to develop new technology. As industrial research became an important component of American industry, some laboratories did take on more significant research activities. By 1910, the inadequacy of Western Union's research support led telegraph engineers William Maver and Donald McNicol to ask "whether men thoroughly familiar with the requirements of telegraphy and of all the conditions to be met with in the technical service, and largely endowed with inventive faculty might not be selected to prosecute investigations relative to the improvement of the telegraph service as relates to the transmission of messages."

RESEARCHERS REPLACE INDIVIDUAL INVENTORS

When Western Union became associated with AT&T that same year, the company moved toward developing a more sophisticated research capability. As late as 1909, the engineering force of the Western Union system consisted of only ten or twelve men, "including inspectors in the field." Between 1910 and 1914, while it was a subsidiary of AT&T, Western Union's engineering department was reorganized and the telegraph company began hiring college-educated men. It also established training courses for colleges and, in coordination with Western Electric's research branch, Western Union engineers developed the multiplex printing telegraph. Two years later, after again becoming independent, the company established a research laboratory, which it housed at AT&T headquarters (formerly Western Union's headquarters). Twenty-five men worked in this new laboratory, which was enlarged in 1918 with a research and chemical laboratory, and again in 1922 with the addition of a mechanical laboratory. These men were responsible for a large proportion of the company's patents as well as for the development of important new telegraph systems.

By the 1920s the scientifically trained industrial researcher was also replacing the individual inventor as a symbol of technical creativity in American society. Americans still responded positively to new technology as an agent of social progress, but they recognized that the industrial corporation had wrought profound changes in their society. Though democratic individualism, represented by the inventor-entrepreneur, had produced an expansive economy and an abundance of material goods, it also produced industrial strife and an economic order represented by the dark side of liberal individualism, the "robber barons." By 1910, political and economic forces had produced a group of industrial giants capable of exerting the kind of economic and political power which only the telegraph and railroads had possessed in the nineteenth century. Yet some prominent political reformers proclaimed the large, integrated corporation to be a "natural" product of economic evolution, as they attempted to manage it "in the best interests of society." Driven by the same belief in scientific rationalization that spurred a rising generation of new corporate managers, these reformers believed that scientific techniques could be used to manage economic and social conflict in the larger society. Because they regarded the corporation itself as a source of the technological and material progress that remained intimately bound up with mainstream American ideas of social progress, these reformers were willing to transfer their traditional faith in democratic individualism and its liberal economic and political system to the corporate economy and bureaucracy of the twentieth century. In the process, the industrial researcher became an appropriate symbol for an age in which many placed their faith in the specialized knowledge of experts and which saw the large, rationally managed corporation as a model for society.

Creating the West Orange Lab

Andre Millard

Reflecting the life and work of a great inventor, today the West Orange labs are a museum and testament to this extraordinary man. Andre Millard, an associate professor of history at the University of Alabama, gives inside views of Edison's strategy for constructing this new complex of buildings. As Millard notes, at the time it was built, this lab was the greatest industrial research facility in the United States and a breeding ground for new technology and new industries of the twentieth century. Here Edison worked at improving the development of the electric light and lowering the costs of electricity to make it widely affordable. The West Orange labs also witnessed the beginnings of motion pictures and recorded music, two of Edison's most influential cultural contributions.

The complex of buildings in West Orange was erected in the late 1880s, when the Second Industrial Revolution was just beginning. As the greatest industrial research facility in the United States, the laboratory was the breeding ground for a new generation of technology and the starting point of some important new industries of the twentieth century. Here Edison worked at spreading his electrical lighting systems all over the industrialized West and lowering the price of electricity until it was available to everyone. The motion-picture camera was invented at the laboratory, along with a host of other important products, such as the Edison storage battery and dictating machine. Edison perfected the phonograph at this facility and manufactured thousands of them in his nearby factories. Two of the twentieth century's most influential service industries—motion pictures and musical

Excerpted from Andre Millard, *Edison and the Business of Innovation*, pp. 2–3, 5–6, 6–10, 16–18, 19–21. Copyright © 1990 The Johns Hopkins University Press. Reprinted with permission from The Johns Hopkins University Press.

entertainment—had their humble beginnings in this cluster of brick buildings.

The experimental rooms and machine shops in the lab are a reminder of the complex technologies introduced by Edison. The impressive library is evidence of the growing importance of science in the technologies of the Second Industrial Revolution—a revolution that was based on the so-called scientific industries of electricity, steel, chemicals, and communications. The rows of technical journals (many of them from outside the United States), scholarly books, and bound patents show that the information age had begun well before the twentieth century, and that Edison saw the importance of keeping up with scientific and technical progress wherever it occurred. He often began his day by reading newspapers and technical journals at his desk in the library.

Now only tourists walk around the library and cross the courtyard to the experimental buildings that serve as museums of Edison's achievements. The lathes and drills in the grimy machine shops are quiet; the lights no longer burn all night in the experimental rooms; and Edison's bunk in the library is never used. The surviving buildings of this once vast industrial complex serve not only as a museum but also as a reflection of the life and work of one of America's greatest businessmen. The West Orange laboratory bore witness to a critical period in the economic history of the industrialized West and it provides an invaluable resource to understand our immediate past. . . .

LEAVING MENLO PARK

The pressure of business forced Edison to leave Menlo Park and set up house in lower Manhattan, close to the headquarters of the Edison Electric Light Company at 65 Fifth Avenue. As a businessman, Edison had to be close to the decision making, yet the influence of the old laboratory remained in the important jobs he gave to men who had worked with him at Menlo Park, the faithful "boys" who formed the initial management of the electrical industry. The Electric Light Company was presided over by Edward H. Johnson, a friend and colleague of Edison's from their days as telegraphers. Samuel Insull, Edison's secretary at Menlo Park and New York, was made manager of the Machine Works. As private secretary, Insull had administered

Edison's business and personal finances and now he ran the financial affairs of the lighting industry. The superintendent of the Machine Works was John Kruesi, a skilled mechanic who had worked with the inventor for many years. Two other laboratory men, Francis Upton and Charles Batchelor, were put in charge of factories. Another crony from the old days, Sigmund Bergmann, was set up in his own manufacturing company.

By 1886 the work of "pushing the system" was well under way. Over fifty power stations had been built in the United States, and many were in use in large European cities. The Edison electric lighting companies were capitalized at around $10 million in the United States. Edison's factories were full of orders and running at top speed to fill the backlog. These manufacturing operations were providing the profits in the electric light business. The money was pouring in. Edison was the hero of his generation, a rich and powerful industrialist, and an inventor of worldwide fame. He was also in love.

His second marriage was to Mina Miller in February 1886. (His first had ended in 1884 when his wife, Mary, died.) Mina came from a well-to-do family in Akron, Ohio, had attended finishing school in Boston, and was a more than acceptable partner for the famous inventor. Marriage inevitably brought changes to Edison's life. He must have been tempted to remain in New York, the center of his business affairs and the home of close associates (such as his chief assistant, Charles Batchelor) and important financial connections (including J.P. Morgan and Henry Villard). But instead of joining the other millionaires putting up mansions south of Central Park, Edison deferred to his wife and moved to West Orange, New Jersey, in the scenic Orange valley, a rural area about twelve miles west of New York City. . . .

BIGGER AND BETTER

An ordinary mortal might have taken time off to savor the pleasures of married life and business success, but Edison was no ordinary man. He was still at the peak of his inventive powers and the flow of ideas had not ceased during the years of perfecting his lighting system. Also, his honeymoon in Fort Myers, Florida, in 1886 and a convalescence from sickness in early 1887 gave him two long breaks to contemplate future inventions. There were still plenty of opportunities in electricity, and other schemes were forming in his imagination: magnetic ore separation could be the technology to revolutionize the iron industry, and the tinfoil phonograph might be the greatest consumer product of the age. He had a wild plan to provide moving pictures to accompany the feeble squeak of the phonograph, but there was no place to develop these ideas. What he needed was another large laboratory, another invention factory, to replace the one he had left at Menlo Park.

Some historians have argued that Edison's idea of the invention factory—the organized application of scientific research to commercial ends—was his greatest invention. He had promised "a minor invention every ten days and a big thing every six months or so" and for once he was as good as his word. The phonograph and the electric light had proved the soundness of this idea. Now he wanted to create "the best equipped and largest laboratory extant and the facilities superior to any other for rapid and cheap development of an invention." The Menlo Park complex had been the largest private laboratory in the United States in the 1870s, and now Edison planned an even bigger facility, one that would enable him to carry out industrial research on an unprecedented scale and reflect his new status as the preeminent American inventor.

Yet Edison was by no means the only inventor in the electrical industry. Charles Brush, Edward Weston, and Hiram Maxim were all pioneers in electric lighting who remained active in the field in the years after Pearl Street. Weston's operations were close to home. He was the first to establish a lighting scheme in Newark, New Jersey, where he built a central station on Mechanic Street, and his arc lamps graced the newly constructed Brooklyn Bridge. Weston was an immigrant from England, and although he had no formal training, he gained the reputation of a scientific inventor—in contrast to Edison who was seen as an inspired tinkerer. Yet Weston's career had some similarities to Edison's: Weston began in the United States as a laborer, worked as a chemist and electrician, and then formed a series of successively larger electrical companies to become a leading figure in the new industry. His patents in the electrical field were almost as valuable as those of Edison.

In 1886 Weston decided to build a private laboratory behind his home on Main Street, Newark. It was finished in 1887, and Edison probably read the laudatory descriptions in the press as he contemplated his own laboratory in West Orange. Weston's lab was described as the largest and best equipped in America. It was depicted as solely devoted to electricity and to "original scientific research and not for the purpose of gain of any money making concern." Perhaps the last comment was aimed at Edison, whose reputation was somewhat tarnished by the unsavory activities of some of the electric lighting companies bearing his name. The two inventors did not enjoy cordial relations, and Weston could be depended upon to snipe at the Wizard of Menlo Park in the press whenever he got the opportunity. These cutting remarks or the publicity surrounding Weston's new lab in Newark could have stung Edison into going one step farther than his rival. If anyone was to have the largest private laboratory in the United States, it would be Edison.

DESIGNED FOR GOOD COMMUNICATIONS

His written plans indicate the grandeur of his concept and reveal something about his method of inventing. The sketch from a lab notebook shows that he was thinking about a structure that would reflect his prestige as a famous inventor and man of substance. This laboratory is an impressive three-story building with a mansard roof. The tower and courtyard are its two distinctive features (often found in the large textile mills of Newark), and these give the invention factory the dignity of a public building. The east wing contains the experimental tables and Edison's own personal room. The north side of this planned lab contains the machine shop and power plant. The quad in the center of the structure enables easy communication between the experimenters in the east and west wings and the machinists in the north wing. The inventor had discovered the vital importance of good communications in industrial research.

The chemical laboratory takes up the whole west wing of this plan, a measure of Edison's love of chemistry and its importance in the application of science to industry. The development of industrial research was closely associated with the progress of chemistry. The first industrial laboratories were established by German chemical companies to carry out testing and basic research, and similarly the first American corporate laboratories were devoted to industrial chemistry. The Pennsylvania Railroad, for example, created a laboratory as early as 1875 to analyze materials. Even Andrew Carnegie, who maintained that "pioneering don't pay," saw the advantages of hiring a chemist to analyze the operation of his blast furnaces. His experience that "9/10ths of the uncertainties of pig iron making were dispelled under the burning sun of chemical knowledge" was repeated by other industrialists. Now that Edison had made electricity more plentiful, he planned to exploit it in ventures such as the electroplating of metals or the production of aluminum. He saw electrochemistry as a profitable new business for the future.

A library was a fixture of all Edison's plans for his new laboratory; it played an important part in every experimental project, which always began with a thorough search of the scientific literature. The first two steps of Edison's method are described thus: "1st. Study present construction. 2nd. Ask for all past experience . . . study and read everything you can on the subject." Not one to explore new fields without considerable preparation, Edison often built on others' work in his inventions, and nowhere was this more evident than in the development of the electric light. Electrical technology was international, and its rapid advance was the result of the transatlantic movement of men, machines, and ideas. Edison had gained immeasurably from the foreign equipment and literature imported into his laboratory (such as the Gramme dynamo from France); they had sometimes been the inspiration for Edison's electrical machines. The experience of the electrical industry had shown that a key piece of information, the key to a breakthrough, could easily be hidden in an obscure scientific journal . . . and Edison planned to take advantage of any new piece of scientific or technical knowledge that came his way. The first function of the invention factory was to act as a net to capture ideas from the many streams of technical information; these turned into a flood as the nineteenth century progressed. The work on electricity had opened up new scientific horizons for Edison and provided the money to acquire the knowledge to explore them. The impressive library he built at West Orange, estimated at about 100,000 volumes, was an important resource for all members of the laboratory.

By early 1887 Edison's ideas for the lab were taking shape. In addition to a machine shop, his plans show supply and apparatus rooms, which were positioned close to the experimental rooms. The supply room served both experimenters and machine shop. It contained metal parts, screws, wire, joints, gears, tubes, and sheets. It would also house the batteries, magnets, and electrical subassemblies that were needed to make up experimental apparatus. The instrument room contained the measuring equipment required in electrical and chemical experiments. The separate galvanometer room for electrical work is evidence of Edison's plans to perfect electric lighting in the future. . . .

A MOVING FORCE

The West Orange laboratory was to be the moving force in the expansion of electric lighting during its second decade, for with no improvement electric light would remain a pinpoint of light in the nineteenth century world, a luxury for the very rich and a novelty for grand hotels and places of entertainment. Increasing the efficiency and lowering the cost of the incandescent lamp were major objectives. In 1887 he planned the new facility at West Orange, complete with a glassblower's room and a vacuum pump room, devoted to further research and testing of electric lights.

Edison bought the land on which his laboratory was to stand in January 1887. The fourteen acres lay next to the main road of the Oranges, at the bottom of the hill that led up to Llewellyn Park. The site was conveniently situated close to Glenmont, and the nearby railroad gave easy access to New York and Newark. Henry Holly, the architect of Glenmont, was retained to design the laboratory. He produced plans for a handsome three-story building 250 feet long and 50 feet wide. Charles Batchelor was given the task of turning these plans into bricks and mortar and spent the summer overseeing the construction. Edison was always around, either coming down from Glenmont or stopping on his way to the temporary laboratory at the Lamp Works in Harrison. The inventor exerted his powerful influence, firing Holly, denouncing bad workmanship, and constantly changing the plans. Yet Batchelor was accustomed to these kinds of distractions and worked on steadily.

Charles Batchelor had been at Edison's side since he joined the inventor's work force in 1871. Born in the north of England, he was one of the many machinists who left the factories of this industrialized Black Country for the textile mills of Massachusetts and New Jersey. Batchelor was sent to install machines in the Clark thread mills in Newark, met Edison, and never returned home. The dark-bearded Englishman had the craft skills that made Manchester the workshop of the world. A master of metal working, he could handle any job—from casting parts of a dynamo to fitting the fragile experimental filaments into incandescent bulbs at Menlo Park. His neat, well-organized notebooks reveal an orderly mind and precise hand. According to one of the laboratory staff, Batchelor was the "sometimes needed, conservative element of the combination," an ideal counterbalance to the mercurial Edison who often got so involved in an experimental project that he forgot everything else. Batchelor was experienced in factory management and well suited to supervise the construction of the large laboratory complex planned by Edison. . . .

AN EXPERIMENTAL LAB

Edison had originally intended to crowd all the experimental areas, supply rooms, and machine shops on the three floors of this building, but the 37,500 square feet of floor space were not sufficient for his ambitious plans. Once the main laboratory was completed, work began on four smaller laboratory buildings, identical in size (100 ft. by 25 ft.) and positioned at right angles to the main building. They were numbered 1 through 4 starting with the one closest to Main Street. Building 1 was devoted to electrical work; the galvanometer room in the early plans for the lab was now made into a separate building dedicated to electricity. It was constructed on a deep foundation of brick and cement to dampen any shocks to the delicate electrical measuring equipment inside. Great pains were taken to avoid metal fittings that might influence the electromagnetic devices used in experiments. This laboratory contained every type of electrical measuring apparatus, including galvanometers, Wheatstone bridges, and many experimental devices. A special rack and control panel was installed in this building to evaluate the performance of incandescent bulbs. This grew into a lamp testing room, which housed four or five experimenters. Several additions were made to the equipment to test more lamps under different operating conditions. The electrical laboratory in Building 1 provided essential testing services for the Edison lighting companies and, by virtue of its superior facilities, set the operating standards for them.

Building 2 was the chemical laboratory. It was fitted with a balance room and lined with shelves containing bottles of chemicals. The front part of Building 3 was used as a store-room for the overflow of chemicals for Building 2, and the rear end was turned into a woodworking shop to make jigs and patterns. The last of the satellite buildings, number 4,

Thomas Edison carefully planned his West Orange, New Jersey, laboratory to make it an efficient place of invention as well as to reflect his prestige as an inventor.

was established as a metallurgical laboratory. It contained rock crushers and graders, assay furnaces, and containers for the many samples of ore that Edison had collected.

These four satellite laboratories indicate the experimental directions that Edison intended to follow: electricity, chemistry, and metallurgy. They complemented the work of the main building (now called Building 5) and completed the physical shape of the West Orange laboratory. The front of Building 1 formed an entrance gateway with the west end of the main building, and the space between it and Buildings 1 and 2 formed a courtyard, the same quadrangle effect envisaged by Edison in his early plans. The open area between buildings was not merely a meeting place; it was an important work space where experiments could be made on large equipment. The laboratory had an open architecture that was consistent with Edison's extravagant plans to add several more buildings. The haphazard addition of a new plant gave the lab an organic pattern of growth.

After the five main buildings were completed in September, Batchelor turned his attention to fitting out the laboratory. The power house was his first job. Then came the dynamo room to power the complex. This was soon equipped with a number of different generators, which could be evaluated while they produced electricity. The laboratory supplied current to Glenmont and other houses in Llewellyn Park and this small distribution system provided a useful test bed to simulate the operation of central stations. It could be used to measure the efficiency of the distribution network of conductors and the accuracy of the meters that recorded output.

The laboratory was wired for electricity throughout and some of the experimental rooms were fitted with outlets of different voltages, yet electrically driven machine tools were still in the future. Batchelor followed current industrial practice in establishing a power house at one end of the main building and running shafts along the first two floors. Leather belts took the power from the drive shafts to the machines below.

The work of equipping the machine shops provided some diversion for Edison and Batchelor who scoured manufacturers' catalogs and purchased a wide selection of machine tools: lathes, drills, grinders, and presses. Batchelor divided them between two floors of the main laboratory building, with heavy lathes, drill presses, and milling machines on the first floor, and smaller lathes, grinders, and polishers on the second. The heavy machine shop on the ground floor was to produce large equipment, like dynamos, for central stations. It was fitted with a traveling crane. The second floor machine shop was called the precision room because the men who worked there were highly skilled mechanics and instrument makers who built experimental models.

At the end of September Batchelor began moving equipment from the temporary laboratory in the Lamp Works, where Edison and a skeleton crew of about ten experimenters continued the development of electric light, ore milling, and the phonograph. During October and November loads of "experimental stuff" were shipped by horse cart from Harrison. As soon as the experimental apparatus was installed, Edison and his men started work. The West Orange lab opened for business in the first weeks of December 1887. . . .

BUILT TO PRODUCE INVENTIONS

Although the Menlo Park lab was the first invention factory, it was not custom-built for the job. The West Orange laboratory was built with the mass production of inventions in mind. Its facilities were purposely laid out to achieve efficient routing of experimental projects, the various elements flowing together from the library at one end of Building 5 through the experimental rooms on the second floor to the two machine shops. Edison's method of invention rested on cooperation between experimenters and machinists. The second floor of the laboratory was organized to facilitate this cooperation on a larger scale than ever before. The location of the precision machine shop next to the experimental rooms of the second floor established a floor plan built around the idea of speed. As ideas occurred to experimenters on the second floor they could quickly draw on the skilled mechanics of the precision room to build the models and devices they needed.

The experimental rooms, where the intellectual effort was concentrated, were the center of the laboratory. They were divided by wooden partitions and could be arranged to suit any project. Edison wanted a flexible floor plan to change experimental directions as he saw fit. The rooms were on each side of the main corridor that led to the precision shop. At the end of the row of experimental rooms on the right side of the corridor was room 5, the photographic studio. This room was kept locked but had an opening in the door to pass through supplies. The historic development of the motion picture camera was carried out in this room. Edison's room was number 12, to the left of the stairs and facing the laboratory's courtyard. Across the hall was the room of Fred Ott, whose precision lathe often gave life to Edison's ideas. It was a short walk down the hall to take advantage of the skilled men and specialized machines of the precision shop. At any time, several experimenters would probably be in this shop, watching the construction of apparatus and swapping ideas and stories with the machinists.

SECOND INDUSTRIAL REVOLUTION LABS

Although Edison claimed that "there is no similar institution in existence," his new laboratory was by no means the only industrial research facility in the United States. In addition to the works laboratories and the testing facilities run by professional chemists, there were also more advanced laboratories to develop the technologies of the Second Industrial Revolution. Alexander Graham Bell established Volta Laboratory Associates in Washington in 1881, which included his cousin Chichester Bell and Charles Tainter. Once the various Bell companies began operation of telephone networks, they discovered a need for engineering services to remedy faults in the system and improve equipment. The laboratories they set up were also charged with testing and the evaluation of new technology. One of the laboratory managers was Ezra Gilliland, a self-taught electrician and an old friend of Edison's from their days as telegraphers. Gilliland soon left the organization to join up with Edison.

The most striking application of science to industry was electricity, and every electrical pioneer had his own laboratory. A few miles down Main Street from the Oranges stood the laboratory of Edward Weston, a two-story building that contained a machine shop, an electrical room with extensive testing facilities, and a chemistry laboratory. This duplicated (on a smaller scale) the facilities Edison erected at West Orange. Despite their association with scientific research, the laboratories of the Second Industrial Revolution were all based on machine shops. Charles Brush, whose arc lights had heralded the electrical age in both London and New York, had laboratories in the machine shops of the telegraph industry in Cleveland. The inventor Elihu Thomson carried out experiments in a "model room" in his factory in Lynn, Massachusetts. He formed the Thomson-Houston company with his colleague Edwin Houston, which later became a serious competitor to the Edison enterprise in the development of electric lighting. Thomson's laboratory was called the model room because its function was to produce experimental devices and patent models. Precision machine tools occupied the bulk of the room, which also contained electrical instruments. With "a few tools and perhaps one or two workmen," Thomson hoped to produce "devices and new appliances . . . to be refined and immediately put into manufacture."

This was also Edison's objective but on a much greater scale. In size and diversity of operations, Edison's West Orange laboratory stood alone in the nineteenth century. None of its contemporaries had a larger work force: the laboratory of the Bell Company employed twenty-nine men in about 1885, the staff of Charles Dudley's laboratory at the Pennsylvania Railroad was about thirty chemists, Thomson's model room and Weston's laboratory employed less than twenty people. In comparison Edison's new laboratory employed about 100 men and the physical facilities dwarfed all other laboratories. As one observer noted: "It is not a factory, as you might suppose, where steam engines or locomotives are made, it is a laboratory and private workshop of a private man." This comment underlines the two essential differences between the invention factory at West Orange and other industrial research facilities: its size and its mission to translate the inspiration of one man into new technology. It was to develop both the practical and the fantastic products of Edison's imagination, from an improved electric meter to the pyrogenerator—a machine to produce electricity directly from coal that would "change the entire motive power and lighting of the world." There was no other facility in the world with comparable resources.

PIONEERS OF INDUSTRIAL RESEARCH

The stated objective of the West Orange laboratory was to conduct experiments and "scientific investigations . . . with a view of making inventions useful in various arts." Despite his many pronouncements to the contrary, Edison was not opposed to basic scientific research provided that it was directed toward some practical goal, however remote. His disdain of what he called "the-o-retical" science came from his lack of confidence in the theory and his belief that research in academe was pointless and slow, the kind of research that Edison, the self-confessed hustler, would not tolerate in his laboratories. This prejudice, molded into his self-promotion as an ingenious tinkerer, has earned Edison an undeserved reputation for trial-and-error methods instead of systematic, scientific research, and denied his laboratories their rightful place as originators of industrial research. By defining industrial research as a science-based activity, some historians have excluded Edison's laboratories from the story of corporate innovation. . . .

At the time the West Orange laboratory was built, there was no clear dividing line between science and engineering, between basic research and applied research. There were few professional electricians and hardly any formally trained electrical engineers. The cutting edge of electrical knowledge was in the operation of lighting systems rather than in the few research laboratories in higher education. In view of the problems of running electric lighting systems, it was unavoidable that Edison's new laboratory had to conduct basic research into phenomena such as electromagnetism. This was carried out with no immediate payoff other than the realization that until more was known about electromagnetism, there was little room to improve the low output and poor efficiency of dynamos. As the eminent electrical engineer Silvanus Thompson noted in 1886, "Until we know the true law of the electromagnet, there can be no true or complete theory of the dynamo."

Edison's invention factories were the pioneers of industrial research because they carried out organized, systematic research directed toward practical goals. Their work encompassed a broad range of activities. If Edison had planned to confine himself to trial-and-error, he would never have insisted on recording every experiment in the laboratory notebooks that were left on every work bench. The master of cut-and-try had indeed made his job easier by assembling a massive storehouse, yet he had also provided the most advanced testing and measuring equipment that money could buy—evidence that the work of this laboratory would not be only trial-and-error experimenting.

The staff of the laboratory used the scientific method in

their experiments, were well versed in theory (such as it was), and kept an exact record of their work. The laboratory notebooks kept at West Orange provide evidence of Edison and his leading experimenters theorizing about fundamental principles, making deductions from these principles, and testing the results by experiment. Some historians have interpreted Edison's activities as borrowing from science rather than creating scientific knowledge. In this he was not alone; many engineers were doing the same in the last decades of the nineteenth century. Edwin Layton has put forward the useful concept of two communities of engineers and scientists coexisting. Instead of one community carrying out separate functions of science and technology, Layton sees two communities that dealt with the same knowledge but had different goals and systems of values. Engineers adopted the theoretical and experimental methods of science to solve technological problems. They expressed scientific knowledge in a different way and put it to a different use than scientists.

The one value of the scientific community that was not in the invention factory was freedom of information. Although Edison planned to benefit from scientific knowledge and encouraged open communication in his labs, he did not allow the results of his work to be freely disseminated. His laboratory staff sometimes carried out research that they wanted to publish as a contribution to the scientific literature. Edison resisted all such entreaties because he feared that the findings might help his competitors. At the same time Edison did not object to using his laboratory as an educational center. He hosted meetings for the scientific community such as a conference on electrical measurement for the American Institute in 1888.

Such inconsistencies make it difficult for scholars to agree on Edison's place in the history of industrial research. The debate whether Edison's method was based on scientific research or cut-and-try will probably never be resolved. Nor will there be agreement on which lab should have the title of the world's first industrial research laboratory. There was no doubt in the minds of the men making their way to West Orange in the fall of 1887. To them Edison's genius had no limit and his ambition no boundaries. Stocked with every conceivable supply and led by the world's greatest inventor the new laboratory was "Heaven . . . certainly one of the finest in the world and the finest in the States."

Using Reverse Salients and Metaphors to Solve Problems

Thomas P. Hughes

Edison's problem-solving techniques were common to many inventors of his day. He did not have Eureka moments in which the workings of entire systems revealed themselves, rather Edison developed an overall conception of how a system was to function and then painstakingly devised and improved—through trial and error—each part of the system until the complete system worked. Author Thomas P. Hughes, who has penned a few books on large technical systems, describes this inventing process in terms of "metaphors" and "reverse salients." Edison's original conception of how the system was to function was usually given in terms of a metaphor, as when he described his quadruplex telegraph in terms of a water system. This gave an overall image to his staff of how he believed the parts of the new system would work in concert, providing all with a mental model of how to proceed. Once the system was devised, Edison and his crew would then tackle each part that didn't function as planned or was lagging behind in performance. Using a military term, Hughes refers to this part of the process as eliminating the "reverse salients" of a system in the same way that an advancing army seeks to eliminate any pockets of resistance that keep some units from catching up to the vanguard of the attack. Edison's tactics were not new to invention, but his conceptualizing of whole systems as he worked often put him ahead of competitors who struggled with perfecting only one invention, like those who toiled on the light bulb but failed to see the networks needed to light a city.

Excerpted from Thomas P. Hughes, *American Genius*. Copyright © 1989 Thomas P. Hughes. Reprinted with permission from Viking Penguin, a division of Penguin Putnam, Inc.

Invention can be seen as the process of solving new problems. Accounts of successful inventors often focus on their problem-solving techniques. Yet their choice of problems provides as much insight—and perhaps more—into the character of the independent inventors and an explanation of their successes—or failures—as does their problem solving. Their independence, or freedom from organizational constraints, allowed them to choose problems that when solved created the nuclei of new technological systems. . . .

Characteristically, independents preferred to create systems, rather than to improve the systems of others. They realized that they could not deploy the facilities and personnel that corporations and government agencies could commit to improving the well-established systems over which they presided. The systems invented by the independents were sometimes striking breakthroughs solving salient problems, such as the controls for the Wright brothers' airplane; at other times independents invented systems that provided alternatives to existing ones, but they would venture this only if the existing ones were new, unrefined, and not yet presided over by a large corporation with massive resources. Lee de Forest and Reginald Fessenden, for instance, invented wireless telegraph systems that competed with the earlier one of Guglielmo Marconi, but the latter's company was not especially large and was handicapped in competing in an American market because it was British. Edison, [Elihu] Thomson, and [Elmer] Sperry invented entire systems of arc or incandescent lighting in the early days of the industry. Joseph Swan, the British inventor whom his countrymen celebrate as the inventor of the incandescent lamp, erred in trying to integrate his incandescent lamp into a system with a generator designed by others for other purposes. As a result, the components did not harmoniously and optimally interact. Unlike Edison, Swan did not have the substantial funding that allowed the invention and development of an entire system. A representative of a company selling the Swan lamp told an Edison representative that Edison's great advantage was in having a coherent system. . . .

PROFESSIONAL INVENTORS EXPLOIT THEIR INVENTIONS

[Alexander Graham] Bell and the Wright brothers can be styled amateur or part-time inventors if we do not take "amateur" to suggest that their inventions were any less imaginative or subtle than those of the full-time, professional inventors. Fessenden and De Forest were full-time inventors notable for their single-minded concentration on wireless. . . . Edison, Sperry, and [Hiram] Maxim, however, can be characterized as representative professional inventor-entrepreneurs in their years of full-time dedication to invention and their establishment of companies to exploit their inventions. Their style of problem choice was characterized by its wide-ranging nature. Maxim invented, among other things, a machine gun, an incandescent lamp, smokeless gunpowder, and a steam-powered aircraft. Among Sperry's more than 350 patents were major contributions to the technology of electric light and power; mining machinery; electric railways; electric automobiles; batteries; electrochemistry; gyroscopic guidance, control, and stabilization; gunfire control; aviation instruments; and others. The range of Edison's inventive activity is also impressive. The more than one thousand patents taken out in his name include those covering the telegraph, phonograph, telephone, electric light and power, magnetic ore separation, storage batteries, concrete construction, and motion pictures. Such a range would have been unlikely in an industrial research laboratory tied to product lines. Thomson, an Edison competitor in the electrical field, took out 696 patents, including major ones on arc lighting, incandescent lighting, electric-generator controls, alternating-current transformers, electric motors, electric welding, electric meters, and X-ray devices.

Prudent drawing on their prior experience also characterized the Edison and Sperry style of problem choice. Unlike the naïve inventors, they did not dream that anything was possible for them. They chose problems most likely to be solved by the particular inventive characteristics they had acquired. Edison learned about the behavior of electrical currents as an experimenting telegraph operator. This experience propelled him through a sequence of related problem choices. It gave him a tacit understanding of the conservation of energy, for he observed firsthand not only the transformation of electricity into magnetism and magnetism into motion, but the fact that motion in the presence of magnetism produced electricity. Edison's insistence that he had thoroughly read and digested the works of Michael Faraday, the British discoverer of electromagnetic induction, seems plausible. He also knew from the work of early-nineteenth-century scientists and inventors that electricity could produce heat and light. The relationship between the resistance of metals and the flow of electrical energy must also have engaged his interest. As a telegraph operator and experimenter, he learned much about electrochemistry from batteries. His experiments with the telephone called his attention to the convertibility of sound waves into mechanical motion and electrical waves. So his sequential inventions of duplex telegraphy, telephone transmitter, phonograph, incandescent-lighting system, and electric railways become comprehensible, for they involve ingenious transformations of energy. Even his venture into iron-ore separation involved electricity and magnetism, and his work on the storage battery recalled the electrochemistry of the telegraph system. In this sense he was an applier of electrical science, but his intimate knowledge of the behavior of electrical devices and his ingenious application of accumulated tacit knowledge distinguished him from most scientists, who tended to be more verbal and theoretical. . . .

REVERSE SALIENTS AND CRITICAL PROBLEMS

After choosing a particular problem on which to work and conceiving of sketchy solutions, often at the instant of a eureka moment, the independent inventor faced a sequence of development problems. These arose in the course of transforming the bright seminal idea into models and seeing them through stages of increasing complexity. At each stage the evolving models had to be tested by experiment . . . to learn whether they could function in increasingly complex environments. Ultimately the inventor would test the invention in the intended-use environment. During this process of developing the invention, the inventor frequently resorted to a problem-identification technique that suggests the image, or metaphor, of a reverse salient in an expanding military front. One of the most horrendous reverse salients in history developed near the French town of Verdun during World War I. The Germans believed that, before a general advance could continue, they had to eliminate this reverse bulge, or reverse salient, in their front lines extending along the Western Front. The French were equally determined to hold this projection, or, from their point of view, salient, into German-held territory. A military front line has salients and reentrants (reverse salients) all along its length.

The reverse salient in an advancing military front proves an apt metaphor for a technological system, because the system, like a military advance, develops unevenly. Some components in a technological system, like some units in the military front, fall behind others. In the case of the military, *ahead* and *behind* can be determined by physical distance. Some components in technological systems can be said to be behind others if the former function less efficiently and act as a drag on the system. A telephone relay that distorts a message in a long-distance system is an example. Components that malfunction and cause breakdowns of a system can also be seen as being behind. Insulators in high-voltage transmission lines that fail and cause electrical shorts provide another example of a reverse salient in a technological system. In other cases, a reverse salient in a technological system can be one that adds disproportionately to the cost of the system. Rare materials in system components are a case in point. Inventors must correct reverse salients in systems they are developing. A perspicacious inventor often is particularly adept in discovering the reverse salients. Realizing that each component in a system affects, and is affected by, the characteristics of other components in it, the inventor looks for the component that has figuratively fallen behind the others. Having decided, for instance, to improve on Marconi's detector, Fessenden and De Forest had to design the other components in the wireless system to harmonize with it. . . . Bell Telephone Company engineers and scientists concentrated on inventing improved relays for an expanding transcontinental telephone transmission. General Electric Company engineers and scientists focused on solving problems involving insulation in high-voltage transmission lines. As with military lines of advance and retreat, the appearance of reverse salients and salients along the expanding front of a technological system is continuous, because the front is in a state of constant flux. As a result, inventors and generals are seldom without problems to solve. "Reverse salient" suggests the fluidity of the course of technological-system development; other metaphors suggesting rigidity and simplicity, such as "bottleneck," do not work so well.

We might consider also what Edison wrote about his invention of a system of electric lighting:

> It was not only necessary that the lamps should give light and the dynamos generate current, but the lamps must be

adapted to the current of the dynamos, and the dynamos must be constructed to give the character of current required by the lamps, and likewise all parts of the system must be constructed with reference to all other parts, since, in one sense, all the parts form one machine, and the connections between the parts being electrical instead of mechanical. Like any other machine the failure of one part to cooperate properly with the other part disorganizes the whole and renders it inoperative for the purpose intended.

The problem then that I undertook to solve was stated generally, the production of the multifarious apparatus, methods, and devices, each adapted for use with every other, and all forming a comprehensive system.

Using Reverse Salients for the Electric Lighting System

Once independents embarked on the voyage of inventing a system, there were beacons all along the way. They concentrated on the sequence of reverse salients as the appropriate problem choice.

Because Edison's extensive notebooks and his papers have been preserved, we have a better understanding of his method of finding reverse salients and solving the critical problems associated with them than we have for other inventors. In the case of the electric-lighting system, he used the reverse-salient technique not only to launch the incandescent-lighting-system project, but also to plot the course of developing it. Edison chose to invent and develop an electric light system in 1878, when he observed how close a number of inventors had come to introducing a practical incandescent bulb, a lamp for which there was a market because the arc lights then in use as streetlights burned too brilliantly for small, enclosed spaces. During the nineteenth century and before Edison began his work, at least twenty different types of incandescent lamp had already been invented. Like other independents, Edison scanned the inventions of earlier inventors seeking systems that were not quite technically or commercially successful, then proceeded to correct by invention the reverse salients and bring the systems onto the market. Like the Wright brothers, he possessed the confidence to take the step that made the difference between failure and commercial success. Larger resources, longer concentration on the problem, and superior knowledge partly explain their successes.

In 1878 he decided that the principal reverse salient in the failed electric-lighting systems was the short-lived filaments in the incandescent bulbs. By autumn he believed he had found the critical problem—to design a rheostat that would intermittently and imperceptibly shut off current to a platinum filament to allow it to cool before melting. Some months later his analysis became more complex and fruitful. Having identified a reverse salient, Edison framed the critical problems that had to be solved to correct the salient. Taking a holistic view of the electric-lighting system, he realized that, even if he solved the technical problem of filament durability, an economic reverse salient remained—the cost of the copper wire needed to transmit energy to the numerous lamps of a large-area system supplied from a central generating station. He foresaw that, if he were unable to reduce the amount of copper wire needed, his system could not compete in cost with urban gas-lighting systems supplied from central stations.

Edison's response to the copper-cost problem testifies to his brilliance as a holistic conceptualizer. Resorting to known laws describing interacting behavior of components in electric circuits, such as Ohm's law, which relates current, voltage, and resistance, he experienced a eureka insight. He foresaw that, by increasing the resistance of the lamp filament, he could reduce the amount of copper in the distribution wires without decreasing the flow of energy. From then on, he and his laboratory associates and assistants pragmatically searched for the right filament material and proceeded to design other system components, such as the generator, to harmonize with the characteristics of the high-resistance incandescent lamps.

EUREKA MOMENTS AND METAPHORS

Eureka moments and instantaneous insights are part of the lore of invention and discovery. Biographers of inventors and analyzers of the act of invention, however, after reverential asides about the mystery of creative genius, tend to pass quickly over such events. On 8 September 1878, Edison experienced a Eureka moment when he discussed with the inventor and industrialist William Wallace the flawed incandescent lamp system of Wallace's collaborator, the inventor Moses Farmer. The durability of Farmer's incandescent bulbs, like those of the other early inventors, was inadequate, but he had found two ways of approaching the problem. After reflection, Edison found these and related insights of his own so promising that he telegraphed an associate, "Have struck a bonanza in electric light. . . ."

He also wrote shortly afterward:

> I have the right principle and am on the right track, but time, hard work and some good luck are necessary too. It has been just so in all of my inventions. The first step is an intuition, and comes with a burst, then difficulties arise—this thing gives out and [it is] then that "Bugs"—as such little faults and difficulties are called—show themselves and months of intense watching, study and labor are requisite before commercial success or failure is certainly reached.

Inventors' imaginations and Eureka moments often involve the use of metaphor. Independent inventors' frequent resort to both verbal and visual metaphor offers us the most suggestive key to understanding the moment of inventive insight. This is not surprising, for metaphor has often been associated with creativity. Metaphor, being far more than a decorative literary device, is one of our most often used and effective ways of knowing. It has been defined as "the use of a word in some new sense in order to remedy a gap in the vocabulary." The word used in a new sense is the principal subject, and the word to which it is compared, and which is used in a literal and conventional sense, is the subsidiary subject. Unable to find a word to designate a sunset sky, someone in the distant past may have said, "the color of the sky is orange." Orange as sky color is the principal subject; orange as color of fruit is the unexpressed subsidiary subject. The principal and subsidiary subjects of a metaphor interact. This means that the reader or hearer of the metaphor will, if the metaphor works, selectively project commonplace characteristics associated with the subsidiary subject onto the principal subject. "A mighty fortress is our God" is an example of an "interaction" metaphor. The metaphor assumes analogies of some features of God and of fortresses. The reaction is to project selectively onto God some fortress characteristics, such as sheltering, power, and endurance. If the creator and the recipient of the metaphor do not share commonplaces about the subsidiary subject, and if they do not select similarly from the array of commonplaces, the metaphor will mislead. (A hearer would be puzzled by the association of the Christian God with the spewing of hot oil and the hurling of projectiles.) . . .

INVENTION BY ANALOGY

To invent machines, devices, and processes by metaphorical thinking is similar to the process of word creation. The inventor needs the intuition of the metaphor maker, some of the insight of Newton, the imagination of the poet, and perhaps a touch of the irrational obsession of the schizophrenic. The myth of inventor as mad genius is not without substance. Metaphor provides for the inventor a bridge from the discovered or invented into the realm of the undiscovered. Edison used metaphors extensively when he resorted to analogy, an explicit statement about the similarities juxtaposed in a metaphor. He worked out the quadruplex telegraph, perhaps the most elegant and complex of his inventions, "almost entirely on the basis of an analogy with a water system including pumps, pipes, valves, and water wheels." The metaphor (analogy) for Edison was "A Quadruplex telegraph will be [like] a water system." The inventor must use the future tense when referring to the primary subject, for it has yet to be invented. Edison had in mind the particular characteristics of a water system that could be projected onto the quadruplex telegraph to be invented. Later, thinking metaphorically, he conceived of the interaction between existing illuminating gas-distribution systems and the illuminating incandescent-light system he intended to invent. The analogy stimulated him to invent a system, rather than only an incandescent lamp.

CHAPTER 3

Lighting the World and Revolutionizing Entertainment

PEOPLE WHO MADE HISTORY

THOMAS EDISON

Edison's Role in the Electric Light

Ira Flatow

Many people believe that Thomas Edison invented
the electric light bulb, yet Ira Flatow, award-winning
host of National Public Radio's weekly science talk
show *Talk of the Nation: Science Friday,* easily dis-
proves that theory by naming other inventors who
created electric light bulbs years before Edison did.
According to Flatow Edison's genius was his concept
of developing "a total electrical system the size of a
city, complete with electric dynamos to produce the
electricity and wires and fuses to distribute and control it." Edison predicted he could create and lay out
this complex network within a few weeks, when in
reality it would take him almost two years. However,
the boast proved fruitful and money flowed in from
financial backers allowing him to found the Edison
Electric Light Company and speed his research.

What do Hiram Maxim, Joseph Swan, Thomas Edison, and
more than a dozen other inventors have in common? They
all invented electric light bulbs. But unless you're British
and insist that Joseph Swan deserves credit for the invention, you've probably never heard of any name associated
with the bulb besides Edison's. Chances are, if you examine
a list of inventors who have toiled to capture electric light in
a glowing glass bulb, you'll be shocked (no pun intended) to
see just how much work was going on in other laboratories
outside Menlo Park in New Jersey.

Edison was certainly not the first to come up with the incandescent light bulb idea. And contrary to popular opinion,
the key ingredient he used for his light bulb—carbon—was
certainly not unique. Carbon had been an ingredient of experimental light bulbs fifty years before Edison.

Excerpted from Ira Flatow, *They All Laughed.* . . . Copyright © 1992 Ira Flatow.
Reprinted with permission from HarperCollins Publishers, Inc.

Why is it then that the world accepts Menlo Park as the bulb's birthplace and Edison as *the* sole light bulb inventor? It's true that Edison received numerous patents for his light bulbs. But so did others. The mid-nineteenth century was an inventor's paradise. . . . To historians who recognize Edison as the inventor the answer involves the difference between having just an idea—an invention—and having a way of implementing the idea. An invention is worthless if it only functions under laboratory conditions.

OTHER LIGHT BULB INVENTORS

At least three or four serious inventors, in England, France, and the United States, were working on the incandescent lamp in the 1870s. They had the right ingredients and had functioning light bulbs. Joseph Swan had lit residences with his British bulb. Hiram Maxim, a serious American inventor and intense rival of Edison's, had filed for incandescent light patents in 1878 and 1879 and had carbon incandescent lamps burning for twenty-four hours at a time. But while Swan, Maxim, and other successful inventors succeeded in producing workable bulbs, theirs functioned only on a small scale, where but a few light bulbs were needed for illumination.

Only Edison designed his lamp, from the beginning, to be part of a total electrical system the size of a city, complete with electric dynamos to produce the electricity and wires and fuses to distribute and control it. Only Edison discerned that the lamp and the system had to work as a unit and had to match. And only when Edison realized that his bulb would have to work outside the lab and be part of a total system did it dawn on him how to create a properly working bulb.

In addition, it was Edison's enormous wealth, influence, and power that allowed him to create the entire system from scratch in his New Jersey laboratories, set up a power station to light New York City with his new bulbs, and influence an eager press and public into believing his bulb to be superior to all others.

THE AMAZING WIZARD

By the time Edison set his mind on the light bulb, he had already become very famous. Sitting and watching a stock ticker spit out Wall Street quotes, he commented how easily an improved version could be made. And he made one in 1869. Shut out of the invention of the telephone—and any royalties from it—by [Alexander Graham] Bell's patent, Edison did the next best thing: He designed an improved carbon transmitter (mouthpiece) that became the mainstay of the phone system. Intrigued with finding a method of recording telegraph messages, Edison invented a means of recording speech. This last invention, the phonograph, brought him instant fame.

Whatever Edison said he would do, he did. The track record of this brash youngster from America's heartland was nothing short of spectacular. From his laboratory in suburban New Jersey, he promised a "minor invention" every few days and a major one every six months or so. He had the phonograph, the stock ticker, and the carbon telephone transmitter to back up his bravado. He also had the heavy financial backing of Wall Street financiers who recognized a "technology factory" when they saw one.

So when the Wizard set his sights on a project, few people doubted he could pull it off. And the next project brewing in Edison's mind that summer of 1878 was finding a way of bringing electric lighting into everyone's home. After observing the workings of an electric dynamo Edison returned home, digested what he had seen, and came to the conclusion that he could install underground wires and light up all of lower Manhattan using yet to be invented incandescent light bulbs. This idea he called "a big bonanza." To the supremely confident—some say cocky—inventor, the light bulb would be a piece of cake. Just a matter of a few weeks, he said. In truth, Edison would sweat for almost two years.

CARBON ARC LIGHTING

Understand one thing at this point. Electric lighting was not a foreign concept; electric lights were common sights. Two well-known ways of making light by electricity existed. In the first, an electric arc was created by bringing two carbon rods close to each other and sending loads of electric current through them. A giant, blindingly white spark would jump across the gap creating an enormous amount of light, on the order of four thousand candlepower.

To get some idea of how bright electric arc lighting is, think of those searchlights you see lighting up the night skies outside movie theaters (they used to be employed to illuminate enemy war planes flying overhead). That intense beam is made by electric arc lighting. A less intense electric arc—

but equally blinding—is produced by welders in their electric arc sets. Notice the kind of eye protection they must wear.

In the 1870s electrical generators were strong enough to produce electric arc lighting. They powered lighthouses and lit up public assembly areas on the streets. But you could hardly bring one into the house. It would blind everyone. Gaslight, the mainstay of illumination at that time, produced on the order of about ten to twenty candlepower. Compare gaslight to the four thousand candlepower of arc lights, and the problem becomes obvious.

The other method of electrical lighting is called incandescent, or light produced by heat. If you take a substance and

THE LIGHT BULB HALL OF FAME

Date	Inventor	Nationality	Filament	Atmosphere
1802	Davy	English	platinum	air
1840	Grove	English	platinum	air
1841	De Moleyns	English	platinum	vacuum
1845	Starr	American	platinum	air
			carbon	vacuum
1846	Greener	English	carbon	air
1848	Staite	English	platinum	air
1850	Shepard	American	carbon	vacuum
1852	Roberts	English	carbon	vacuum
1856	de Changy	French	platinum	air
1859	Farmer	American	platinum	air
1860	Swan	English	carbon	vacuum
1872	Lodyguine	Russian	carbon	nitrogen
1875	Woodward	Canadian	carbon	N/A
	Kosloff	Russian	carbon	nitrogen
	Konn	Russian	carbon	vacuum
1876	Fontaine	French	carbon	vacuum
1877	Maxim	American	platinum	air
1878	Sawyer	American	carbon	nitrogen
	Maxim	American	carbon	hydrocarbon
	Lane-Fox	English	platinum-iridium	air-nitrogen
	Farmer	American	carbon	nitrogen
1879	Jenkins	American	platinum	air
	Hall	American	platinum	air
	Edison	American	carbon	vacuum

pass enough electricity through it, it will become hot enough to give off light. That's great. But in the process you run the danger of melting or burning up the substance. Every inventor who had tried to make an incandescent lamp—with inventions dating back to 1823—wound up with a melted puddle of metal or a material that caught on fire. For example, platinum, which had a high melting point, did not catch fire but got too hot and melted. Carbon, which did not melt, continually caught fire even in a partial vacuum. . . .

EDISON BRAVADO

To Edison, a veteran of the world of telegraphy, victory in the lamp war was simply a matter of finding the right kind of switch to regulate the temperature of the burner. As an expert in switches (after all, what are telegraphs made of?), Edison boasted he'd have the problem licked in just a few weeks. Without even an operating light bulb to exhibit, Edison bragged to the newspapers on October 20, 1878, "I have just solved the problem of the subdivision of the electric light."

The inventor's supreme confidence in his own brilliance was enough to control the stock market. Talking about the death of gas lighting, speculators drove down the price of gas stocks. Backers were falling over themselves to jump on the bandwagon. J.P. Morgan and the Vanderbilts opened their coffers, and out flowed the cash used to found the Edison Electric Light Company. The new company financed the expansion of Menlo Park and assured any and all funding needed to develop the new lamp.

With renewed life, Menlo Park kicked into high gear. Technicians busily modeled new lamps. Engineers fashioned new electric generators. Dozens of new regulator switches were attached to platinum burners, each designed to cut off the power should the temperatures go too high. The burners themselves were remodeled and reshaped; the aim was to find the best shape that provided the most light while producing the least heat.

Work was going like gangbusters at the lab. Things couldn't be busier. There was just one detail that couldn't be overcome—the lamps didn't work. Nothing the technologists did could solve the problems built into the lamps. Either they flickered too much from the rapid on-off switching of the heat-sensitive regulators, or the platinum melted. If, responding to the heat problem, the current was turned down, the light became too faint. The design was just too laden with bugs. It was hard keeping such bad news from upsetting the investors. By November 1878, when word of continuing failures was out, Edison was forced to admit that he needed a new line of attack. And some new brain power. He hired a young physicist from nearby Princeton, Francis Upton. Upton didn't bring a new magical bag of scientific tricks. But he brought the scientific discipline that the self-educated Edison lacked. Edison was a "try, try again" inventor; he would blindly try a new burner, test it, throw it away when it didn't work, and try a new one: a very unselective, inelegant, "brute force" process. Upton's more scientific mind led him to learn from the research of his rivals. Why waste time repeating their mistakes?

A Change in Tactics

Immediately Edison's staff began searching through old patents, gaslight journals, and the works of their competitors. Whereas Edison had previously been preoccupied with building one prototype after another until he found one that worked, he now realized how little he understood about the materials he was working with. And to his credit, he stopped the inventing process and had Upton and his associates concentrate on learning everything they could about the lamp materials. They tested different combinations of platinum and other metals, recording their electrical and heat characteristics.

Designing the System

Then, in the first quarter of 1879, Edison made a major breakthrough. He realized that the kind of metal he needed in his lamp could not be platinum or anything similar. Platinum offered a very low resistance to electricity. To get it to burn brightly, he would have to pump a lot of electricity through it to create the "electrical friction" inside the burner that created heat. If hundreds—even thousands—of light bulbs were to be made out of platinum and hooked up to a power station, the station's electricity would quickly be drained by these low-resistance light bulbs.

Instead, what was needed was a light bulb whose burner was more resistant to the flow of electricity. Then not very much electricity—current—had to flow through it to create the heat. Instead, the pressure (voltage) of "pushing" the electricity through the resistant wire would create the electrical friction for heat and light. Rather than a lot of electricity, a lot of voltage would be needed, on the order of about one hundred volts per lamp.

Apparently, this thought had not occurred to most of Edison's rivals. While they each had been working to perfect the light bulb, they did not stop to look at the entire lighting system that would have to supply the power. It would be the needs of the entire system that dictated the burner, not the whim of technicians sweating in a laboratory. Adding up the number of homes that needed to be serviced, Edison calculated the specifications for the light bulb. By lengthening and thinning the platinum wires, Edison was able to increase their resistance. By sucking all the air out of the bulb (or as much as his pumps allowed him to), he could extend the

ACHIEVING THE IMPOSSIBLE

Laboratory assistant Francis Jehl recounts the momentous occasion when—despite the many negative opinions of scientists that it couldn't be done—Edison, Charles Batchelor, and Jehl all stood watch while an electric bulb brightly burned for almost forty-five hours.

We now come to October 19, 1879, a Sunday morning when another sewing-thread carbonized filament lamp, finished the day before, was placed on the pump for extraction of the air. . . .

On this particular Sunday the only work to go on was that of evacuating and treating the lamp, which . . . required about ten hours; and the only other man present was Batchelor who, with Edison, prepared new filaments for further tests during intermissions in their attendance on the pump. . . .

As the life test alone would decide the question of success or failure, Sunday passed without unusual excitement. We had tested many lamps before, none of which had attained the success expected by Edison; hence the lamp now under test might yet exhibit some of the antics of its predecessors. Lamps that had appeared fairly healthy as they came from the pump had developed deficiencies when put to the test. . . .

Without much comment Edison now requested the writer to put the new lamp on the stand and to connect it for the life test. That Sunday night, long after the other men had gone, Edison and I kept a death-watch to note any convulsions or other last symptoms the lamp might give when expiring.

The lamp, however, did not expire! In the morning we were

time elements glowed before they burned out.

While waiting for the right burner to be invented, Edison designed and built the rest of the system: dynamos to produce high-voltage electricity; meters, switches, and fuses to control it. He even hired a glass blower to design special pumps to evacuate the bulbs.

But all to no avail. Despite round-the-clock work by the legions of Menlo Park, by the fall of 1879 it appeared that even the Wizard had met his match. The platinum bulb stubbornly refused to keep burning. High-resistance ones or low-resistance ones, they lasted but a few hours.

CARBON IS THE ANSWER

It was at this point that Edison's research staff turned to carbon. Edison was no stranger to carbon. Menlo Park pro-

---

relieved by Batchelor, Upton, and Force. The lamp continued to burn brilliantly all that day, passing the twenty-four hour mark. We were stirred with hope as each hour passed, more and more convinced of progress. Bets were made and general good humor existed all round. All sorts of discussions of problems yet to be solved were the order of the day. The night of the 20th of October again brought quiet to the laboratory as the watch continued, this time composed of Edison, Batchelor and me. During the night between the 20th and the 21st, Edison, judging from the appearance of the lamp still burning without flaw, seemed satisfied that the first solid foundation of the future of electric lighting had now been laid. The lamp held out heroically that night and the following day until, between one and o'clock in the afternoon of Tuesday, October 21, 1879, it had attained more than forty hours of life—the longest existence yet achieved by an incandescent lamp. . . .

In Edison's own words: 'We sat and watched it with anxiety growing into elation. It lasted about forty-five hours, and then I said, "If it will burn that number of hours now, I know I can make it burn a hundred!"'

The great German historian Emil Ludwig has said: 'When Edison, the father of the American Nation, the greatest living benefactor of mankind, snatched up the spark of Prometheus in his little pear-shaped glass bulb, it meant that fire had been discovered for the second time, that mankind had been delivered again from the curse of night.'

Francis Jehl, *Menlo Park Reminiscences.* Dearborn, MI: Edison Institute, 1937, pp. 351–57.

duced batteries, wires, and other electrical devices out of carbon. Edison's telephone transmitter (what we call the mouthpiece today) was made from carbon.

Carbonizing paper and cardboard had become routine at Menlo Park. Edison's researchers had experimented with carbon on and off in 1877 and 1879, only to have given up on it after the burners had failed. In addition, many of Edison's competitors had used carbon in their experiments years before he did. A *Scientific American* article of July 1879 mentioned how English inventor Joseph Swan had designed an incandescent lamp using carbon shaped into the form of a cylinder. Edison admitted to having read this article. (Swan defenders claim Edison stole this idea from Swan. Edison backers claim Edison read the article after he designed his own carbon filament.)

In any event, carbon seemed to be the perfect material. Carbon offered the desired electrical resistance. That October Batchelor started the tedious process of finding the right form and shape of the stuff. He tried making carbon spirals, but they crumbled. He tried molding sticks, but they cracked.

Batchelor then turned to carbonized cotton thread and made an important discovery: On October 22, he wrote in his notebook that the carbon-thread "filament"—a thin long piece of carbon—had burned for thirteen and a half hours. A great triumph. In addition, it had a relatively high resistance to electricity. Batchelor was on the right path.

What about other plant materials? Would they work even better? The search was on. Batchelor tried almost anything he could get his hands on: paper, thread, fishing line, cardboard, cotton soaked in tar.

Edison sketched out a patent application. His drawing depicted the carbon filament in the shape of a spiral. Filed with the patent office in November 1879, this light bulb design was never successfully put into production. The filament was too brittle. But the patent described a key difference between Edison's light bulb and those of his competitors. Edison's filament would be heated in a bulb containing a super-high vacuum, produced by vacuum pumps Edison had helped to modify to his own standards. By pumping out extra air, Edison was able to slow down the rate at which his carbon filament oxidized (burned up). This achieved longer bulb life.

By New Year's Day 1880 Edison was proudly showing his imperfect lamp to the public. People flocked to Menlo Park to witness carbonized cardboard that burned but was not consumed. Company insiders knew that Edison had not found the best filament material. And it wasn't for lack of trying. They literally scoured the world. Finally, following the Fourth of July holiday, the successful material was unceremoniously announced: bamboo. Bamboo plucked from a common fan was tested and found to burn for an hour and a quarter. It was strong and sturdy enough to stand up to the shaking the filament would take in use.

By August a better quality bamboo, called Japanese bamboo, proved to burn longest. Called the best lamp ever made from a vegetable product, this carbonized bamboo filament burned for almost three and a half hours. It filled the bill for a commercially viable product. And the commotion its discovery caused at Menlo Park? Just another day at the office.

By the end of the year bamboo lamps were burning for 240 or more hours. . . .

TAKING CREDIT

Edison's patent would be followed by years of court battles over who deserved to be credited with the invention of the light bulb. In the strict sense of the meaning of the word invention, Edison can hardly claim to be the bulb's sole inventor. His invention contained no unique materials. He merely improved upon the work of others. On New Year's Day 1880, two months after Edison's famous "event," a letter appeared in the British journal *Nature,* submitted by Joseph Swan and alluding to the hullabaloo about Edison. What's the big deal, he wrote:

> Fifteen years ago, I used charred paper and card in the construction of an electric lamp on the incandescent principle. I used it, too, in the shape of a horse-shoe, precisely, as you say, Mr. Edison is now using it.

Swan was England's Edison. Or to put it more correctly, Edison was America's Swan. A tinkerer and born inventor, Swan not only showed great interest in the light bulb but made key improvements in the science of photography. Twenty years Edison's senior, Swan was experimenting with light bulbs while Edison was still a toddler. By 1848, at the age of twenty, Swan had already begun experimenting with a carbon/vacuum light bulb. And by 1877 he turned his full attention to mastering the light bulb. His publication in *Scientific American* of experiments with a carbon cylinder was certainly read by

Thomas Edison holds his electric lamp. This invention brought great publicity and fame for Edison.

Edison. But there is no reason to believe that Edison's key light bulb breakthrough—making the carbon into a thin filament, not a rod—was influenced by Swan's work. If anything, Swan swiped the filament idea from Edison. Swan never claimed to have invented the carbon filament.

Having installed hundreds of light bulbs in some of England's most prestigious homes (Sir William Thompson's home glowed with 150 bulbs) and landmarks (the Royal Institution), Swan started his own company. This caught Edison's attention—more correctly, his lawyers' attention. In 1881 they went into English court to sue Swan for patent infringement. Fighting on his own turf, Swan proved to be a formidable enemy. Bowing to good business sense, Edison couldn't lick 'em, so he joined 'em. A new company, Edison-Swan United, was born and sold light bulbs under the trade name Ediswan. Together, the transcontinental giants put all light bulb competitors out of business.

THE BIRTH OF THE GREAT WHITE WAY

Even after the spectacular triumph of the electric light bulb, the world did not rush to embrace this new technology. Remember, no power lines, no house wiring, no power plants existed. All this took time to come on line. In 1885 the British *Electrician* considered the electric light "at this moment a luxury." Gas was in no danger of being replaced. Only the super-rich could afford the shiny glass bulb. In Europe the incandescent lamp numbered among its elite environs the chateau of the Baron Alphonse de Rothschild and the palace of Prince Manko-Negoro. The castle of the Marquise of Bute was illuminated by the glow of 400 electric lamps. In England, 150 Swan lamps glowed in Didlington Hall, Brandon; C.P. Huntington's mansion at Astely Bank glowed in the light of the new lamps.

In the United States, Macy's in New York City became the first store to use incandescent lamp lighting in 1883, after having installed arc lights in 1879. In 1888 the Hotel Everett on Park Row in New York City became the first American hotel to be lighted by incandescent lamps. Its main dining room, reading rooms, parlors, and lobby shone brightly under the glow of 101 electric lights.

New York theaters were the first to take advantage of the lights' ability to spell out "boldly in letters of fire" the names of the featured program. The Great White Way began to go incandescent in 1895.

By 1882 Edison Electric Light Company's Pearl Street Station was up and running in New York City. This early electrical system, running on direct current, would serve as a model for the rest of the country.

AC/DC: The War of Electric Currents

Robert Silverberg

A recipient of numerous Honor Book awards, Robert Silverberg explains how one of the greatest inventions of all time, the system of power distribution that gave electric light to the world, also brought about one of the fiercest controversies over which electric current should prevail—alternating current or direct current. Scientists were aware of these two types of electric current since the beginning of the electrical age. Because alternating current didn't seem useful to early experimenters, AC was converted into non-pulsating direct current. Edison's first generating machines were DC dynamos and he clung to DC power even after other companies were proving the technological advantages of moving to alternating current. George Westinghouse was the chief rival who was determined to create his own electrical empire based on AC power and nudge Edison out. His success heralded the doom of direct current. Ultimately, when Edison was unable to acknowledge that the future of electricity was with AC, the executives of Edison General Electric eased him out of the company.

The existence of two types of electric current had been known since the dawn of the electrical age. Hippolyte Pixii's generator of 1832 had had a rotating magnetic field that cut the conductors first in one direction and then in the other. This produced a series of interrupted electrical pulses as the magnets swung back and forth; the flow of electricity reached a maximum in one direction, then decreased, moved toward a maximum in the other direction, and reversed again to begin a new cycle.

Excerpted from Robert Silverberg, *Light for the World: Edison and the Power Industry.* Copyright © 1967 D. Van Nostrand Company, Inc. Reprinted with permission from the author.

Such an "alternating" current did not seem useful to the early experimenters. Ampère had suggested a simple device called a commutator, which converted the oscillating or alternating current into a non-pulsating "direct" current, and commutators became standard features on the dynamos of the arc light era.

Edison's first generating machines were direct-current dynamos, but his early commitment to d.c. was accidental, to a large extent. For the purpose of providing incandescent lighting, it did not matter whether Edison used d.c. or a.c. The dynamo technology of 1878 was almost exclusively a d.c. technology, and so he chose to make no departure from it. Before long, though, he was irrevocably wedded to the d.c. concept as an essential part of his system.

What was important to Edison as he created his system was not the type of current he used, but the voltage. The Edison system was based on power that traveled at 110 volts all the way from the generating station to the consumer. The great advantage of this was its safety. Current at 110 volts and at the low amperage sufficient for electric lighting could do no harm; a customer who came in contact with an unshielded line would receive a mild shock, no more. The danger of fire was low, too. Sensitive to the problems inherent in getting a new kind of illumination across to a suspicious public, Edison wished to avoid any possibility of spectacular electrical disasters, so he opted for the safest form of distribution.

However, low voltages had a built-in drawback: they limited the distance of transmission. Current moving with such a modest force could be carried no more than a mile or two from the generating station; then the drop in voltage became so great that the outlying lights dimmed. In addition, much of the power would be dissipated in the form of heat. Under Edison's low-voltage transmission system, Edison's own great concept of the central station was seriously impaired, for 110-volt service required a chain of power stations at close intervals in order to supply any large city with electricity. At best an Edison station could serve some sixteen square miles.

Ideally, the solution was to have power leave the generating station at a high voltage, and then to step it down to a safe 110 volts before it reached the customer. But this was technically impossible on the Edison system. The young Edison would have looked for some way to *make* it possible;

the middle-aged Edison simply accepted the situation as a regrettable innate flaw in his design, and left it at that. But there was a way—with alternating current.

A NEW TRANSFORMER

The germ of the long-distance a.c. transmission system lay in the original work of Faraday. His first successful experiment had made use of two coils wound on an iron core; by stopping or starting a current in one coil, he induced a current in the other. Although he did not realize it, the basis of the transformer, or voltage-changer, could be found in this experiment.

Seven years later, in 1838, the American Joseph Henry used Faraday's two-coil arrangement as a step-down transformer. One coil consisted of many turns of wire, the other of only a few; high-voltage power entered the first coil, and was stepped down to a low voltage in the second.

The transformer received little further attention until 1882, when Lucien Gaulard of France and John D. Gibbs of England produced a transformer specifically designed to reduce the voltage of a.c. power en route from the generator to the consumer. Gaulard and Gibbs obtained an English patent on their work in 1883, but in practice it had serious mechanical defects and could not be used without modification.

The modifications were quick in coming. In 1885 three Hungarian inventors found a way to employ the Gaulard-Gibbs transformer in long-distance power installations. Their device, called the "Z.B.D. transformer" after the initials of its inventors, went into immediate use in Europe. It permitted power first to be boosted to very high voltage as it left the generator, then to be stepped down again as it reached the consumer—with remarkably little energy loss over great distances. The higher the voltage used in transmission, the less the loss on the line.

Rights to the Z.B.D. system were offered to Edison in 1886. He sent Upton to Europe to inspect the equipment, and at Upton's suggestion Edison paid $5000 for a three-year option, against a total price of $20,000. But Edison could not bring himself to veer from his low-voltage d.c. transmission system. In November, 1886 he received a report from a Berlin engineering firm to the effect that the Z.B.D. system was troublesome, costly to install, and dangerous to work with. That was all Edison needed to hear. He allowed the option to lapse, and angrily rejected the suggestions of his associates that he give the Hungarian transformer a further trial. Edison's adherence to his own original system had become something deeply personal, a matter for the emotions, not the reason. He clung to his 110-volt concept despite all advice to the contrary.

Yet younger men all over Europe and America were excited by the new development. High-voltage transmission suddenly was the technological darling of the moment. Of course, it would require a changeover from d.c. to a.c. power. Since transformers functioned only with a changing current, the output of d.c. generators could be neither stepped up nor stepped down with transformers. High voltages required the use of a.c. equipment. And that produced certain new problems. Alternating current could not be used for driving electric motors; it seemed to demand two or three times as much coal per kilowatt hour as direct current; and it rendered obsolete most of the existing capital plant of the power industry. Nevertheless, the forward-looking men of that industry were confident that someone would invent a feasible a.c. electric motor and that the generating cost of a.c. could be made comparable to that of d.c. As for the obsolescence of existing equipment, that would cease to matter in time. Alternating current was sure to win universal acceptance.

Edison—nearly alone—fought the new trend.

His option on the Z.B.D. patents gave him the exclusive right to use the new transformer in the United States until 1889. Since that was the case, rival manufacturers had no choice but to go back to the defective Gaulard-Gibbs device and attempt to modify it themselves in a way that circumvented the Hungarians. The most eager of these rivals was George Westinghouse of Pittsburgh, who had gone into the electric business in 1885.

THE WESTINGHOUSE CLASH

Westinghouse, one year Edison's senior, had founded his industrial fortunes on his invention of the air brake for railways. Bold, ambitious, even reckless, he dreamed of an electrical empire to rival Edison's, and by liberal use of cash had attracted some of the best engineers of the day away from the ever more conservative Edison organization.

The new Westinghouse Electrical & Manufacturing Company sought to steal a march on Edison by getting control of that segment of the electrical field that Edison scorned: high-voltage alternating current equipment of 1,000 volts or more. For that Westinghouse needed a practicable transformer. Westinghouse bought the American rights to the Gaulard-Gibbs transformer and assigned the job of making it work properly to a young engineering consultant, William A. Stanley. The flaw in the Gaulard-Gibbs system was that it employed a number of transformers to be connected in series, so that they could not work independently. Stanley found a patentable way of connecting transformers in parallel and making each transformer automatically regulate itself, thus permitting independent control. On March 6, 1886, the first commercial alternating-current lighting system went into operation in Great Barrington, Massachusetts, using the Stanley transformers. . . .

Westinghouse, in 1886, also purchased the United States Electric Lighting Company, which had control of the contested Maxim incandescent lamp patents. Now he proposed to compete in both spheres of the electrical industry. Through Westinghouse Electric he would manufacture high-voltage equipment; through United States Electric he would set up power companies that, by taking advantage of the economies of long-distance transmission, would outstrip the Edison companies. Where he could, Westinghouse would rely on the non-Edison technology of a.c. Where he could not, he intended to invade the Edison patents, whose validity was under attack in the courts. In an advertisement exceptional for its blandly self-congratulatory tone Westinghouse declared:

> We regard it as fortunate that we have deferred entering the electrical field until the present moment. Having thus profited by the public experience of others, we enter ourselves for competition, hampered by a minimum of expense for experimental outlay. . . . In short, our organization is free, in large measure, of the load with which [other] electrical enterprises seem to be encumbered. The fruit of this . . . we propose to share with the customer.

That is, having allowed Edison to bear the burden of developing the electrical industry, Westinghouse planned to undersell him by making use of his pioneering work.

In March of 1887 Westinghouse began to move into New York City, Edison's home grounds, with an a.c. incandescent lighting system. He organized the Safety Electric Light and Power Company and licensed it to use the Westinghouse system of generation and distribution of electricity by alternating current. Safety Electric began to buy into an existing arc light company, United States Illuminating, which held several important street and park contracts. Soon Safety Electric controlled United States Illuminating; it changed its name in 1889 to United Electric Light and Power Company and began to spread the Westinghouse system into those parts of Manhattan that Edison Illuminating had not yet reached.

Naturally the older company fought back. In 1888 it denounced the Westinghouse system in a pamphlet that declared:

They cannot make it safe.

They cannot make it reliable.

They cannot make it run twelve 16-candlepower lamps per horsepower.

They cannot make its lamps even.

They cannot make its lamps last a reasonable time.

They cannot make it sell by meter.

They cannot make it run motors.

Some of these charges were true at the time; others, particularly the accusation of unsafeness, were not. But the men who had made such a deep financial and emotional investment in d.c. could not abide the thought that their system was obsolescent.

Edison himself, though no longer directly concerned with the fortunes of the Edison Illuminating Company, was seriously perturbed by the spread of a.c. It was an attack on his technical judgment, he felt; he was worried, also, about Westinghouse's talk of using power at 5,000 or even 10,000 volts. Contemporary insulating techniques did not seem adequate for such voltages, Edison felt. To Edward Johnson he wrote:

Just as certain as death Westinghouse will kill a customer within 6 months after he puts in a system of any size. He has got a new thing and it will require a great deal of experimenting to get it working practically. It will never be free from danger. . . .

None of his plans worry me in the least; only thing that disturbs me is that Westinghouse is a great man for flooding the country with agents and travelers. He is ubiquitous and will form numerous companies before we know anything about it. . . .

The problem of the electric motor also hindered the spread of a.c. in 1887. All existing motors worked on d.c., and d.c. alone; no one yet knew a way of adapting them for a.c.

use. Since the electrical industry was coming to depend for its revenues more and more on industrial power use, less and less on lighting, a practical a.c. motor was essential if the new system were to last.

Elihu Thomson built one of the first a.c. motors in May of 1887. It had a laminated magnet consisting of many disks of metal pressed together, and a laminated armature with three coils. The Thomson motor attracted considerable attention when it was displayed before a scientific group, but it did not go into production at once, and the aggressive Westinghouse gained a leading position with the a.c. motor of Nikola Tesla.

THE GENIUS OF TESLA

Tesla, a towering, mystical genius out of Yugoslavia, had once been part of the Edison organization but had slipped away. As an electrical inventor be was extraordinary, very likely superior in vision even to Edison. But he was a romantic, brooding figure of little practical awareness who could never have become a permanent part of the Edison research team. There was room in Edison's entourage for only one genius at a time; besides, Tesla believed passionately in the alternating current.

In 1882, in Budapest, Tesla was seized with a vision of an alternating-current motor: a rotating magnetic field that carried the armature around with it. The Tesla motor employed two alternating currents at once; the currents were equal in the frequency of their cycle of minimum-to-maximum amplitude, but were out of phase relative to each other. With one current or the other always at a maximum, the motor worked continuously. It was a brilliant idea, a landmark in engineering. But in 1882 there was no a.c. power source to drive Tesla's motor. . . .

Tesla went to Edison's Fifth Avenue office . . . presented his letter, and was treated to a discourse on the problems of Pearl Street.[1] Edison would hear no talk of alternating current; he put Tesla to work at once on routine electrical work. When Tesla solved a knotty problem with unexpected cleverness, Edison saw his merit and gave him harder assignments—

---

1. In the 1880s, Pearl Street Station was the first Edison station to generate a public supply of electricity. Initially it ran at a deficit, but it did establish the Edison direct-current stations worldwide. Unfortunately, the 1890s gave way to alternating current and Edison lacked the flexibility to make this transition.

without, however, raising his pay beyond that of a beginning technician. Feeling underpaid, and angered by Edison's refusal to consider his theories, Tesla came to the inevitable collision with his employer and resigned after a year. From the spring of 1886 to the spring of 1887 he supported himself as a day laborer, digging ditches and taking on occasional electrical jobs.

Then he found backers, and set up the Tesla Electric Company. Though their financial support was modest, Tesla was able to carry on his research and to apply for patents. Between November and December, 1887, Tesla filed for seven patents on his motor and on an electrical distribution system; so radically different were they from anything in existence that the applications were granted in only six months. Tesla was invited to explain his ideas at a meeting of the American Institute of Electrical Engineers on May 16, 1888. He had "arrived."

Now he held patents on a revolutionary power system. His high-voltage lines could carry power hundreds of miles with relatively little energy loss or voltage drop. His motors were far more efficient than the small d.c. motors then in use, and could handle much greater loads. But the Tesla Electric Company lacked the capital to make use of the patents. Inevitably, Tesla was summoned to meet George Westinghouse. Westinghouse offered the inventor a million dollars in cash for his patents, plus a generous royalty arrangement, and hired Tesla as a consultant.

Though the unpredictable Tesla soon quarreled with Westinghouse and returned to private research, his patents had passed into the manufacturer's control. Now it was Westinghouse, and not Edison, who held the technological advantage. Westinghouse could make use of the newest and most exciting ideas in the field; Edison, relegated to the role of grim defender of the past, was forced to rely on the great work of 1878–83 at a time when that work had passed into obsolescence. As often happens when a great man must occupy an untenable position, Edison grew more convinced that he was right each time Westinghouse added new proof that he was wrong. Thus began the famed "Battle of the Currents."

Edison set out to prove that a.c. was a menace to the public. He rigged an a.c. generator at West Orange that supplied current at 1,000 volts, and before invited audiences of reporters and other guests staged grisly demonstrations in which hapless dogs and cats were nudged out onto wired sheets of tin and electrocuted. The stray animals of upper New Jersey perished at a ghastly rate in this gruesome promotional campaign.

Then, in February of 1888, Edward Johnson issued a manifesto titled, "A Warning from the Edison Electric Light Company." It summarized the results of the animal executions and provided a long list of the fatalities caused by arc lights, which used high voltages. The pamphlet sideswiped Westinghouse and Thomson-Houston by branding them as "patent pirates" who were out to gain quick wealth by introducing a newfangled and risky kind of electricity to the American home.

Westinghouse issued relatively restrained denials, pointing out that the mishaps of arc light companies in 1880 had nothing to do with his own incandescent system of 1888, and that in any event high voltages would be used only in transmission lines; current entering the home would be stepped down to a voltage no greater than that favored by Edison. . . .

Edison's promotional campaign—sparked by the ingenuity of Samuel Insull—swung into a high level in the autumn of 1888. Edison lobbyists asked state legislatures for laws limiting electric circuits to 800 volts, and nearly succeeded in Ohio and Virginia. In New York, Edison took a different and much more bizarre approach: he persuaded the legislature to legalize the electric chair for the execution of condemned criminals—and saw to it that the fatal chair used Westinghouse equipment! What better way to dramatize the lethal nature of alternating current? . . .

ELECTRIC CHAIR HELPS DECIDE THE OUTCOME

A human being was available for this research: one William Kemmler, a condemned murderer. The state authorities were eager to try Mr. Edison's death chair, and so Kemmler was sentenced "to suffer death by electricity at Auburn Prison within the week beginning Monday, June 24, 1889." . . .

Edison expressed the belief that 1000 volts of one-ampere current would be ten times as much as was needed to kill any man with the Westinghouse alternator. . . .

After lengthy debate, Kemmler's execution date was set for August 6, 1890. The warden of Auburn Prison was empowered to invite twenty-one witnesses. Most of the guests selected were scientific men, among them Edison—who, however, did not care to be present at Kemmler's death.

An ordinary commercial Westinghouse machine capable of producing a current at 1500 volts was used. It was driven by a steam engine in the prison basement; the power lines were run out of a window of the dynamo room to the roof of the jail and along the roof to the death chamber. A current varying in force from 800 to 1300 volts gave Kemmler his place in the annals of penology; the witnesses unofficially reported that the death had been slower and less pleasant than Edison had predicted.

None the less, electrocution became the rule in New York State, and Edison, at some loss in dignity, managed to frighten many Americans into thinking that a.c. was a public menace. Some of his own men, particularly Frank Sprague, pleaded with him to halt his campaign, but Edison had gone too far now to back down. All his prestige was pledged to direct current. Out of bitterness and testiness he had elevated his original shortsightedness to the status of an inflexible policy; it was the worst mistake of his career.

Through 1888 and 1889 it became increasingly apparent to most men in the field that the future of electricity lay with a.c. By the time William Kemmler went to his death in the summer of 1890, that fact seemed certain to virtually everyone but Edison. Among the converts to the new creed were the executives of Edison General Electric, although they did not dare suggest to Edison that he had outlived his usefulness in electrical engineering. A series of complicated developments grew out of Edison's vested interest in the outmoded system of electrical generation and transmission, and when the dust settled, Edison had been quietly shown to the exit.

The Phonograph: Entertainment vs. Commercial Use

Paul Israel

Having a background only in telecommunications, Edison and other major players in the phonograph industry weren't prepared to imagine or create an entertainment industry. This new market was completely lost on Edison. Managing editor of the multivolume documentary edition of the Thomas Edison Papers at Rutgers University and coauthor of *Edison's Electric Light*, Paul Israel sheds insight on the inventor's vision for the phonograph. Edison felt the phonograph's most important use would be by businessmen for dictation since so many of his previous inventions had found industrial applications. As Israel asserts, leisure time was a new concept and its rapid growth shifted the manufacturing economy from producer to consumer goods. By the end of the 1890s, Edison's most successful businesses would be his phonograph and motion picture companies that targeted consumers.

Over the course of the [1890s], the new phonograph that Edison developed during the first months of work at his new laboratory led him into the entertainment industry. Although he had always envisioned entertainment uses for the phonograph, Edison designed his improved wax-record phonograph, the first new product of the West Orange laboratory, as a business machine rather than as an entertainment device. Edison and the other major figures in the early phonograph industry shared a background in telecommunications; they were ill prepared to imagine and create an entertainment industry. When Edison began work on motion pictures at the end of 1888, with his phonograph as a model,

Excerpted from Paul Israel, *Edison: A Life of Invention.* Copyright © 1998 Paul Israel. Reprinted with permission from John Wiley & Sons, Inc.

he had an even less clear understanding of the potential new entertainment market for films. He later remarked that "[we] knew we had an interesting and novel apparatus, [but] we generally regarded it more or less as a curiosity with no very large practicable possibilities." Inventing the technologies of entertainment, as it turned out, was not the same as inventing their commercial use. . . .

ENTERING THE CONSUMER ENTERTAINMENT BUSINESS

The growth of leisure time and in the consumption that came with it helped to shift the manufacturing economy from producer to consumer goods. As Edison's experience shows, the transition could be difficult. His prior experience was with producer technologies. His telegraph, telephone, and electric lighting systems, his electric pen, and his early phonographs were all developed and sold primarily for business use. By the end of the 1890s his two most successful businesses would be his phonograph and motion picture companies, which catered to consumers rather than businesspeople. Yet, in the 1890s Edison continued to devote most of his own time to electric lighting and to his process for extracting low-grade iron ore in iron and steel mills. In the 1900s, drawing on the income from these consumer goods, he continued to focus his own efforts on producer markets, developing improved methods for making the cement used in buildings and a storage battery for automobiles. Edison's personal involvement in his new consumer entertainment businesses remained quite limited until the 1910s, and when he finally did take a larger hand in their operations, his participation was of dubious benefit to his companies.

Edison's development work on phonographs and motion pictures was also a product of his very different understanding of their potential markets. Edison expected his phonograph to fit into an expanding market for business machines such as typewriters and telephones. He therefore put the full resources of his new laboratory to work on the problem of an improved dictating phonograph. At the same time he devoted some of these resources to development work on sound recording and record duplication for entertainment purposes. In contrast, the work on motion pictures remained a minor project at the laboratory with a small staff of researchers who worked on it part-time. Edison planned a large factory and sales campaign for the phonograph, but his manufacturing and marketing plans for motion pictures were relatively haphazard.

Edison had begun to plan the development of a new dictating phonograph with his inventive partner, Ezra Gilliland, in October 1886. Unlike his earlier phonograph designs, the new machine would be designed for use by a single person working in the quiet of an office. Thus, the recording would be made by a person speaking into a flexible tube rather than shouting into a mouthpiece, and the recorded sound would be heard when a listener would hold the tube up to his or her ear. It would not be amplified and broadcast into the room by a funnel. Edison and Gilliland hoped that this would reproduce the human voice "about as loud and clear as a good telephone on a short circuit." In his notebook, Gilliland described the new phonograph as "a small compact instrument suitable for office use" that would be run by a small electric motor. He also proposed recording on a polished glass or metal cylinder covered with "shellac, gum or wax or something of that nature which can be applied by a brush." By turning to such recording surfaces, Gilliland and Edison were clearly influenced by a new competitor to Edison's tinfoil phonograph.

This was the graphophone developed by Charles Sumner Tainter at Alexander Graham Bell's Volta Laboratory in Washington, D.C. Tainter, a skilled machinist who at one time had worked for Charles Williams in Boston, had been working with Alexander and his cousin Chichester Bell to improve the phonograph since 1881. They had begun by experimenting with a small 1878 Edison tinfoil phonograph, but Tainter soon suggested that wax would be a good recording surface, and an experiment in which they filled the phonograph cylinder's grooves with wax showed promise. Although the Volta associates experimented with a wide variety of recording methods and surfaces, wax became the focus of their experiments. Because the phonograph was just one of many inventions under development at the laboratory, it was not until 1885 that Tainter finally devised a wax-cylinder phonograph that showed commercial promise. This machine used a wax-covered paper cylinder and listening tubes for hearing the recording, which was made by speaking into a funnel. Unlike Edison's and Gilliland's proposed design, it was hand-cranked like the original tinfoil phonograph. In naming their new machine the graphophone, the Volta associates paid homage to Edison's phonograph by reversing the letters in its name.

COMPETITION INSPIRES RENEWED EFFORTS

In the summer of 1885, as they progressed to the point where they began to consider commercial development, the Volta associates decided to approach Edison. Bell's father-in-law, Gardiner Hubbard, contacted Edward Johnson and Uriah Painter, his associates in the Edison Speaking Phonograph Company, and proposed joining the Bell-Tainter phonograph interests with those of Edison and the company on a fifty-fifty basis. However, after three months of discussions, Edward Johnson, who was negotiating on Edison's behalf, remained uncertain whether to recommend joining forces "for an invention that might or might not prove ultimately of real practical value." Although Tainter's demonstration of a new machine during the first week of October produced better results than ever before, Johnson advised waiting for further developments. By the end of the year the Bell-Tainter group decided to move ahead on their own and formed the Volta Graphophone Company. As the graphophone proceeded toward commercial introduction, Edison decided that it was time to return to the phonograph. Although he never acknowledged it publicly, the graphophone was clearly the source of inspiration for this renewed effort and provided an initial model for the new phonograph design.

Neither Edison nor Gilliland did much work on the new phonograph until after Edison had begun to make plans for his new laboratory. It was an exhibition of a Bell-Tainter graphophone at the St. James Hotel in New York City in early May 1887 that spurred their renewed interest in developing this machine. The influence of the graphophone is evident from [Edison's chief assistant] Charles Batchelor's description of Edison's new plan for "making a phonograph that will be able to lift out cylinder as well as stop and start at will etc." The graphophone on exhibit recorded on a removable paper cylinder coated with a 1/8-inch layer of ozokerite wax, and it had a stop motion that enabled an operator to start and stop it while continuing to supply power to the drive mechanism with a foot treadle. Several other features were designed to improve the quality of recording and playback: the foot treadle had a governor that provided uniform rotation speed to the cylinder; a funnel concentrated sound waves onto the diaphragm and needle that cut the recording into the wax surface; the record was reproduced by a second diaphragm whose needle was attached by a thread to reduce pressure and wear-and-tear on the wax; and a listening tube made it possible to hear dictation quite clearly.

Aware that the soft ozokerite wax of the graphophone cylinder tended to dull and clog the recording stylus and wear down under the pressure of the reproducing stylus, Edison initially focused his research on finding a better recording wax surface and developing a reproducer that would not wear down the recording. With Gilliland unable to assist him because of an illness that kept him away from the laboratory for several weeks, Edison relied on Batchelor, whom he set to work "making cylinders of plumbago, mixtures, and steatite" so that "the dust falls away leaving in shaving etc." Within a short time they discovered that waxes, particularly paraffin mixed with resin, did indeed provide a better recording surface, and they focused their research in this direction. . . .

A DEVICE CONSTANTLY IN NEED OF IMPROVEMENT

Little is known of the work on the phonograph prior to the opening of the West Orange laboratory in the fall. Although Edison wrote George Gouraud on July 21 that he already had "a much better apparatus" than the graphophone and was "building the factory to manufacture" it, there is little evidence to support these claims or his optimism that "in the course of a couple of months I will be prepared to put this improved instrument upon the market." Electric lighting and the construction of the new laboratory rather than the phonograph occupied most of Edison's time for the remainder of the summer. By the beginning of October, however, he had made sufficient progress to offer Gouraud all foreign rights for his new phonograph and to place Gilliland in charge of manufacturing it. . . .

If Edison had made any significant improvement over the graphophone, it was the spectacle-shaped frame he had devised for the recorder and reproducer. This device facilitated changing between the two operations and allowed the recording and reproducing diaphragm and needles to be removed for repair, adjustment, or replacement. Nonetheless, this device had a thumbscrew adjustment that required considerable trial and error to set properly and that Gilliland attempted to improve by adding a spring adjustment. After Sigmund Bergmann saw the machine during the first week of January, he wrote Painter, "Unless you have money to throw away I would advise you to wait a while as they admitted to me that they were not yet finished experimenting."

Although reluctant to admit it publicly, Edison realized that his new phonograph required considerable improvement. With the resources available in his new laboratory, he would be able to duplicate the kind of research and development effort that he had undertaken eight years earlier at Menlo Park when he turned his electric lighting system from an experimental into a commercial product. As he had done with the electric light system, Edison subdivided the work of improving the phonograph and its recording cylinders among his experimenters. Arthur Kennelly and the galvanometer room staff were in charge of experiments on motors and batteries; Jonas W. Aylsworth was given the task of developing better waxes for the recording cylinder; Theo Wangemann, an experimenter and also an accomplished pianist, was assigned the task of making experimental recordings of both voices and music; and Dr. Franz Schulze-Berge, a German Ph.D. who had worked for a decade in Hermann von Helmholtz's physical laboratory before joining Edison, experimented on processes for duplicating records. Before moving to the third floor of the main building to take charge of the research on electroplating and duplicating phonograph cylinders, Schulze-Berge had conducted electrical experiments in the galvanometer room under Kennelly. Edison focused his own efforts on the phonograph itself, although he kept a watchful eye on all phases of the research and frequently offered suggestions and conducted experiments. . . .

INTERCHANGEABLE PARTS

The "perfected" phonograph, as Edison termed it, was designed with manufacturing in mind. Ten years earlier Edison had suggested that "a practical, marketable machine . . . can only be built on the American principle of interchangeability of parts like a gun or a sewing machine." At the time he thought that such a machine would have to "be simple and easily made and one that will be hard to improve, otherwise we will be changing and improving all the time, which lessens profits." Now, however, he saw interchangeability as a way of allowing him to make continual improvements in the phonograph. By using special-purpose machine tools operated by semi-skilled workers who carefully gauged each part as it was manufactured, Edison felt that he could ensure that "any new designs will be adapted to instruments already sent out, requiring only the removal of the part intended to be replaced—nothing else will be interfered with." Edison believed that his manufacturing system would allow him to beat the Graphophone Company, which had started a factory in Bridgeport, Connecticut, because "Tainter [was] not practical man: don't know how to make cheap."

To establish phonograph manufacturing using the American system of interchangeable parts, Edison and Batchelor organized the Edison Phonograph Works at the beginning of May and began to build a factory next to the laboratory. Whereas the small-scale hand operations of Edison's Bloomfield factory were capable of producing only twenty-five to thirty-five phonographs per day, Edison expected the new factory to produce two hundred per day. Because so much of his own money was tied up in the electrical manufacturing shops, Edison tried to interest Henry Villard in the enterprise as part of his general effort to have Villard become the primary backer of all his enterprises. When that effort fell through, Edison himself had to become the primary financier for the factory, which cost nearly $250,000 to build and equip, including special tools and machinery, before manufacturing began in earnest in the fall.

Production of phonographs had continued at the Bloomfield factory during the winter, and by mid-March Gilliland informed Edison that "we are within two weeks or less, of having machines ready for market." However, as the general agent for the Edison Phonograph Company, Gilliland also expressed his concern that there was "not one contract closed with any agent and no printing or advertising matter of any kind," and he told Edison that "the commercial end of the Phonograph business needs my personal attention badly and I think from this time forward I shall give it all of my time." Having learned from Edison's complaints about his independent efforts to improve the phonograph, Gilliland also decided that it would be essential for him to get Edison's approval for "every step I take." By the end of March Edison arrived at the basic form of the "Standard Phonograph," and although the commercial machine would be delayed for several months as he continued to make improvements, it was clear to both men that the new design was vastly superior and they agreed to begin promoting it and securing sales agents. . . .

ENVISIONED FOR BUSINESS AND PLEASURE

Edison and Gilliland both believed that the phonograph's most important market would be businessmen who would use it for dictation. Yet, contrary to what has generally been written about his phonograph business, Edison did not fail to recognize the potential for an entertainment market nor did he actively oppose such use. Certainly, the articles published under his name in *North American Review* about his original phonograph of 1878 and his "perfected" phonograph of 1888, both pointed out such uses. Indeed, in 1888 he claimed that

> through the facility with which it stores up and reproduces music of all sorts, or whistling and recitations, it can be employed to furnish constant amusement to invalids, or to social assemblies, at receptions, dinners, etc. Any one sitting in his room alone may order an assorted supply of wax cylinders, inscribed with songs, poems, piano or violin music, short stories, anecdotes, or dialect pieces, and by putting them on his phonograph, he can listen to them as originally sung or recited by authors, vocalists and actors, or elocutionists. The variety of entertainment he thus commands, at trifling expense and without moving from his chair, is practically unlimited.

Edison not only suggested that his phonograph be used for entertainment, he actually became involved in two efforts to develop them for this purpose. The first of these was a talking doll that he set Batchelor to work on in February 1888. Edison had originally proposed the use of the phonograph for toys in 1877 and an unsuccessful effort had been made in this direction in 1878. In the mid-1880s William Jacques, a Bell Telephone researcher, and his partner Lowell Briggs developed a talking doll after learning of the improvements in the Bell-Tainter graphophone, and in October 1887 they approached Edison about the manufacture and sale of this device. Edison agreed to the formation of the Edison Phonograph Toy Manufacturing Company, and Batchelor began trying to improve the mechanism and records for the doll. Unhappy with Jacques's management of the toy company, Edison placed his own man in charge, and in 1889 he began manufacturing the dolls at the Phonograph Works. Although he planned to have a large shipment of dolls ready for Christ-

With the invention of the phonograph Edison went to work making it serve as a source of entertainment. He founded a company to create toys, and one of the first products was this talking doll.

mas 1889, the talking doll continued to have serious technical shortcomings, particularly because of the fragility of its small record, and production did not begin in earnest until the following January. Although more than 3,000 were made and tested by the end of March 1890, Edison withdrew them from sale the following month because of complaints over the reliability of the phonograph mechanism. He entirely suspended manufacturing in October and refused to commit any of his own resources to it, especially after the toy company became embroiled in legal disputes. . . .

WHEELING AND DEALING

As Gilliland began to focus on the commercial end of the phonograph in March 1888, a new promoter entered the talking machine business. Jesse H. Lippincott, who had made a considerable fortune in the glass industry, arranged with the Graphophone Company for an exclusive license to market its machine. Soon afterward, Gilliland showed him the new phonograph; concerned that it could affect his graphophone business, Lippincott determined to gain control of Edison's machine. He commenced negotiations with Gilliland, offering to purchase the Edison Phonograph Company for $500,000. Gilliland broached the idea to Edison through Edison's attorney John Tomlinson. At the end of June, after extensive negotiations, Edison finally agreed to the sale. The course of the negotiations and the agreement itself indicate that Edison retained his producer-goods frame of reference. While willing to give up control of the marketing of his phonograph Edison was adamant about retaining exclusive manufacturing rights. This had been characteristic of his early years as an inventor-manufacturer in the telegraph industry, and his experience in electric lighting suggested that manufacturing would be the most lucrative business in a new industry.

Unknown to Edison, the negotiations also involved a private deal between Lippincott, Gilliland, and Tomlinson. Lippincott agreed to purchase Gilliland's agency contract in exchange for $250,000 of stock in a new company he was forming to exploit the two talking machines. Tomlinson received part of this settlement, ostensibly because he had an interest in Gilliland's contract but possibly also for his role in arranging the deal. Fifty thousand was to be paid upfront with an option to buy the additional $200,000 within four months of Edison's signing his agreement with Lippincott. Edison finally learned about the cash settlement with Gilliland and Tomlinson in September when Lippincott had difficulty making his required payment to the inventor. Edison became enraged upon learning about it, contending that the other men had been looking out for their own interests and not his when they got him to agree to the sale. By the time Edison learned about their secret arrangement Gilliland and Tomlinson were in Europe, where Gilliland was exhibiting the phonograph. Edison immediately cabled Gilliland: "I just learn you have made a certain trade with Lippincott of a nature unknown to me. As you did not have permission to sell from Company I have this day abrogated your contract and notified Mr Lippincott of the fact and that he pay any fur-

ther sum at his own risk. Since you have been so under-
handed I shall demand refunding all money paid you & stop-
page of further payments and I do not desire you to exhibit
phonograph in Europe." Protesting his innocence, Gilliland
replied "You certainly are acting without knowledge of facts
and are doing me great injustice have in this and at all other
times worked faithfully in your interests. Shall return at
once." Edison, however, refused to see him and permanently
severed connections with the man who was his oldest and
closest friend. He also removed Tomlinson as both his personal lawyer and counsel for his companies. The fallout with
Gilliland and Edison's strained relations with Johnson,
which were exacerbated by conflicts over the electric lighting
business between several of Edison's close associates, had
arisen in part because Edison continued to treat them as in-
feriors rather than equals, even when they played crucial
roles in his inventive or business enterprises. . . .

PHONOGRAPH VS. GRAPHOPHONE

Lippincott's plan for marketing the phonograph was one
with which Edison was quite familiar and of which he
seems to have approved. Rather than sell phonographs as
the sewing machines or typewriters were sold, Lippincott
drew on the model of the Bell Telephone Company by
proposing to rent instruments through exclusive state territories. It may be that this plan was influenced by the Bell
Telephone interests connected with the Graphophone Company, who also clearly saw the graphophone as a business
machine. Edison, with his experience in the telephone industry and earlier in the telegraph market-reporting industry, which also leased instruments, would have found this a
plausible scheme, especially as businessmen would be familiar with it and might feel more comfortable if the phonograph company was responsible for maintaining the instruments. To carry out his scheme, Lippincott organized the
North American Phonograph Company and immediately began organizing some thirty local subsidiary companies that
would be assigned territories within which they would market the instruments to customers who would be given a
choice between the phonograph and the graphophone. . . .

Edison's superior research facilities enabled him to respond to complaints from local companies and to make improvements to the phonograph that virtually drove the

graphophone from the market. But the market itself remained very limited. In June 1891, at the second convention of local phonograph companies, they reported renting only a little over three thousand machines. Just one out of fifty of these instruments was a graphophone. By the end of the year, all but a few graphophones would be replaced by Edison's improved phonograph. However, many businessmen still considered the machine too complex for themselves and for their clerks.

EXPERIENCE WITH A CONSUMER MARKET

Even as the business market stagnated, the local companies were finding profit by using their phonographs for entertainment purposes. Beginning in May 1889, North American Phonograph Company had begun to offer recordings made at the Edison laboratory and duplicated by the Phonograph Works, and a few of the local companies had begun using musical recordings to promote the phonograph. By the 1891 convention, the companies were using one out of every three phonographs in a coin-in-slot amusement device. Many agreed with the editor of the *Phonogram*, who complained in January 1891 that this diminished their ability to sell them to businessmen: "Those companies who fail to take advantage of every opportunity of pushing the legitimate side of the business, relying only on the profits derived from the 'coin-in-the-slot,' will find too late that they have made a fatal mistake . . . as it has the appearance of being nothing more than a mere toy, and no one would comprehend its value or appreciate its utility as an aid to businessmen and others for dictation purposes when seeing it only in that form." Edison, however, thought that the business of making duplicate records would become "a trade that will net us ten thousand dollars a year" and sought to control it, although he was satisfied to leave the making of original recordings to the local companies. . . .

THE STRUGGLE TO REGAIN CONTROL OF THE MARKET

Writing to the managers of his English phonograph company in 1893, he said that "Our experience here shows that a very large number of machines go into private houses for amusement purposes—that such persons do not attempt to record nor desire it for that purpose they simply want to reproduce. It has always been my idea that one of the greatest

fields for the phonograph was in the household for reproducing all that is best in oratory & music but I have never got
any one to believe it until lately." Nonetheless, Edison still
expected the manufacture and sale of phonographs and duplicated records, not the production of original recordings,
to be the primary business of his phonograph company.

When Edison began his effort to regain control of the
phonograph business in 1894, he had been planning to market a new electric phonograph with a large cylinder capable
of recording "1/2 hour for music & 1 hour for talking that
records and reproduces music with as near absolute perfec-
tion as can be." By the time he finally succeeded in reorga-
nizing the business, however, he found that the market had
shifted because of the introduction of cheap spring-driven
machines better suited to a mass market for home entertainment than his expensive and cumbersome electric
phonograph. Edison's experiments with spring motors for
the tinfoil and early wax-recording phonographs had led
him to conclude that they could not produce the even and
constant cylinder rotation required for quality recording and
playback. He thus chose to use electric motors that overcame the problem, but also significantly raised the cost of
the phonograph and required users to deal with the expense
and difficulty of maintaining the chemical solutions of primary batteries. In the mid-1890s several local phonograph
companies, facing declining income from their phonograph
parlors and in the market for business machines, began to
adapt spring motors to the Edison phonograph to offer
cheap instruments suitable for home entertainment. . . .

To compete with the cheaper machines being marketed
by the Columbia Phonograph Company, Edison decided to
develop a spring-motor phonograph to sell "for about $40.00,
thus placing the instrument within the reach of everybody
as a formidable rival to the limited music box." . . .

After Edison redesigned the motor to operate with a
single spring and patented a much better speed regulator for
it, National Phonograph began selling machines using it as
the "Home" phonograph, a name much better suited to the
consumer market. . . .

Phonograph model design during this period relied primarily on engineering refinements rather than new inventions in sound recording technology. As we have seen,
throughout his career, dating back to his days as a telegraph

manufacturer, Edison had been concerned with just this kind of product improvement, and his experience helped to ensure that Edison phonographs remained the industry standard. . . . To maintain the growing market for entertainment phonographs, however, Edison also needed to improve the reproduction quality of both records and machines. During the next few years he devoted considerable effort to refining the technical quality of sound recording. As a result, even though his machines tended to be somewhat more expensive than those of his competitors, during the early years of the phonograph boom their technical superiority combined with the name Edison often made them more desirable to consumers. But as the novelty of hearing recorded music wore off and consumers began to pay more attention to the artists and their music, Edison began to face considerable competition because he failed to recognize that musical recordings involved art as well as technology. . . .

TRYING TO BALANCE TECHNOLOGY AND AESTHETICS

Edison's name could produce short-term profits, but his early experience with both phonographs and motion pictures suggest some of the problems that would continue to confront him and his companies as new competitors entered the field. With his background in producer goods, Edison felt most comfortable as a manufacturer selling to businesspeople. He knew how to respond to complaints about technical problems. He was less certain about the aesthetic issues associated with the consumer market. . . .

As was the case with motion pictures, Edison would continually struggle between his tendency to focus on technology and the necessity of meeting the tastes of consumers. When technological issues regarding the design of phonographs or the quality of sound recordings dominated consumers' concerns, Edison was well prepared to satisfy them, but he and his companies often struggled when these concerns turned to aesthetic issues. Nonetheless, the ability of Edison, his laboratory, and his shops to produce technologically superior machines continued to provide important competitive advantages for the Edison phonograph and motion picture businesses.

Motion Pictures: The New Revolution

Thomas Alva Edison

Thomas Alva Edison's diary was published post-humously in 1948 and is one of the best accounts of his discoveries in the field of motion pictures. The vision he had for movies was in education rather than in entertainment. He felt the combination of camera and film could teach the world what it needed to know in the most direct manner. He even predicted that textbooks would become obsolete, replaced by motion pictures in school. When movies started specializing in amusing films, he decided not to take an active part in production, explaining he was an inventor not a theatrical producer. Still, Edison felt that nothing else had the potential for "great and permanent good to humanity" as the motion picture.

They say they are spending a million dollars nowadays to make just one big picture. If I had been told in the days of our first movie studio that anybody would spend a million dollars to produce a single film, I don't know whether I would have swallowed it or not. It would have been some effort.

It may seem curious, but the money end of the movies never hit me the hardest. The feature that did appeal to me about the whole thing was the educational possibilities I thought I could see. I had some glowing dreams about what the camera could be made to do and ought to do in teaching the world things it needed to know—teaching it in a more vivid, direct way.

I figured that after the novelty wore off, the camera would either be taken up by the big educators and pushed as a new agency in the schools—or that it would be developed mostly along straight amusement lines for entertainment and commercial purposes. I guess up to date the entertainment and

Excerpted from Thomas Edison, "Moving Pictures and the Arts: Money and Movies," in *The Diary and Sundry Observations of Thomas Alva Edison*, edited by Dagobert D. Runes. Copyright © 1948 Philosophical Library, Inc. Reprinted with permission from the Philosophical Library.

commercial purposes have won.

I don't know about the quality of the entertainment always, but I suspect there has been good money in it—for those who knew their business. When the industry began to specialize as a big amusement proposition I quit the game as an active producer.

A good many people seemed to wonder why I did so—maybe they still wonder. But the answer is simple enough. I was an inventor—an experimenter. I wasn't a theatrical producer. And I had no ambitions to become one.

If, on the other hand, the educational uses of the camera had come more to the front, as I had hoped, and I had seen an opportunity to develop some new ideas along those lines, my story as a producer might have been very different. I should have been far more interested in going on.

COMBINING MOVIES AND SOUND

Do you know that one of my first thoughts for the motion picture camera was to combine it with the phonograph? In fact, that was what primarily interested me in motion pictures—the hope of developing something that would do for the eye what the phonograph did for the ear.

My plan was to synchronize the camera and the phonograph so as to record sounds when the pictures were made, and reproduce the two in harmony. As a matter of fact, we did a lot of work along this line, and my talking pictures were shown in many theatres in the United States and foreign countries. I even worked on the possibility of an entire performance of grand opera, for example, being given in this way.

Another thought I had was that such a dual arrangement might record both the lives and the voices of the great men and women of the world. Can you realize the tremendous impetus this would be to the study of history and economics?

They are producing pictures of this kind now, I understand, by photographing and reproducing the sound waves. We were working, of course, from an entirely different angle—but we had the first of the so-called "Talking Pictures" in our laboratory thirty years ago.

We might have developed them into a greater commercial circulation if we had kept on—but I was interested in the educational and not the entertainment field. When the educators failed to respond I lost interest. What I had in mind was a bit ahead of the times, maybe. The world wasn't ready for the kind of education I had pictured.

MOVIES WILL REPLACE TEXTBOOKS

Maybe I'm wrong, but I should say that in ten years textbooks as the principal medium of teaching will be as obsolete as the horse and carriage are now. I believe that in the next ten years visual education—the imparting of exact information through the motion picture camera—will be a matter of course in all of our schools. The printed lesson will be largely supplemental—not paramount.

Let's see how visual education might work out in a practicable way. Suppose we take the development of the memory through the medium of the eye. Most of us have never learned how to use our eyes properly—and still fewer of us have ever learned how to remember properly the impressions that our eyes do register. Perhaps I can illustrate what I mean.

In the early days of the motion picture camera an especial problem for us was to find what kind of pictures people were most interested in. We were pioneers in a brand-new field. You must remember that at that time only a small percentage of the public had ever seen a motion picture film of any sort. And we soon discovered that our problem wasn't so much that of the showman as that of the experimenter, the educator.

An important fact that we ran up against right at the outset was the need to make our arrangement of scenes just as obvious and simple as possible. We found that if we didn't keep to an easy straight continuity it was difficult for many of the spectators to follow the picture at all. They hadn't been trained to visualize more than one thought at a time—and it seemed hard for some of them to do that. The average memory faculty had not been developed beyond the most elemental lines.

If one of the pretentious motion pictures of to-day, with its elaborate titles and multitude of characters and scenes, had been exhibited at that time it would probably have been a conspicuous failure. Half of the audience would have been hopelessly confused before it was finished.

If the motion picture has done nothing else it has been the greatest quickener of brain action that we have ever had. It has stirred up sluggish brain-cells as all of the printing presses in the world could not do.

It is easy enough to understand why, and yet this angle has probably never occurred to most of us. The motion picture has a definite physical impression to present to the eye, but it is an impression so swift that in order to register and apply it properly brain-cells that had not been used to hurried exercise had to learn to function far beyond any limits to which they had been accustomed. The automobile got us used to physical speed. It was the motion picture that got us used to mental speed. . . .

HOW MOVIES BEGAN

It was in 1890 that we decided that we were far enough advanced in our plans for the development of animated photography to warrant a special building for our work, but it was such an ungainly looking structure when it was done, and the boys had so much sport with it, that we called it "The Black Maria."

Our studio was almost as amazing as the pictures we made in it. We were looking for service, not art. The building itself was about twenty-five by thirty feet in dimensions, and we gave a grotesque effect to the roof by slanting it up in a hunch in the center and arranging shutters that could be opened or closed with a pulley to obtain the greatest benefit from the light.

Then, in order to make certain of as long a working day as possible, we swung the whole building on pivots, like an old-fashioned river bridge, so it could be turned to follow the course of the sun. We covered it with tar-paper outside, and painted it a dead black inside to bring our actors into the sharpest relief. It was a ghastly proposition for a stranger daring enough to brave its mysteries—especially when it began to turn like a ship in a gale. But we managed to make pictures there. And, after all, that was the real test. . . .

We didn't use artificial lights in those days. We had to depend altogether on nature. Therefore, it was a case of literally having to follow up the sun so as to extract all the benefit we could from every fugitive ray. Crude methods, the modern film producer may say, but they gave us results and fairly continuous results, too.

The phonograph first suggested the motion picture camera. I had been working for several years on my experiments for recording and reproducing sounds, and the thought occurred to me that it should be possible to devise an apparatus to do for the eye what the phonograph was designed to do for the ear.

That was the broad purpose, but how to accomplish that purpose was a problem which seemed more impossible the longer I studied it. It was in 1887 that I began my investigations, and photography, compared to what it is to-day, was in a decidedly crude state of development. Pictures were

---

THE FIRST TICKETS TO MOVING PICTURES

Alfred O. Tate, one of Edison's private secretaries, relates in his Edison biography the amusing events that led to the first moving picture public exhibition for a fee.

Many statements have been made concerning the first exhibition of moving pictures. The fixing of this date depends upon whether the exhibition was made publicly for a fee or privately during the course of the development of the art. . . .

It was not until the advent of the translucent, traveling photographic film that the art became practical and its commercialized initiation can be authentically established by the date when moving pictures, employing this method, first were shown publicly for a fee. That is the date that now, authentically, I am going to establish. . . .

The North American Phonograph Company, under the direction of Thomas R. Lombard, was preparing an exhibit of the phonograph. Lombard had seen a demonstration of the Kinetoscope at the laboratory, and it occurred to him that a profitable enterprise could be conducted if a number of them could be procured for exhibition at the World's Fair.

He consulted me and the proposal was placed before Edison, who approved it and agreed to construct twenty-five Kinetoscopes, and to sell them at the price of three hundred dollars each. . . .

The first installation [of the Kinetoscope] was to be made in New York, and in preparation for this I leased a small store. . . .

Here the ten machines were placed in the center of the room in two rows of five each, enclosed by a metal railing for the spectators to lean against when viewing the animated pictures. . . . In the window there was a printed announcement or advertisement whose legend I cannot now recall, and a plaster bust of Edison painted to simulate bronze. . . .

By noon on Saturday, the 14th day of April, 1894, everything was ready for the opening of the exhibit to the public on the following Monday. . . . I locked the door on the inside and we

made by "wet" plates, operated by involved mechanism. The modern dry films were unheard of.

I had only one fact to guide me at all. This was the principle of optics, technically called "the persistence of vision," which proves that the sensation of light lingers in the brain for anywhere from one-tenth to one-twentieth part of a second after the light itself has disappeared from the sight of the eye. . . .

all retired to the office in the rear to smoke and engage in general conversation. We had planned to have an especially elaborate dinner that evening at Delmonico's, then flourishing on the southeast corner of Broadway and Twenty-sixth Street, to celebrate the initiation of the Kinetoscope enterprise. From where I sat I could see the display window and the groups who stopped to gaze at the bust of Edison. And then a brilliant idea occurred to me.

"Look here," I said, pointing towards the window, "why shouldn't we make that crowd out there pay for our dinner tonight?". . .

I said to my brother, "you take charge of the machines. I'll sell tickets and," turning to Lombard, "you stand near the door and act as a reception committee. We can run till six o'clock and by that time we ought to have dinner money."

We all thought it a good joke. Lombard stationed himself at the head of the row of machines, my brother stood ready to supervise them, and I unlocked and opened the door and then entered the ticket booth where printed tickets like those now in use were ready to be passed out. And then the procession started. . . .

If we had wanted to close the place at six o'clock it would have been necessary to engage a squad of policemen. We got no dinner. At one o'clock in the morning I locked the door and we went to an all-night restaurant to regale ourselves on broiled lobsters, enriched by the sum of about one hundred and twenty dollars.

From that day forward the public exhibition of moving pictures through the medium of a translucent photographic film, substantially the same as that in use today, was maintained without a break until the Kinetoscopic method was adapted for screen production. I am the only surviving member of the group that introduced them in this form to the public on that memorable 14th day of April, 1894.

Alfred O. Tate, *Edison's Open Door.* New York: E.P. Dutton, 1938, pp. 282–87.

This fact served as the basic principle for various mechanical toys, creating the illusion of pictures that moved before the eyes of the beholder. A very simple contrivance of this kind was a spinning cardboard, revolving on a string. On one side was the picture of a man, and on the other side the picture of a galloping horse. As the card was spun, the man apparently leaped into the saddle of the horse, whereas what actually happened was that the revolutions of the card brought the second picture into view before the eye had lost the mental image of the first. I presume the inventor of the novelty made a good sum. He deserved to. . . .

CELLULOID, THE NEW, DRY FILM

There were many problems connected with the first motion picture camera, but before everything else came the question of making a unit machine—that is, one where all of the exposures needed could be made with the same apparatus and through the same lens. And this at once brought up the second difficulty. Obviously, it was quite impossible to construct any single camera capable of the proper speed and mechanism required for the purpose, and use glass plates for the exposures. I saw at once these would have to be discarded entirely, and any experiments would have to start from a brand new point of departure.

We tried various kinds of mechanisms and various kinds of materials and chemicals for our negatives. The experiments of a laboratory consist mostly in finding that something won't work. The worst of it is you never know beforehand, and sometimes it takes months, even years, before you discover you have been on the wrong line all the time. First we tried making a cylindrical shell, something like an ordinary phonograph cylinder, and sensitizing the surface in the hope of obtaining microscopic photographs which could be enlarged.

These impressions would have been no larger than the point of a pin, if successful, and, of course, our plan involved a tremendous magnifying process to produce results. But we couldn't find a substance for coating the cylinder that was sensitive enough for our need. The old dry albumen that had been used by photographers we found would not do at all. Then we tried a gelatine bromide of silver emulsion, and for a little while it looked like it might work.

The first minute impressions were all right, and seemed

clear enough for our purpose, but as soon as we undertook enlargements we saw we were stumped at the start. The bromide of silver was so coarse that all of the details of the negative were blotted out even in an eighth-of-an-inch size. We had to begin again, and this time we tried a different kind of mechanism with the idea of making larger pictures.

And again we found that we were wrong. Celluloid by this time was on the market—and we conceived the idea of a drum, over which a sheet of prepared celluloid was drawn, with the edges squeezed into narrow slots in the rim, like the old tin-foil phonograph. We had to take our pictures spirally, and they were so limited in size as a result that only the center of each could be brought into focus.

It was along about this point that George Eastman came into our experiments. I heard that he was working on a new kind of dry film, and asked him to come down and talk it over. The result was that his representative went back home to see what he could do in making a narrow strip of sensitized film that would operate on a roll. Without George Eastman I don't know what the result would have been in the history of the motion picture. The months that followed were a series of discouragements for all of us. While he was busy with the problem of chemicals we were busy with the problem of mechanics.

It is almost impossible for the layman to appreciate the extreme niceties of adjustment we had to overcome. Try to realize that we were dealing always with minute fractions of seconds. For instance, allowing forty-six exposures per second, as we did at first, we had to face the fact that the film had to be stopped and started again after each exposure. Now, allowing a minimum of 1/100 part of a second for every impression that was registered, you can see that practically half of our time was already gone, and in the remainder of the time we had to move the film forward the necessary distance for the next exposures.

And all this had to be done with the exactness of a watch movement. If there was the slightest variation in the movement of the film, or if it slipped at any time by so much as a hair's breadth, this fact was certain to show up in the enlargements. Finally we completed a mechanism that allowed the film to be moved in the uniform ratio of one-tenth part of the time needed for a satisfactory exposure, and permitted from twenty to forty such exposures per second.

It looked as though we were finished, and we tried the first roll of film jubilantly. Success was in our hands. But we had counted too soon.

The strips had been made in a one-half inch width that we thought was ample, but it was not enough. We had to make a larger size, allowing a one-inch surface for the emulsion, with a one-half inch margin for the perforations needed for the locking device that we used for starting and stopping the film.

This meant, of course, adjusting our mechanical apparatus also to carry the new-sized roll; but we did it at last, and soon the first of the new cameras was ready to show what it could do.

BIRTH OF THE KINETESCOPE

I didn't apply for the patent until two years later. I was very much occupied with other matters, and while we all congratulated ourselves on what we had accomplished, and knew we had an interesting and novel apparatus, we generally regarded it more or less as a curiosity with no very large practicable possibilities. It probably seems strange to the

Edison operates his film projector. This early invention was the forerunner to the modern motion picture.

world now, but such was the fact, even after we had exhibited our first pictures.

These were shown originally in an apparatus that we christened "The Kinetescope," consisting of a cabinet equipped with an electrical motor and battery, and carrying a fifty-foot band of film, passed through the field of a magnifying glass. They attracted quite a lot of attention at the World's Fair in Chicago in 1893, but we didn't think much of it until we found that two Englishmen, who had been interested in the exhibit, finding that I had carelessly neglected to patent the apparatus abroad, had started an independent manufacture on a considerable scale.

Of course, it was too late then to protect myself, and I concentrated my efforts in devising a mechanism that would project the pictures on a screen before an audience. This consisted largely in reversing the action of the apparatus for taking the original pictures.

The main trouble we found here was the question of "flicker" and eye strain. It was necessary primarily to find and establish a uniform speed both for photographing and projecting the pictures. If we kept the number of exposures down too low it made the action jerky and hard to follow on the screen. Nearly all of our first pictures allowed from thirty to forty exposures per second, although the number has since been reduced down to from fifteen to twenty.

THE MISSION OF THE MOVIES

I consider that the greatest mission of the motion picture is first to make people happy . . . to bring more joy and cheer and wholesome good will into this world of ours. And God knows we need it.

Second—to educate, elevate, and inspire. I believe that the motion picture is destined to revolutionize our educational system, and that in a few years it will supplant largely, if not entirely, the use of text-books in our schools. Books are clumsy methods of instruction at best, and often even the words of explanation in them have to be explained.

I should say that on the average we get only about two per-cent efficiency out of school books as they are written to-day. The education of the future, as I see it, will be conducted through the medium of the motion picture, a visualized education, where it should be possible to obtain a one-hundred-per-cent efficiency.

The motion picture has tremendous possibilities for the training and development of the memory. There is no medium for memory-building as productive as the human eye.

That is another basic reason for the motion picture in the school. It will make a more alert and more capable generation of citizens and parents. You can't make a trained animal unless you start with a puppy. It is next to impossible to teach an old dog new tricks.

I do not believe that any other single agency of progress has the possibilities for a great and permanent good to humanity that I can see in the motion picture. And those possibilities are only beginning to be touched.

CHAPTER 4

Working Through Failures and Moderate Successes

Edison's Optimism and Persistence

Gene Adair

Biographer and former teacher Gene Adair provides an overview of some of Edison's inventions that did not herald success, yet reminds us that he never allowed his failures to discourage him. Although he lost several million dollars attempting some inventions, he good-naturedly shrugged it off and went on to his next project.

In 1918, Edison left the movie business altogether. Meanwhile, the center of the film industry had shifted from the East Coast to the sunnier climates of Southern California, where the name Hollywood quickly became synonymous with the movies.

In addition to the development of motion pictures and the phonograph, the work at West Orange included a dizzying array of other research. At one time or another, there were experiments with X rays, electric-train motors, flying machines, cheap housing made from poured concrete, and electric automobiles. These projects show the diversity of Edison's interests and the amazing fertility of his mind, even though many of them did not get very far.

UNDETERRED OPTIMISM

Though experimental failures never dampened Edison's enthusiasm for invention, neither did setbacks of another kind. When fire destroyed much of the West Orange complex in December 1914 (though it spared the main laboratory), Edison scarcely blinked. Looking on as the spectacular flames consumed his factory buildings, Edison turned to his son Charles and said: "Where's Mother? Get her over here, and her friends too. They'll never see a fire like this again." Within days, he was rebuilding.

Excerpted from Gene Adair, *Thomas Alva Edison.* Copyright © 1996 Gene Adair. Reprinted with permission from Oxford University Press, Inc.

ELECTRIC CARS YIELD BETTER STORAGE BATTERY

Edison's relentless determination was especially apparent in his efforts to develop an improved storage battery. (Storage batteries, unlike so-called primary batteries, can be periodically recharged.) In the late 1800s, lead-acid batteries were the only kind of storage battery in use; they depended on a chemical reaction involving lead, lead peroxide, and a sulfuric acid solution to produce the electric current. Edison believed that a better storage battery—something lighter, longer lasting, and more efficient than the lead-acid type—was possible, and throughout the early 1900s, his laboratory struggled to produce one. By 1909, after many a costly and frustrating experiment, a battery based on a reaction between nickel oxide, iron, and a potassium hydroxide solution was perfected. It found a variety of uses—in devices such as miner's lamps, train lights, and railroad signals—and became one of Edison's best-selling products. However, the main use Edison had originally intended for it, to power electric cars, faded when gasoline-powered automobiles, such as those produced by Henry Ford, came to dominate the growing car market between 1908 and 1910.

Edison's hopes for the battery brightened in 1912 when Ford asked him to adapt the battery to a car ignition system. Ford was looking for a better way to start his Model T than the familiar, arm-wrenching hand crank. Unfortunately, Edison's battery lacked sufficient power to start the motor and failed entirely in cold weather. But even though Edison's battery did not suit Ford's purposes, the inventor and the auto maker became good friends and later took vacation trips together.

STORAGE BATTERY BRIEFLY POWERS NAVY SUBMARINES

Edison's storage battery also attracted the attention of the United States Navy, which was especially interested in using it to power its submarines. This interest intensified when World War I erupted among the European nations in 1914 and threatened to involve the United States as well. The navy not only tested Edison's batteries on its new experimental submarine, the E2, but in 1915 made the inventor chairman of the Naval Consulting Board.

Unfortunately, the E2 experiments had a tragic outcome. In 1916, hydrogen gas escaping from the batteries ignited, causing an explosion that killed five sailors. Although it was clear that the crew had ignored basic safety precautions, the batteries were blamed for the mishap. Any hopes Edison had for producing submarine batteries ended right there.

Despite the accident, Edison remained an active advisor to the navy and was instrumental in planning a naval research laboratory, which he modeled after the facility at West Orange. After the United States entered the war in 1917, he concentrated his experimental efforts on ways of detecting enemy submarines. The experiments produced no practical results, however, and the navy was not interested in any of Edison's other ideas. By the time the war ended in 1918, the inventor was disillusioned with the naval bureaucracy. . . .

During the first two decades of the 20th century, the West Orange complex grew into a major industrial operation. In 1900, Edison's factories employed about 3,000 workers; by 1920, more than 10,000 employees staffed his assembly lines. The laboratory, which formed what today would be called a research and development department, became only a tiny (if still vital) part of the total organization.

In running this industrial empire, Edison was not always the most progressive of bosses. With some of his men—especially those who had been with him a long time—he could be generous and would keep them on the payroll even after they stopped being productive. Yet, with most employees— the younger, college-trained researchers as well as the countless workers who assembled his phonographs, storage batteries, and other products—he was tough and uncompromising. He kept wages low—a lab chemist might make as little as $20 a week, while a factory worker as little as $1.50 a day. Long opposed to unions, he had little sympathy for the grievances of labor. When a strike occurred in 1903, for example, he had wasted no time in breaking it. As someone to whom work meant everything, Edison had trouble understanding why others could not be as dedicated to their jobs as he was.

THE SEARCH FOR NEW SOURCES OF RUBBER

Despite his advancing age, Edison refused to slow down. He even had a lab built at his winter home in Fort Myers, Florida, so that he could work during the months when he was away from West Orange.

Among the last projects in which the inventor was personally involved was an effort to find a domestic source of rubber. Because of World War I and the disruptions it caused in international trade, American businessmen realized the dangers of relying on foreign sources of raw materials. After the war ended, fears abounded that British and Dutch interests were conspiring to monopolize the rubber supply. These concerns prompted Edison, with financial help from Henry Ford and the tire maker Harvey Firestone, to begin an intensive search in the late 1920s for a homegrown plant that would yield a good supply of rubber.

Edison planted hundreds of shrubs and trees around his home in Fort Myers and enlisted the aid of dozens of botanists, both professionals and amateurs, in collecting plant specimens. His obsession with the project, which was typical of how he approached everything he ever did, caused Mina to note: "Everything has turned to rubber in our family. We talk rubber, think rubber, dream rubber."

Edison continued working on the rubber project right up to the eve of his death and did manage to produce a high strain of rubber from the goldenrod plant. By this time, however, the British and Dutch attempts at monopoly had collapsed. Rubber prices dropped, and the fears about a short supply faded. Yet, although the project had little impact in the end, it kept Edison busy and happy. He had officially retired in 1926, leaving the administration of his company to his son Charles. Searching for rubber gave him an ongoing sense of purpose. . . .

TRAITS OF EDISON'S GENIUS

The most famous saying attributed to Edison—that genius is "one percent inspiration and ninety-nine percent perspiration"—summed up the inventor's lifelong belief in doggedly working through the problems of any given project. Yet the statement underestimates the role of inspiration in Thomas Edison's work. That special creative spark, the ability to conceive of things no one else has thought of, was definitely present in Edison, and it was a critical factor in his success.

Closely linked to Edison's creative gifts were his unfailing optimism and extraordinary confidence in himself. That confidence, which included a flair for brash showmanship and which often surfaced as unrestrained boastfulness, helped Edison over many a rough spot. It kept him going in the face of experimental setbacks and competition from rivals, and it reassured conservative investors who might otherwise have withdrawn their support.

In the end, probably no one can say exactly why Edison so towered above all other inventors. But the world can only be grateful that he did.

The Great Ore Mining Bust

William Adams Simonds

Edison had an idea for a new process to extract pure iron from exhausted mines in the Appalachian region. At the time it was believed that iron ore was becoming scarce, yet there was an ever-growing demand for it. Edison boasted that the thousands of acres he leased near Ogdensburg, New Jersey, would keep America supplied with iron ore for many years to come. Edison worked in the mining fields with his men blasting and crunching their way through the mountains, but "Baby Ogden," as the project was called, was a losing venture for almost a decade. Edison's competitors located huge quantities of ore in the Mesabi Range in Minnesota that needed little excavation to be useable, and could be mined at a considerable savings despite the distance from the Eastern smelters. Edison could not compete, and the Baby Ogden had already depleted several million dollars of Edison's total wealth. But the inventor's optimism shrugged off the expense as he turned to other ventures. William Adams Simonds, a biographer of Edison as well as Henry Ford, gives this account of the failed operation.

Increasing demands for steel to keep pace with the progress which had been made by industry in so many different fields convinced Edison that time was ripe to put to practical test his theories of magnetic ore-milling. The chief eastern iron deposits in the Lake Champlain region of New York and in eastern Pennsylvania could not suffice much longer for the requirements of industry.

Thanks to his foresight, he controlled many thousands of low-grade ore deposits in northern New Jersey. The Ogden

Excerpted from William Adams Simonds, *Edison: His Life, His Work, His Genius.* Copyright © 1934 The Bobbs-Merrill Company; copyright renewed © 1962 William Adams Simonds. Reprinted with permission from Scribner, a division of Simon & Schuster.

mine, his largest, had been worked in earlier days. Going there, he set up headquarters with W.S. Mallory as vice-president, and "Johnny" Randolph, office boy in Menlo Park days (now John T. Randolph), as secretary.

At first, laborers refused to stay at the mine because of the poor accommodations. Edison studied the difficulty. "If we want to keep men here, we must make it attractive for the women. Let us build houses with running water and electric lights, and rent them at a low rate."

That day he designed a suitable cottage, and fifty were constructed immediately. Their comforts were described attractively in advertisements inserted in the New York papers, and more than six hundred and fifty applicants presented themselves in response. A new town sprang up, named "Edison."

A New Way to Mine

Edison had not been at the mine long before he decided that entirely new methods must be evolved if he was to succeed in getting out the ore cheaply enough to interest eastern ironmasters. His daring conception caused experienced mining men everywhere to express doubts. He proposed to tear down the mountain bodily and grind its boulders to dust; and from the dust to extract the iron and prepare it for shipment to the mills; all at such a low cost that the venture might be profitable.

Two shifts of five men each would handle twenty thousand tons of ore a day, blasting the rock by dynamite from the mountain, crushing it, reducing the iron to cement-like proportions, separating it from rock and earth and making it into bricklets.

Except for steam shovels, engines and dynamos, the rest of the machinery had to be devised by himself; for nothing existed to perform the kind of work he demanded. Ordinarily, ore-bearing rock was blasted to comparatively small-sized boulders before crushing. Because of the expense, he refused to use dynamite except for the initial blast, planning enormous rolls to crush the large rocks.

He was warned that the blow against the rollers when a boulder dropped into them would tear any engine to pieces. He replied: "I shall bring the rollers up to a high speed, and then, just before the boulder is dropped in, cut the engine loose. The momentum of the rollers will do the rest."

At the scene of the blasting the rock was loaded on skip

cars, carried by gravity down-grade, and broken into smaller pieces through five sets of rolls, of which the largest were six feet in diameter—their moving parts weighed about seventy tons.

The giant rolls, "rock-crackers," had to be seen and heard to be appreciated.

> It was only as one might stand in their vicinity and hear the thunderous roar accompanying the smashing and rending of the massive rocks as they disappeared from view, that the mind was overwhelmed with a sense of the magnificent proportions of this operation—Pieces of rock weighing more than a half a ton would be shot up in the air to a height of twenty or twenty-five feet.

The broken fragments next fell into an intermediate set of rolls four feet in diameter, then through two sets of three feet, and a last one of two feet, whence they were transported by conveyor to an adjoining mill to be pulverized by "three-high rolls" to the consistency of fine sand. After screening, the particles were lifted to a tower and dropped past magnets in a fine stream, the ore being drawn off to one side and the sand passing on.

After separation, the iron ore passed on and joined with a resinous binder in a mixing house, whence it was carried to briqueting machines, pressed into molds and moved by slow conveyors into baking ovens. While still hot, the briquets were loaded into railroad cars for shipment to the steel furnaces.

This brief description hardly does justice to the immense labor the inventor performed at Edison. For five years he worked there, returning to West Orange only for week-end visits. He made his home in a plain clapboard structure nicknamed "The White House." Grimy and exhausting as was the work, Edison thoroughly enjoyed it.

"I never felt better in my life than during the years I worked here," he told T.C. Martin. "Hard work, nothing to divert my thought, clear air and simple food made life very pleasant." ...

ALWAYS INNOVATIVE

Many stories have been told of Edison's activities at the mine. He asked an engineer to submit sketches for special machinery to cover one of the operations and received three, none of which was satisfactory. "It's too bad," the engineer remarked, "because there is no other way we can do it." Edison said nothing, but on his return from week-ending at Orange, laid on the engineer's desk sketches showing forty-eight other ways of accomplishing the same operation. . . .

In his efforts to interest blast furnace men in his ore, Edison approached John Fritz of the Bethlehem Steel Company. Fritz realized the merit of the undertaking and said: "I am willing to help you. I mix a little sentiment with business, and I will give you an order for one hundred thousand tons."

Edison remarked that Fritz sat "right down and gave me the order.". . .

COMPETITION FORCES CLOSURE

When a test of the Edison briquets had indicated considerable increase in the yield, Edison began to plan a larger works in a more favorable location. The cost of coke presented an obstacle to eastern steel manufacturers; in that item the Pittsburgh builders had a price advantage of about

THE CHALLENGE OF SUCCESS AFTER FORTY

In this article, Bernard Finn describes some of the challenges Edison faced when, after ten years of successful inventing, he moved his staff into the new West Orange lab that was ten times larger than Menlo Park. Electrical technology was changing and since Edison was unqualified to follow some of the fields that were opening up, he pursued the ones that had served him well in the past.

The great inventor had failed to foresee the effect of changes in the world around him. Thus, his work in the second half of his life never attained the level he reached in earlier years. . . .

By the mid 1880s, the nature of electrical technology was changing dramatically. The telephone, alternating current power systems, and newly discovered radio waves all required elaborate concepts, often mathematical in form. In response to these changes, universities introduced programs to educate a new generation of students in electrical engineering and corporations established research laboratories to keep pace with possibilities of the rapidly expanding technology. Edison had been a principal contributor to the arrival of the new age, but his education and training left him unqualified to pursue the fields that were opening up.

Rather than try to acquire additional skills (notably in electronics), Edison concentrated in those areas that had served him well in the past. He made important contributions to an improved phonograph, motion pictures, and storage batteries;

one dollar a ton. By erecting a plant nearer the fuel deposits of eastern Pennsylvania, Edison hoped to lower transportation costs.

Even while he planned, the fate of his entire enterprise was threatened!

For several years, northern Indians had repeated tales of mountains of iron on the Minnesota shore of Lake Superior. When the white man finally investigated, he found a heap of solid red ore rising one hundred and fifty feet above ground, so exposed that it could be shoveled out with practically no excavating. There was iron enough to last the Pittsburgh steelmakers for many decades.

True, it was eleven hundred miles away, nine hundred of them over water. Special ore ships were designed to bring the mineral from the northern wilds to the southern Erie shore. Loaded on cars at Mesaba Monday morning, it was in

less successfully, he established processes for iron ore separation and the manufacture of concrete houses. In his final years, he searched for a domestically available plant that might serve as an efficient source of rubber. Nothing quite came up to the level of what had been achieved with the much smaller group at Menlo Park.

Finally, Edison's concept of a large research laboratory was flawed. At Menlo Park, he could be at the center of virtually all projects, directing and inspiring his colleagues. He thought he could do the same at West Orange, but, in the larger setting, a different style was required. The leader of such a laboratory needed to have management skills and provide direction, but did not have to be the sole source of ideas. Indeed, the modern research laboratory would decentralize the process, providing common services for multiple workstations. This is the type of industrial laboratory that would emerge early in the 20th century, notably at General Electric and the Bell Laboratories.

Edison had thought he could extrapolate from his earlier years in plotting his life after 40. He was in error, because he did not foresee the effect of changes in the world around him or in his own personal needs. Still, it is unlikely that he had many regrets over the remaining 44 years leading to his death in 1931. As he said shortly after he had lost several years of effort and more than $2,000,000 in the iron ore extraction process, he had "a hell of a good time."

Bernard D. Finn, "Thomas Alva Edison After Forty: The Challenge of Success," *USA Today*, July 1994, pp. 84–93.

Edison poses next to his model of a concrete house. Edison's patented system of cast-iron molds made it possible for the concrete of an entire house to be poured in a single day.

steel rails or bridges by Saturday night.

The resourceful Pittsburgh barons led by Carnegie and his associated Phipps, Frick and Schwab, were able to ship their ore more cheaply than Edison could hope to extract it. When the price of pig iron dropped below ten dollars a ton, he recognized the inevitable. Nature and a canny Scotsman had found a cheaper way to supply the demands of the market, against which odds he was wise to suspend operations. When the price dropped still lower, he told Mallory they would have to close the works.

A Costly Yet Valuable Experience

It was a difficult decision to reach, for Edison was more enthusiastic over the operation than ever. However, the plant was several hundred thousand dollars in debt, with no prospect of paying it off. On the way back to West Orange, the future was discussed.

"I have never been connected personally with a company," said Edison, "which failed to pay its debts. The Concentrating Works will be no exception."

"There was nothing in Mr. Edison's manner," said Mallory, "to show that he was specially disappointed, his every thought being for the future, and as to what could be done to pull us out of the financial situation in which we found ourselves, and to take advantage of the knowledge we had acquired at so great a cost."

It was estimated that fully two million dollars had been expended at Edison, of which the inventor personally had put up fully three-quarters, derived largely from the sale of his General Electric stock.

"Well," said he, "it's all gone, but we had a hell of a good time spending it!"

Several lines of endeavor were considered; probable financial returns from the phonograph works were estimated. Edison believed the experience and knowledge gained in ore-reduction could be applied to some practical use, possibly in the manufacture of cement. Then there was the storage battery which, despite the labors of many inventors, was still in a primitive stage.

The upshot of their conference was that they decided to invade both fields—Edison to conduct experiments seeking a battery which would not be self-destructive—Mallory to build a plant for manufacture of Portland cement according to a new process.

The Elusive Storage Battery

Matthew Josephson

After his flop with ore mining, Edison discovered the Automobile Age had started. These vehicles were powered by an assortment of engines: steam, gasoline, and electric motors. Edison felt the gasoline engine was unscientific and wasteful compared to the electric motor. Therefore he began a quest to build a better storage battery. Newly developed batteries were tested and production started. Soon reports were coming in that Edison's battery containers leaked and production stopped immediately. He took back all defective batteries at his own cost and suffered huge financial losses. Edison's storage battery company was out of money, so revenues from his motion picture company were used to finance continued experimentation. In 1909 the battery was finished and production began. Twelve months later a million dollars' worth of the long-life batteries had been sold—a profitable beginning for this Edison company that has continued to this day.

When Edison had first gone up to the Jersey highlands in 1890 to crush magnetite rock, the world was given over to the Bicycle Craze. Everywhere, from St. Petersburg to San Francisco, people were tasting a new freedom of movement; young and middle-aged, bold men in knickerbockers and daring ladies in bloomers dashed about on their pneumatic-tired velocipedes, down the open roads, to the country, the fields and the flowers, and the open sky, at a speed of ten miles an hour; while those who plodded along in horse-drawn vehicles looked at them envyingly.

But a decade later, when Edison came down from his hills, beaten but undaunted, the Automobile Age had begun. The

Excerpted from Matthew Josephson, *Edison.* Copyright © 1959 Matthew Josephson. Copyright renewed 1987 by Carl Josephson. Reprinted with permission from Harold Ober Associates Incorporated.

fascination of rapid movement was more intoxicating still at twenty, or even thirty miles an hour, thanks to the horseless carriage. In light coupés or phaetons powered by all sorts of steam and gasoline engines, or electric motors, some three thousand Americans were already "burning up the roads"— living man's dream of devouring distance in self-propelled chariots. The first crop of steam cars and gas buggies were noisy, hot, and bothersome; they stank and gave much trouble mechanically; yet every year they gained in following.

Edison, on occasion, tried the early gas buggies and steamers, and kindled to them at once. For him, the faster the better. Although these vehicles had been imported from Europe since the 1880s, one heard nowadays of "automobile inventors" who were attached to almost every carriage shop in the Middle West.

ENVISIONING ELECTRIC CARS

Edison allowed that the horse was doomed; the future would belong to the motored carriage. Like others, he foresaw a future in which millions would ride to their business or their pleasure in self-propelled carriages and trucks. He also ventured to predict that most of them would be driven by electric motors and storage batteries.

Why electric cars? A survey made in New York at the end of 1899 showed that of a hundred motorcabs in use in the downtown area, ninety were powered by storage batteries. Compared with cars using steam engines, which were heavy, or gas engines, then most unreliable, the electric runabout was clean, light, and quiet. Carriage builders were producing "electrics" in goodly number, by installing lead batteries and small motors in a Studebaker or Columbia vehicle. But who knew as much as Edison about electrical machines? It was the right time, he judged, to enter this field and contrive a product more practical than any other.

After his ore-separating venture was over, he had entertained all sorts of plans for new lines of activity. "I have enough ideas to break the Bank of England," he used to say. The phonograph shops and the motion picture studio were humming with business by 1900. Another project was the Edison Portland Cement Company, which would use his big rock crushers for grinding cement and limestone. He also contemplated a novel engineering scheme for the construction of low-cost concrete dwellings, a plan that needed several years of preparation. But, though he worked at or directed these and a good many other smaller affairs concurrently, there was always some one ruling idea that dominated his thoughts for a given period, and engaged his hopes above other ventures. Now it was the electric car—and its *sine qua non*, the storage battery. He saw the "commercial need" for the new product he had fixed upon. Like the incandescent lamp, it would conquer the masses for him once more. Hence the great plunge into the storage battery project. A cautionary thought should have come to him.

ENCOUNTERING HENRY FORD

Three years earlier, at a festive gathering of members of the Association of Edison Illuminating Companies (the trade association of electric utilities using his system) at Manhattan Beach, New York, he met by chance one of that anxious breed of automobile inventors, a thin, long-legged young man with pale-blue eyes, named Henry Ford. Ford was then employed as chief engineer at the Detroit Edison Company's powerhouse, and had been introduced to Edison by the head of that company, Alexander Dow. "There's a young fellow," said Dow, "who has made a *gas* car." (The worthy Mr. Dow, in those days, kept pestering Henry Ford, who was a good electrician, to make an electric car instead.) The electrical men present had in fact been discussing with Edison the possible economies of charging storage batteries for the use of streetcars and private vehicles, during low-traffic hours at the lighting plants. But Ford was one of those who clung steadfastly to the gasoline engine. It was his first meeting with Edison.

For long years Henry Ford had fairly worshiped Thomas A. Edison as the greatest of inventors and regarded him as the example whom he, a mechanic of inventive disposition, desired above all to emulate. Now he was invited to sit next to this great man. He was shy, and usually dull in conversation. But when asked to describe the components of his first automobile model, the young engineer became animated, and Edison, cupping his ear, listened with keen interest.

The older man plied Ford with questions. Edison, who could be curt and discouraging to aspiring inventors, was impressed with what he heard. He brought his fist down upon the table and said, "Young man, that's the thing! You have it!— the self-contained unit carrying its own fuel with it. Keep at it." Such a simple gas engine powered with what Edison called "hydrocarbon," as cheap as kerosene, and soon to be available everywhere along the road, would be most practical if it were perfected. At that period the unlettered Ford did not even know, as he recalled, what the word hydrocarbon meant. But previously he had met with much discouragement in his part-time work on his "quadricycle." The fact that America's greatest inventive genius had given him prompt and positive encouragement was worth worlds to him. . . .

BUILD A BETTER BATTERY

But while Edison had given Henry Ford excellent advice, he himself soon forgot all about it. In talking of automobiles he had remarked that electric runabouts had a radius limited to the vicinity of power stations; the lead-sulphur storage batteries then available were heavy, difficult to recharge correctly, and corroded quickly. But the years passed and those petrol engines were still as balky and stinking as ever. Edison, therefore, must develop an electrically driven car. As portable power plants for carriages the contemporary storage batteries also gave trouble. But Edison would build a better battery—who else? One that would weigh little, give great power, last forever! And small enough to be carried in a valise—a package of power that could be used in a thousand different ways to lighten man's burdens.

Edison "proceeded to each new undertaking, no matter how difficult, with the expectant joy of a naive child," one of his expert chemists observed at about this time. From 1900 on, he had eyes for nothing but the "miniature reservoir of electric force" that he must create. . . .

The whole idea of the "secondary" or storage battery had fascinated scientists for a century, ever since the time of Volta's primary cell. The voltaic cell, working by chemical action, changed chemical energy into electricity, but exhausted itself regularly and required renewal of its components. The possibility of a secondary cell, which, after having accumulated electrical force and having been discharged, could be recharged an almost indefinite number of times, by being "reversed," had also been present in men's minds for many years now. The first reversible, or "storage," battery had been invented in France, in 1859, by Planté, and marked a sensational advance in the electrical art; twenty years later the Faure battery of lead and sulphuric acid was perfected, a veritable "box of electricity," that stored energy and gave it back.

On first inspecting the Faure storage battery, Lord Kelvin exclaimed that it embodied the realization of dreams he had scarcely hoped would be realized in his lifetime.

As soon as there were practicable generators producing current economically, electrical scientists saw in the storage battery a most useful auxiliary, a portable reservoir of power. But the lead and sulphuric acid storage battery of the eighties and nineties, despite the helpful energy it yielded, remained heavy and corrosive. Edison had experimented with lead batteries many years before and thrown them aside. The claims for them were exaggerated. He once remarked, "When a man gets on to accumulators [storage batteries] his inherent capacity for lying comes out."

In looking at the problem of the horseless carriage in 1900 he had concluded that the gasoline engine was "unscientific" and wasteful compared with the electric motor. But in considering the batteries available as motive power, he was led to the conclusion that they also were inefficient. Their lead-acid components were scientifically incompatible and unnatural; they were too heavy; the corrosion of metal by acid constantly limited durability and efficiency. "I guess I'll have to make a battery," he said.

He defined the problem and the objectives for himself: to attempt an entirely new voltaic combination that would make his "box of electricity" light, durable, undeteriorating, quickly chargeable, and economical. Such an instrument, he felt in 1900, would "open up a new epoch in electricity." In his notebooks he wrote, "The object . . . to produce a practicable battery which will permit the storage of a larger amount of energy per pound of material than possible with the type of battery using lead electrodes."

His idea at the start was to use an alkaline solution as his electrolyte, so that his metals would not be corroded. The negative element would be some form of iron, or iron oxide. On the choice of the positive element he was less decided; he would hunt for it. In his first experiments he worked with copper oxide in various combinations, then examined hundreds of other materials. . . .

As in the early 1880s, during the electric light investigations at Menlo Park, he got together a staff of expert technicians to assist him; by 1901, he had a force of about ninety persons, among them several accomplished physicists and chemists, with Dr. J.W. Aylsworth as head of the chemical

department. Without regard for cost, samples of every
known material were assembled, and every possible tool or
device that could be of aid. Having gathered personnel and
equipment, he gave the signal for the hunt to begin. Hundreds of tests were made of various grades of copper and
finely divided iron, and the results set down painstakingly in
laboratory notebooks. This project was very different from
ore separating, or from improving the motion picture camera; it was like the old days at Menlo Park, with its all-night
sessions when time and labor meant nothing. The number
of experiments mounted up into the hundreds, then to the
thousands; at over ten thousand, Edison said, "they turned
the register back to zero and started over again." A year,
eighteen months went by, and they had not even a clue. . . .

THE ANSWER ELUDES HIM AND THE SEARCH CONTINUES

As [Edison's assistant A.E.] Kennelly pointed out, the chemical processes going on in those battery cells under the hundreds of different combinations tried were really of a
tremendous complexity. If you tried, for instance, to make
the negative electrodes (iron) lighter, you increased the rate
of deterioration. If you added something else, such as copper
oxide, it created new variables. Then there were the tricky
problems posed by the electrolyte, an alkaline solution of 25
per cent caustic potash (KOH); this would not corrode metals, like sulphuric acid, but the cell capacity tended to drop
off quickly. It seemed to need something to improve its conductivity. What that missing factor was would take a long
time to find out. Then there was also a great drag hunt over
a wide field for the right combination of metals to make up
the positive electrode. They tried cadmium-copper, cobalt,
magnesium, and, after many trials, nickel hydrate in various
forms. In this area Edison and his associates began to get
better results, and they felt a little more cheerful.

In the search for an improved positive electrode, Edison
carried on his experiments by taking carbon strips and filling their pores with every conceivable substance that might
serve as the positive element of an electrical couple. After
charging, he tested for a galvanometer deflection on dis-
charge, but usually got no results. Many photographs of the
1900s show him standing at a laboratory table about fifteen
feet long and covered with some four hundred test tubes,
each containing different electrolyte solutions, in which he

tried his various electrical couples. That was what was so time-consuming. The tests of these different nickel-and-iron couples were made in terms of milliampere hours, and some of the early tests showed only around 300 milliamperes. Gradually, as the material was improved, the figure crept up to 500 milliamperes; and at last in 1903, while Edison was away on a trip to Canada seeking a good source of nickel, the figures went up to 1,000 milliamperes. Aylsworth, who was in charge of the tests, remembered afterward how vastly pleased Edison was to learn of this advance upon his return to West Orange.

Nickel hydrate, the most promising of materials tested for the positive electrode, was, however, a poor conductor; in order to get the desired electrical action, through an improved contact, Edison considered and tested a great variety of conducting substances that might be mixed and packed into the pockets of his battery cells with the nickel hydrates. But that was not easily found either. Sometimes the nickel gave trouble; sometimes it was the pure iron that was most mischievous. Very little was known then of any of these metals in their chemically pure state. In 1903 Edison built a small plant for the manufacture of batteries at Glen Ridge, a few miles outside of Orange, where he kept a team of trained men working for long months to refine various grades of iron and nickel, so as to learn what he could.

At sixty, stout and round-faced and deafer than ever, Edison had nonetheless changed very little in spirit and method since he had invented the carbon filament lamp thirty years earlier. There was the same abandonment to unending studies, no matter how difficult. His temper, to be sure, was a little shorter nowadays, sometimes violent when a clumsy mechanic upset things; but he continued to show an unfailing patience in the face of repeated disappointments. In fact, it was a rule with him never to show grief or bitterness, even when some long-prepared experiment proved to be a failure. The only difference in method was the larger organization he used; his staff of ninety, including trained scientists, technicians, draftsmen, and plain mechanics, was a pretty big laboratory around 1900. . . .

Walter Mallory, his loyal companion of the ore-milling adventure, used to come down about once a month from the new Edison cement works, and ask Edison whether he were making any progress in the storage battery experiments.

When, after several months, he still heard that nothing had been accomplished, he thought he would offer his condolences. But to his surprise, Edison flashed his fine, sudden smile and said emphatically, "Why, man, I've got a lot of results. I know several thousand things that won't work!"

To his chief chemist Aylsworth, he once revealed something of his deep inward torment, however, when he said with much feeling, "In phonographic work we can use our ears and our eyes, aided by powerful microscopes; but in the battery our difficulties cannot be seen or heard, but must be observed by our mind's eye."

Finally, a Breakthrough

He gave the utmost care to the design of an entirely new battery form, to the size and shape of the containing pockets of its plates; and, after making many of his rough sketches and having them drafted precisely and built up as models, he evolved a novel structure of nickel-plated steel, the positive pockets being packed with nickel hydrate and the negative being of iron oxide. The difficulty experienced in obtaining a good electrical contact in the positive element, it was remarked at the time, put lots of gray hairs in Edison's head. Finally, after many trials, he decided upon a certain form of graphite, that was mixed with the nickel hydrate filling the positive pockets, and found this satisfactory.

At last, in 1903, he was ready to test his batteries in actual usage. He installed them in carriages with a small electric motor and chain drive, and ran these vehicles over the rough country roads near Orange. Records were kept on test sheets and closely scanned. In his laboratory Edison also set up an electrical apparatus that jolted his battery cells up and down, day and night, in simulation of heavy road usage. He wanted his battery to be able to withstand abuse, to be foolproof.

Tom Robins, the conveyor belt inventor, dropped in at the library one day in 1904, just as Edison was getting ready to manufacture his new product. As the two men sat talking there was a loud crash just outside the window, as of some heavy object that had fallen; then another, and after a minute, another. Robins was alarmed, but Edison never turned a hair. After a while a workman came in and said, "Second floor O.K., Mr. Edison." Edison nodded and ordered, "Now try the third floor." To the wondering visitor he gravely explained that he was testing the endurance of his storage battery—by having packages of them thrown out of the windows of the upper floors of his laboratory. "For a scientist, Edison used some mighty peculiar methods," Robins reflected.

PRODUCTION BEGINS

At Silver Lake, in the summer of 1904, the manufacturing plant was made ready, special machine tools were set out, and 450 workmen were engaged. Production slowly got under way, and in the first season several thousand cells of the first battery model, the "E," were turned out. The demand far exceeded what Edison could supply; merchants and transport concerns had the first Edison storage batteries installed in light delivery wagons and, at the outset, found their electric carriages and trucks highly convenient.

With his usual self-confidence Edison had started a rousing publicity campaign for his "revolutionary" storage battery, even before he was ready to manufacture it. Once more, he did a thorough advance-agent job, whetting the public's curiosity to a high pitch, so that when "The Wizard's Newest Marvel" finally arrived—so the battery was heralded in the press—people really believed it was such. Thus, in authorized interviews during 1903, and early in 1904, he announced that there would soon be "a miniature dynamo in every home . . . an automobile for every family." Men had said that no commercially successful battery could be made without lead. "The new battery means that another impossible thing has been accomplished." Lead batteries deteriorated rapidly even when they were not being used; they contained destructive acids; they leaked and were dead after a few months' use in an automobile. The new Edison battery had great power, weighed next to nothing, had neither acid nor lead, would not deteriorate when not in use, was almost endlessly rechargeable, and could withstand almost any mistreatment. He concluded:

> Yes the new battery will settle the horse—not at once but by degrees. The price of automobiles will be reduced. . . . In fact I hope that the time has nearly arrived when every man may not only be able to light his own house, but charge his own machinery, heat his rooms, cook his food, etc., by electricity, without depending on anyone else for these services.

In short, he had "revolutionized the world of power" the newspapers reported; he had brought forth the "age of stored electricity," with independent power sources that were destined to change sea travel, land transport, warfare, and agriculture. The outlook for the ill-smelling gas buggies seemed dark indeed!

Edison posed before news photographers standing beside a spanking little red sulky, which had nickel-iron batteries and an electric motor. It was so easily run, he declared, that his twelve-year-old boy Charles could drive it. With that he leaped on board and sped away at twenty miles an hour.

In more restrained terms, Dr. Kennelly, presenting a paper before the Institute of Electrical Engineers in New York, reported that storage capacity in the nickel-iron battery had been raised to 14 watt-hours per pound, or 233 per cent above the contemporary lead battery models; weight, at 53.3 pounds per electrical horsepower-hour, was reduced by about half.

DEFECTIVE BATTERIES CAUSE FACTORY SHUTDOWN

However, bad reports soon began to come in from the first users; and then the reports grew steadily worse. After all the effulgent propaganda, it was a shock to learn that the battery containers leaked on being used in vehicles; that the cells were of uneven performance, and usually dropped about 30 per cent in power. Defective batteries returned to the factory were broken up and examined. The electrical contacts in the positive (nickel) element were found to be unreliable, although Edison had thought he had corrected this weakness by introducing graphite in the positive pockets.

The truth about this fiasco was spreading; it was even reported in European technical publications and newspapers. What was to be done? All the exuberant advance publicity, the habitual Edisonian optimism, had but made things worse. Moreover, Edison this time had raised $500,000 through friendly investors by giving a bond and mortgage on his other manufacturing properties; and these funds had all been exhausted by the work of research and the cost of setting up the factory.

This new crisis might have been something to laugh over, if it hadn't been so nearly disastrous for Edison. He recognized that his nickel-iron battery still needed prolonged study before it could be marketed. But if he shut down his plant and set to overhauling the whole job in his laboratory, he faced a very heavy financial loss. Still worse, and most humiliating to him, would be the public admission of failure, after his sweeping claims of success.

After a brief discussion with his financial associates, he

made his decision swiftly. He would shut down production at once and take back all the batteries that had proved defective, at his own cost. Distribution of several thousand cells had already been initiated by agents in England and Germany as well as America. Some of the carriage companies, such as Studebakers', wanted him to continue delivering his batteries as long as they worked in some fashion. One of his associates questioned his wisdom in stopping manufacture, saying, "It is right to get an ideal thing, if possible, but the batteries, as we have had them, are so far in advance of lead batteries, that everybody is eager for the time when they will be on the market."

To such objections Edison replied flatly, "I stopped manufacturing because the battery was not satisfactory to myself. . . ." And again, "The factory will not start up until I find out why the cells lose capacity."

It was an act of courage. He had always shown pride in the quality and performance of the products he marketed. Now he not only reimbursed buyers for the defective batteries they turned in, but, since the Edison Storage Battery Company had used up all its capital, he financed it thereafter out of his own pocket. Fortunately the motion pictures—thanks to [Edison's first feature film] *The Great Train Robbery*—were now booming. At his command, virtually his whole laboratory force set to work to overcome the irregularities that had shown themselves in the first nickel-iron battery, the cause of which, at first, seemed extremely obscure. The new series of experiments brought forth more variables, and were to engage the labors of Edison and his staff for five years more.

RENEWED EFFORTS TO NOT GIVE UP

The new succession of experiments and tests was "record-breaking," according to one of his principal laboratory assistants, Walter E. Holland, who adds, "I might almost say heartbreaking too, for of all the elusive, disappointing things one ever hunted for that was the worst." Edison vowed that he would find the right way to make a battery—"If it takes me seven years and $1,750,000"—alluding here to the cost of his recent education in iron ore milling.

In chemical work he certainly followed his old methods of "cut and try," the way of the empirical inventor. Could he have used more precise theoretical calculations to shorten his labors? There was actually in the possession of chemical scientists very little exact knowledge of positive and negative electrode combinations, or of electrolytes, the liquid solution in which they were immersed. There was very little that could then be "predicted" theoretically. There was all too much "magic" in the storage battery—as there still is. If the field of possible electrode combinations has been narrowed a great deal by now, this is due largely to the work done *empirically,* and the information gathered, by Edison and his associates and by others who came after them.

One chemist and his assistant were put to the task of improving the leaky containers, and working out a superior welding job. Another group worked over the refinement of the iron element; while still another, with Edison participating directly, was occupied in building up the conductivity of the nickel hydrate, the admixture of graphite particles having proved to be unsatisfactory. Many different materials were tested, by being given repeated charges. The results were awaited during long periods; some solutions would seem promising, then would "fade away." By the summer of 1905 Edison could report that he had again made a "vast number of experiments, now reading 10,296," and that he "had found out a great many things."

In the winter of 1905, while working under great stress, he became very ill, and underwent what was then a fairly dangerous operation for mastoiditis. After this piece of radical surgery, he woke up the next day and growled for his newspapers. Henceforth he would be almost stone-deaf. Though the annual winter vacation at Fort Myers would have benefited his health, and he longed to go, he returned instead to his laboratory to watch the testing of hundreds of new combinations for battery cells and examine the test sheets being compiled for them.

Though the road seemed to lead through all the turnings of an immense labyrinth, Edison insisted on preserving a mask of outward composure and good cheer.

When an associate came to him one day and in forthright language declared that a long series of tests had proved negative and the whole venture was a waste of labor and money, Edison rounded on him and cried angrily, "Is that all you have to say for yourself?" and then walked out of the room. To another who also assured him that a certain series of experiments gave progressively worse results, and that they simply posed "a problem without solution," he replied with spirit, "I've been in the inventor business for thirty-three years, and my experience is that for every problem the Lord has made He has also made a solution. If you and I can't find the solution, then let's honestly admit that you and I are damn fools, but why blame it on the Lord and say He created something 'impossible.'" . . .

Nevertheless, the ten years' hunt for a good storage battery was a prevailingly somber period, Edison's associates recalled, despite his ideas about keeping up morale. Age was coming upon him; his long, thick hair grew very white, while his well-defined eyebrows remained very dark, accentuating his pallor.

The year 1907 was one of profound business depression. Even the phonograph business was hard hit. The Edison company had clung to the cylinder record too long, while Berliner's disk record, produced by Victor Talking Machine, gained in popularity month by month.

In that year also, the newspapers reported that a Rolls-Royce car with a six-cylinder gasoline engine had passed a 10,000-mile endurance test. In Detroit, Henry Ford, working with a will as fierce as Edison's, perfected a cheap 15-horsepower 4-cylinder engine for his Model N car, precursor of the celebrated, raven-hued Model T. The Model N went twenty miles on a gallon of fuel and cost only $600. "Hundreds of persons," it was reported, rushed to buy Ford's small car. Had Edison missed the bus? . . .

In the years 1905 to 1908, Edison applied for a long series of patents covering refinements in his storage battery, especially the process of making metallic film or flake out of the nickel by electroplating. He and his associates had gone far in the study of both iron and nickel in a state of very high purity. They had managed to obtain nickel film or flake as light as thistledown—about four one-hundred-thousandths of an inch in thickness. This was accomplished by electroplating thin layers of copper and nickel on a metal cylinder, then dissolving away the copper in a chemical bath, leaving nickel film so fine that tiny segments of it, about 630 layers, could be packed alternately with nickel hydrate in a cell pocket that was only four inches in height, the nickel flake replacing the graphite formerly used in the positive pockets as a conductor. The development of the nickel-flake process gave Edison an improved electrical contact and conductivity, and the lightness of weight he wanted, while extending capacity and wattage.

The whole structure of the storage cell was redesigned, so that instead of building its numerous "windows" out of flat pockets, Edison used seamless tubes of thin nickel-plated steel, perforated with minute holes through which the electrolyte could seep in freely. Alternate charges of the nickel flake and nickel hydrate were then fed by machine into the tubes, and packed or tamped down under pressure of four tons to the inch. Whereas formerly the active materials used to cause swelling of the pockets, the shift to the tubular structure made for a great improvement in battery performance.

In starting on this big experimental problem of the "completely reversible" battery in 1900, Edison had had a very good initial concept or "intuition" about using nickel as his positive element, and a noncorrosive electrolyte solution of potash. But refining upon that idea—"the last ten per cent"— had taken a fearful amount of time and study. Among chemical scientists there was then only a dim knowledge of how the tiny electrified atoms of oxygen called *ions* ("wanderers") detached themselves from the iron oxide, passed through the alkaline solution, and deposited themselves upon the nickel, thus producing the high oxide of nickel. By prolonged experimenting Edison and his co-workers brought about one improvement after another, and helped to clarify this problem.

His electrolyte, made of the caustic potash solution, at first had tended to drop off gradually in capacity, from cycle to cycle of charging and discharging. But some time in 1908, after they had tried hundreds of different additives, trials were made with a small amount of lithium hydroxide ($LiOH$); introducing lithium had the effect of raising capacity and then holding it steady over a long period. According to present-day chemical technicians, this step constituted "a real piece of magic" that could never have been calculated theoretically in Edison's time, and whose mechanism is still not clearly understood. All that is known now (1959) is that lithium ions mysteriously improve conductivity and alter the oxidation tendency of the nickel flakes. Edison's empirical work, therefore, was successful in the end and helped to create for later men a wider base of information to calculate from. His ten-year campaign to master the imponderables of the storage battery has remained famous in the history of battery technology. It was really a beautiful work in applied science, carried out at the cost of a million dollars of his own money.

NEW BATTERY PUTS COMPANY "IN THE BLACK"

"At last the battery is finished," Edison wrote in the summer of 1909, with evident relief, to the head of the Adams Express Company, who had been waiting to use his improved product for delivery wagons. It seemed "an almost perfect instrument." A year later factory production was resumed on a large scale; in the first twelve months thereafter a million dollars' worth of the new A battery cells was sold, beginning a profitable career for the Edison Storage Battery Company that has continued to this day.

Several important carriage works, among them Anderson's of Detroit, hastened to produce electric runabouts and light trucks, known as the Detroit Electric, that were powered by an array of Edison cells. In the Eastern states the similarly equipped Baker Runabout also had some vogue between 1911 and 1914. Department stores used such electric trucks for years. Light electric town cars were popular for a period because they were noiseless and fumeless; their radius was about sixty miles a day between chargings, and their Edison batteries—unlike lead batteries that needed long periods for recharging—could be fully recharged in seven hours. . . .

The nickel-iron-alkaline battery was generally acknowledged to possess special merits over the heavier lead-acid affairs, because it resisted decomposition, was well-nigh completely reversible, and showed a long life. Edison had hoped, above all, that it would be adaptable for automotive traction, and even for streetcars, a model of which was operated for a while on Main Street, West Orange, on a branch line of the Erie Railroad. However, to the inventor's deep disappointment, automobile traction proved to be just what it was *not* suited for. Nor was it useful as a starter battery. Its voltage capacity tended to be lower than that of contemporary lead batteries (about 1.19 against 1.50 volts per cell), so that one needed more Edison cells for a given task—which offset their advantage of lighter weight. The Edison battery was also affected by cold temperatures, its alkaline electrolyte becoming weak and slushy, though not freezing. When winter came it was common for many Edison-powered vehicles to become stuck in snowdrifts or on muddy roads. Meanwhile the far-ranging gas buggies of Ford and others, with their cheap, improved combustion engines, swept all before them.

On the other hand, the beautifully constructed Edison battery was found particularly useful where dependability and long life were important, as for stand-by purposes at power plants, and for railway signaling; or to provide current for miners' lamps, train lights, and other railway and marine appliances. Though the electric automobile had only a brief vogue, a remarkably wide field of usage was developed in industries such as mining and quarrying (for firing blasts), on merchant vessels, and ships of war. Edison batteries were also used at first to manipulate naval torpedoes; later a model was developed for driving submarines when submerged, with diminished risk of exposing the crew to injurious gases.

When demonstrating the use of his cells in a submarine, Edison told Navy officials, "Keep it clean, and give it water, and at the end of four years it will give its full capacity."

"Four years?" they queried in astonishment. "Yes," he replied, "four years, eight years; it will outwear the submarine itself."

During World War I the Edison battery also entered into wide use in the growing field of radio telegraphy. In short it won acceptance as the most rugged of industrial storage batteries.

Was it worth the tremendous expenditure of effort? Edison used to profess that his inventive work was guided only by the criterion of commercial success or practicability. But the profits were rather on the moderate side, in the end, when measured against the "punishment" he had taken in that series of heart-breaking experiments lasting nearly ten years. As he himself sometimes suspected, whatever he might say overtly, he really "lacked the commercial temperament." The thought of calling a halt at some midway point and cutting his losses was never tolerated. Why did he go on and on? "I always invent to obtain money to go on inventing," he said simply. A few more of Nature's secrets had been wrested from her, though not as many as was hoped for. It was not for profit that he labored so hard—he scarcely needed more money nowadays—he was driven by his will, and by the "spirit of workmanship," to contrive and create. As one of his laboratory confreres remarked after they had finished their task, "Secrets have to be long-winded and roost high to get away when the Old Man goes hunting for them."

CHAPTER 5

Legend and Legacy

PEOPLE
WHO MADE
HISTORY

THOMAS EDISON

Our Debt to Edison

Henry Ford

An extraordinary automobile inventor in his own
right, Henry Ford had great admiration for the Wizard, which is evident as he acknowledges Edison's
numerous contributions to the world. Ford cites that
nearly every important factor in America's prosperity
either directly or indirectly traces back to some invention by Edison. Edison's discoveries made modern industry in America possible. For example, creating a generating and distribution system for the
electric light freed people from the limitations of
daylight and added extra active hours to every day.
This lengthened the amount of time people might
use consumer goods, which in turn increased the
need for products, thereby creating more jobs. This
ripple effect had an impact on factories, which,
thanks to Edison's light could carry on as efficiently
at night as during the day. His inventions also were
fundamental to the practical introduction of the telephone and to the extension of the telegraph as an inexpensive method of communication, both of which
have aided business and the consumer alike. Any
one of his inventions might have taken another inventor's lifetime to create, but Edison, who relied on
his invention factory, was able to commit his time
and energy to one invention after another.

It is the fashion to call this the age of industry. Rather, we
should call it the age of Edison. For he is the founder of modern industry in this country. He has formed for us a new
kind of declaration of independence. The Declaration of Independence stated certain principles of political liberty. The
Edison declaration is not in words. It is in the nature of a kit
of tools, by the use of which each and every person among
us has gained a larger measure of economic liberty than had

Excerpted from Henry Ford, *Edison As I Know Him*, written in collaboration with
Samuel Crowther. Copyright © 1930 Samuel Crowther.

ever previously been thought possible.

We are only learning to use the tools and the methods that he has given to us. Already our general prosperity leads the world, and this is due to the fact that we have had Edison. Nearly every important factor in our prosperity directly or indirectly traces back to some invention by him. He is not only fundamental in our present prosperity but he has further discoveries and inventions of which we can avail ourselves when the need comes.

A great part of what Edison has done is now so much a part of our lives and so commonplace that we forget we owe it to him. His work has not only created many millions of new jobs but also—and without qualification—it has made every job more remunerative. Edison has done more toward abolishing poverty than have all the reformers and statesmen since the beginning of the world. He has provided man with the means to help himself.

EDISON'S CONTRIBUTIONS

The work of Edison falls into two great divisions. The first has to do with his direct contributions of inventions—of tools. The second has to do with his example in linking science with our everyday life and demonstrating that, through patient, unremitting testing and trying, any problem may eventually be solved. It is certainly useless and probably impossible to determine whether his actual accomplishments or the force of his example has been the more valuable to us.

These statements may seem extravagant—as arising out of my own great admiration for the man. In truth, the statements fall short of the facts. Our prosperity of today would be impossible were it not for the mobility of our artificial power and the facility of our communication and transportation. Behind all of these is Edison. Look at some of his work in brief summary and from the viewpoint of its effects:

(1) The invention of the incandescent lamp freed us from the limitations of daylight and added many active hours to every day. People need more things during the long electric day than they could need during the short natural day or the somewhat longer days of the candle, the lamp or the gaslight. None of these forms of artificial illumination approaches the convenience of the incandescent light. Lengthening the time in which people might consume naturally increased the volume of consumption and therefore created more jobs. We

gain in wealth not simply by production but by the production of goods that are consumed. The incandescent light not only increased the volume of consumption but it gave light to the factories so that production could be carried on as efficiently at night as by day with a consequent cheapening of production through the use of less capital equipment.

(2) The incandescent lamp would of itself have been only an interesting toy if Edison had not taken over the solution of the whole problem and created a new system for both the generation and the distribution of electricity. He evolved a dynamo which turned into electricity ninety percent of the applied power instead of the forty percent which was then the record of the best dynamos. And then, through his invention of what is called the "three-wire system," he saved nearly two-thirds of the copper which would have been necessary to distribute the current on the existing two-wire systems. Without his more efficient dynamo and the great savings he effected in copper, the cost of electricity to the consumer would have been so great that it could not have been considered as other than a luxury. He started electricity on its way to being a commodity.

(3) The provision of a whole new system of electric generation emancipated industry from the leather belt and the line shaft, for it eventually became possible to provide each tool with its own electric motor. This may seem only a detail of minor importance. In fact, modern industry could not be carried on with the belt and line shaft for a number of reasons. The motor enabled machinery to be arranged according to the sequence of the work, and that alone has probably doubled the efficiency of industry, for it has cut out a tremendous amount of useless handling and hauling. The belt and shaft were also very wasteful of power—so wasteful, indeed, that no factory could be really large, for even the longest line shaft was small according to modern requirements. Also high-speed tools were impossible under the old conditions—neither the pulleys nor the belts could stand modern speeds. Without high-speed tools and the finer steels which they brought about, there could be nothing of what we call modern industry. That means that we could not have the present combination of high wages and low-priced goods. The present-day low-priced automobile, to mention only one out of thousands of commodities, would be a high-priced luxury article without the aid of the electric motor in its manufacturing.

HIS INVENTIONS REVOLUTIONIZED MODERN INDUSTRY

Electricity as a servant of general utility began with Edison. No one has as yet been able to comprehend how far-reaching this use of electricity really is, for it goes through every phase of our lives. But, in addition, Mr. Edison's inventions and developments were fundamental to the practical introduction of the telephone and to the extension of the telegraph as a cheap and general method of communication. He also made the typewriter a practical office machine and performed the largest single work in the development of the storage battery.

These inventions, the purport of which I have sketched, have made modern industry possible. Without them we could not have volume production and without them we could not have the large corporation, for it depends upon volume production, quick transport and quick communication. These things have vitally changed all of our lives, but also and in a different way our lives have been changed by the phonograph and by the motion picture, and for both of these Edison is primarily responsible. In each he was the pioneer. He was also a pioneer in radio work, but he did not follow it through because of other and more pressing matters.

SO MANY INVENTIONS FROM ONE MAN

In the field of building and construction he did pioneer work in the processes of cement making, in the composition and mixing of concrete and in the devising of methods by which buildings might be constructed by pouring liquid concrete instead of putting them up brick by brick or block by block. This involved the developing of a concrete which could be poured without having all the larger solid matter sink to the bottom, leaving a mass of unequal strength.

He perfected a method of pouring the entirety of a good-sized cottage in a single mold and by a single operation. But in this, as in many other things, he was ahead of his time. Many buildings are now being poured in part and eventually we shall see building revolutionized.

For the future he has provided many inventions which we shall work into or which we may turn to in necessity. Chief among these is his process of extracting iron from low-grade ore. This he developed and put into operation in New Jersey at a cost to him of several million dollars. Then came the discovery of the high-grade ores in the Missabe region. But his process gives us an absolute assurance that at no time shall we ever suffer from the lack of cheap iron. He has insured to us iron for all time; he can profitably use ore which would otherwise be worthless on account of the expense of getting out the small percentage of iron.

Once Edison has fully demonstrated the practical utility of any invention and has sketched its possible developments, he begins to lose interest and prefers to turn over the actual development to others and to engage himself with something new. I do not know of a single one of his inventions, the development and manufacture of which could not have taken the whole life of any other man.

In fact, the development and elaboration of his inventions is today taking the entire time of many thousands of men, but fortunately for the country his mind is too restless and too inquiring to be held to a single subject—once he has overcome all the difficulties which have baffled everyone else. He finishes his task, puts his product into actual manufacturing, sketches the eventual development in a peculiarly unerring way, and then opens up on another subject which has been pressing for his attention.

ALWAYS SEEING THE POTENTIAL

For instance, as far back as 1878 he wrote down the following possible applications of the phonograph—which he had just then completed. It will be noted that some of these applications have already been made and that none of them today seems extraordinary. But imagine this vision in 1878! Here is the list:

1. Letter writing and all kinds of dictation without the aid of a stenographer.

2. Phonographic books, which will speak to blind people without effort on their part.

3. The teaching of elocution.

4. Reproduction of music.

5. The 'Family Record'—a registry of sayings, reminiscences, et cetera, by members of a family in their own voices, and of the last words of dying persons.

6. Music boxes and toys.

7. Clocks that should announce in articulate speech the time for going home, going to meals, et cetera.

8. The preservation of languages by exact reproduction of the manner of pronouncing.

9. Educational purposes: such as preserving the explanations made by a teacher, so that the pupil can refer to them at any moment, and spelling or other lessons placed upon the phonograph for convenience in committing to memory.

10. Connection with the telephone, so as to make that instrument an auxiliary in the transmission of permanent and invaluable records, instead of being the recipient of momentary and fleeting communication.

Of the typewriter, which was brought to him to be improved and perfected, he said:

The typewriter proved a difficult thing to make commercial. The alignment of the letters was awful. One letter would be one-sixteenth of an inch above the others; and all the letters wanted to wander out of line. I worked on it till the machine gave fair results. Some were made and used in the office. A few of us were very sanguine that some day all business letters would be written on a typewriter.

Why Edison?

Robert Conot

In this thorough and thoughtful account of Edison, biographer Robert Conot paints an accurate picture of a
rugged individualist and inventor who has influenced
the lives of so many people. Edison was a single-
minded man who worked only to obtain money to
feed his passion for inventing. A visionary whose
business was thinking, Edison didn't see an invention
as an end in itself but one more discovery on the rung
of an unending ladder of searching. Lionized by the
press and called a wizard and God-like genius, this
humble man who usually found it difficult to credit
his staff for their major contributions to his inventions made a generous comment at the 50-year
golden jubilee when he said, "In honoring me you are
honoring that vast army of thinkers and workers of
the past without whom my work would have gone for
nothing." His vision of a world run by electricity has
been fulfilled. He made new discoveries where many
felt there were none. If Thomas Edison had not existed, undoubtedly another great mind would have
conceived his electric light and power system; yet this
one-of-a-kind inventor most likely advanced the use
of electricity by at least a generation.

Why Edison?

How did the offspring of such an ordinary family become
the most extraordinary inventor in history?

Had Charles Dickens met him as a trainboy, he would
have seen little more in Al than in any other ambitious
American youth, a character far too commonplace to be the
subject of a novel. As for Horatio Alger, he would have noted
Al's lack of thrift, his disbelief in religion, his uncouthness,
and some of his other less-than-admirable qualities, and
concluded he was destined to come to no good end.

Excerpted from Robert Conot, *A Streak of Luck.* Copyright © 1979 Robert Conot.

It was, in a way, typical of the contradictions in Edison's personality and life that, though he was the great-grandson of a Tory who had almost lost his life in the American Revolution, he took Tom Paine for his idol. Rebellion was one of his most notable early characteristics—rebellion against his disciplinarian mother, against a stern and unforgiving church, against a dull and rigid school. From boyhood to old age he could not bear to have anyone tell him what to do, but remained undisciplined and iconoclastic. . . .

Had he been a well-rounded person of more physical talent, had he had more success in school or as a telegrapher (not to speak of as a locomotive engineer!), he might have felt less pressure to prove himself, and turned out to be just another nineteenth-century middle American. "If I had not had so much ambition and had not tried to do so many things, I probably would have been happier, but less useful," he remarked shortly before his death.

His poor hearing forced him to rely more on his sense of sight, provided incentive for him to become an excellent reader, and reduced the ordinary distractions and disturbances of the world. When he withdrew into the semisilent universe of his mind, he wove imagination, ingenuity, and technical knowledge into new configurations. "The man who doesn't make up his mind to cultivate the habit of thinking misses the greatest pleasures in life," Edison said. "The brain that isn't used rusts." He attributed the cause of people's troubles to one source: "It is all because they won't think, won't think!" Every room in the laboratory contained the quotation from Sir Joshua Reynolds: "There is no expedient to which a man will not resort to avoid the real labor of thinking."

A RUGGED INDIVIDUALIST

"My business is *thinking*," Edison declared.

But Edison was not only a thinker; he was a visionary. And as such his thoughts were often unorthodox. His experiences with conventional institutions and accepted modes of doing things were of such negative character that he was convinced there must be better ways. This exposed him, like most searchers for new paths, to the criticism of the establishment and the derision of his peers. When his critics turned out to be wrong a significant percentage of the time, his faith in his own certitude and his exclusion of all opinion that did not conform to his ideas became ever more pronounced.

From an early age, Edison had an adversary relationship with many of the people with whom he came into contact. He irritated them by upsetting the established order with his innovative sallies. They could not understand why, if an operation or mode of proceeding was good enough for the rest of the world, it was not good enough for Edison. Edison's brashness and disinclination to be diplomatic aggravated his poor relations with people in authoritative positions—had he been forced to make a living by working on a job he would have fared badly. He seldom cultivated friendships, but looked upon acquaintances as dispensable, to be used for his own advantage and advancement, then forgotten. He was what Herbert Hoover extolled, "the rugged individualist." His ethics and his standards were his own; and when they conflicted with his drive for success, they could be overridden.

The Edison who came to New York was an ambitious, aggressive, rebellious, single-minded, self-centered, imaginative, creatively intrepid youth with a half-dozen years of experience in the country's fastest-growing industry. He invented to make money, and to prove himself to his critics. Once he had the money, he did not spend it on drink, because alcohol disagreed with him; he did not spend it on girls, because he was shy and not a womanizer; he did not speculate on Wall Street, because one of his earliest and most profound experiences in New York was watching what happened to those who did; he did not spend it on luxuries for himself, because they meant nothing to him; he did not save it up, because he lacked any inclination for thrift. Instead, he reinvested it in his business.

"I always wanted to obtain money to go on inventing," he said. And however much he wasted, piece by piece he built up his inventive facilities. Although the Menlo Park laboratory was small and primitive by today's standards, in 1876 it was unique. Edison was the only inventor with his own fully equipped laboratory, the only one who could afford to maintain a staff. Neither Michael Faraday nor Joseph Henry had facilities comparable to Edison's. Alexander Graham Bell's laboratory was rudimentary. William Sawyer in New York and Joseph Swan in England were competing against a well-ordered if not well-organized enterprise.

At a time when modern science was still in a natal stage, inventors were forced to do nearly everything for themselves. Obviously, a successful operation necessitated significant wherewithal, which, among inventors, only Edison possessed and was willing to spend. With [Charles] Batchelor and his other associates Edison composed an in-

EDISON'S INTEREST IN THE OCCULT

In this excerpt from his article on occultism, Martin Gardner shows Edison's fascination with the occult and mentions some predictions Edison made for the future of certain inventions—his own and those of others.

Edison was fascinated throughout his long life with the occult. In his thirties he became intrigued by the writings of that amusing mountebank Madame Helena Petrovna Blavatsky, the great guru of theosophy. Edison attended meetings in New York of the theosophical society and was awarded some sort of diploma. A firm believer in PK (psychokinesis), he tried to start pendulums swinging by mind control, but the results were negative. He also attempted to confirm telepathy by experiments with electric coils around the heads of human receivers and transmitters. Ebon quotes from Edison's diary: "Four among us first stayed in different rooms, joined by the electric system. . . . Afterwards we sat in the four corners of the same room, gradually bringing our chairs closer together toward the center of the room, until our knees touched, and for all of that, we observed no results."

It was Edison's good friend Henry Ford who introduced Edison to the magician Berthold Reese. . . . "Dr." Reese, as he liked to call himself, traveled widely around Europe performing what magicians call "mental magic" for celebrities and royalty. He liked to wear on his tie a huge diamond pin given to him by the King of Spain, and an even larger diamond on a finger ring. Many leading parapsychologists believed he had extraordinary psi powers.

Reese specialized in what is called "billet reading." He would ask someone to write something on a piece of paper, which he would fold and either hide or destroy. Reese would then pretend to read the message by ESP. His methods were well known to honest magicians of the time. There are scores of ways to accomplish billet reading. . . .

Edison was the most famous person to be totally bamboozled by Reese. Like so many scientists who tumble for psychic charlatans, Edison considered himself far too intelligent to be

ventive *team*. If Edison wanted to experiment with an alloy, he usually had to make it himself. When he needed an efficient vacuum pump, he had to design it, construct it, then redesign and reconstruct it over and over. If electrical measuring instruments were required, [Francis] Upton had to devise them.

fooled, and of course it never occurred to him to seek explanation from a magician. When an article in the *New York Graphic* unveiled some of Reese's techniques, Edison was furious. He sent the newspaper a letter in which he said:

I am certain that Reese was neither a medium nor a fake. I saw him several times and on each occasion I wrote something on a piece of paper when Reese was not near or when he was in another room. In no single case was one of these papers handled by Reese, and some of them he never saw, yet he recited correctly the contents of each paper.

Several people in my laboratory had the same kind of experience, and there are hundreds of prominent people in New York who can testify to the same thing. . . .

There is evidence that Edison thought he himself had ESP. At any rate, there is no question that his powers of precognition were poor. Here are some of his failed predictions that I found in *The Experts Speak* (1984), an amusing anthology by Christopher Cerf and Victor Navasky, and elsewhere: . . .

"It is apparent to me that the possibilities of the aeroplane, which two or three years ago was thought to hold the solution to the [flying machine] problem, have been exhausted, and that we must turn elsewhere."

"The radio craze . . . will die out in time so far as music is concerned. But it may continue for business purposes.". . .

"In fifteen years, more electricity will be sold for electric vehicles than for light."

Edison's worst prediction had to do with what was called the "war of the currents." Nikola Tesla and others believed that alternating currents were the best way to transmit high voltage electricity over long distances. Edison stubbornly insisted that only direct current should be used. "There is no plea which will justify the use of high-tension alternating currents, either in a scientific or a commercial sense. They are employed solely to reduce investment in copper wire and real estate. . . . My personal desire would be to prohibit entirely the use of alternating currents. They are as unnecessary as they are dangerous.

Martin Gardner, "Thomas Edison, Paranormalist," *Skeptical Inquirer*, July/August 1996, pp. 9–12.

INVENTION YIELDS MORE INVENTIONS

Edison was able to establish not only continuity, so that discoveries made in the development of one invention could be applied to another, but scope. The phonograph was an outgrowth of multiple lines of investigation. Edison sustained the experiments on the incandescent light for over a year without coming close to obtaining a lamp of practical value, yet in the end triumphed and produced not only a commercial light but a generator and a vacuum pump considerably in advance of their time.

Since Edison did not regard an invention as an end in itself but rather as one more discovery in a never-ending search, invention followed invention like the steps on a ladder. The amazement with which he was regarded, even early in his career, was epitomized by the *London Standard* in October, 1878:

> Why a man should tear himself to pieces to concoct a string of inventions is a problem which may interest the psychologist. It seems as inevitable for Mr. Edison to invent as for a fish to swim. It is his nature, or it may be described as an all-devouring passion, which nothing can satiate. We appear to behold a union between the restless spirit of American enterprise and the scientific genius of the present age. Mr. Edison invents with the same impetuous ardor that his countrymen speculate. There is the same disdain of precedent and the same determination to "go ahead." . . .

No other inventor has approached the number of patents issued to him singly or jointly—1093—and they exhibit a notable unity:

Telegraph	150	Ore Separator	62
Electric Pen and		Cement	40
Mimeograph	5	Motion Pictures	9
Telephone	34	Battery	141
Phonograph	195	Automobile	8
Electric Light and Power	389	Miscellaneous[1]	35
Railroad	25		

SELF-EDUCATION WAS KEY TO HIS SUCCESS

Although Edison had no more than four years of schooling—in a day when few but privileged children went beyond

---

1. Among the miscellaneous patents are three for typewriters, one for vacuum preservation, one for an auto giro (a cross between a helicopter and an airplane, having a rotor for lift and a propeller for forward motion), three for chemicals, three for military projectiles, two for radio, and one for rubber.

grade school—he was not uneducated. He emerged from his years as a newspaperboy and telegrapher with a wide span of general knowledge. His on-the-job training in telegraphy, supplemented by his inquisitiveness and experimentation, gave him an excellent grounding in practical electricity. When, subsequently, he learned chemistry, he developed into the outstanding empirical chemist-electrician of his age. Time and again his interdisciplinary self-education proved the key to success.

Complementing his expertise as a chemist and an electrician was his ability as a promoter. He had picked up from his father the art of scheming. From his association with newspapermen he learned the importance of the press. He was not only a good inventor, but always managed to convince potential backers he was better than he was; and when he projected himself into the newspapers, he was never short of superlative. He proceeded on the well-established theory that successes will be remembered, while failures are forgotten. He acted on the basis that a promise can bring practical advantage, so it is self-defeating to worry whether the promise can be kept. The genesis of the quadruplex, the carbon-button telephone transmitter, and the phonograph made the disappointment of other, unfulfilled expectations seem insignificant. Every success augmented the mystique growing up about him, and added to his standing with the financial community— from the time that Marshall Lefferts and George Harrington began to back him, his ties with Wall Street made him unique as an inventor.

PRACTICAL AND TOPICAL INVENTIONS

In keeping with his background and experience, Edison's inventions were distinguished by two primary characteristics.

They were *practical*; that is, they were intended to earn money. "A scientific man busies himself with theory. He is absolutely impractical. An inventor is essentially practical," Edison asserted. "Anything that won't sell, I don't want to invent. Its sale is proof of utility, and utility is success." Although he was occasionally diverted by phenomena like "etheric force," he did not pursue them—he could not, in truth, afford to pursue them. When the phonograph proved inapplicable for recording telephone conversations and sales of the machines lagged, Edison lost interest until Tainter threatened to transform the invention into a commercial instrument. Although he was a pioneer in wireless transmission, he did not follow up the experiments after the rather unsuccessful Grasshopper operation or renew them after Marconi demonstrated long-distance transmission was practicable, because he failed to perceive that any substantial revenues could be derived. Since, for a long time, motion pictures appeared to have only limited profitability, Edison during his entire career took out only nine patents in the field. In comparison, he obtained sixty-two patents for ore separation, which he expected to be the source of fabulous wealth.

In addition to being practical, his inventions were *topical*. He worked either in the mainstream of technology, as with the telegraph, or jumped into a developing field, as with the telephone, the incandescent light, the X-ray, the electric automobile, and, at the very last, the domestic production of rubber. When he himself was ahead of everyone else, as with the phonograph, wireless telegraphy, and the kinetoscope, he paused until commerce caught up to him. . . .

By dealing in the practical and topical, he was able to interest men whose motive was profit, and to obtain backing. His contacts, his ability to raise money, his exploitation of people, his ambition, his imagination, his dedication—these were the ingredients of his success. There was one more, perhaps the most important of all: his persistence.

SUCCESSFUL INVENTOR, FAILED BUSINESSMAN

Conversely, many of the elements that were the ingredients of his success as an inventor were the cause of his failure as a businessman.

His disinterest in tailoring his products to customers' preferences and demands, his disdain of economics, his jealousy of the inventions and products of others, his stubborn assertion of his own correctness against all contrary opinion, his insistence on being different from everybody else, his unwillingness to cooperate and compromise, his impatience on the one hand and tendency to procrastinate on the other, all contributed to his lack of commercial success.

Despite his talent for press agentry, he understood little of the psychology of dealing with the public. His privateering approach . . . alienated people and was self-defeating when he destroyed the confidence and good will of men with whom he had to conduct business. His persistence in continuing failing ventures after all reasonable probability of their success was exhausted was a blueprint for bankruptcy.

Not only was it virtually impossible for Edison to reach a disagreeable decision, it was difficult for him to come to *any* decision. The process of arriving at a logical choice was something he had not learned in his self-education. That was why in experimenting he tried whatever seemed reasonable. Either a mechanism or a chemical reaction would work or it would not. *It* made the decision. Not he.

THE LEGEND BEGINS

As his fame increased, there was a surge of interest in his background. Edison, however, was close-mouthed about his personal life. When he rattled off anecdotes, he used them as a means of defense against too close an inquiry into his family relationships and business transactions. Men like MacKenzie strove to expand the importance of their association with him, and told exaggerated tales. George Bliss, using largely third-hand material, was the first to attempt to put together an account of Edison's life, which he presented before the Chicago Electric Society early in 1878. Soon afterward, he reported chagrinedly to Edison:

"Ashley writes me that my article is a romance and all that I have ever heard about you isn't so." A few months later, nevertheless, a Chicago publisher, Rhodes & McClure, expanded on the Bliss biography in a slim volume. Edison was credited with such feats as using the whistle on a locomotive to send Morse-code messages across the St. Clair River, a tale that was appropriated from the 1860 visit to the United States by the Prince of Wales, when the prince's guide, Colonel Wilson, had used two locomotives to signal back and forth across the Mississippi. Edison's experience at Stratford was embellished by grafting on a portion of another telegrapher's story of his service on the Grand Trunk Railroad, an account that appeared in *The Operator* under the title of "Brian Born's Hard Luck" adjacent to Bliss's life of Edison. Yet Bliss's "romance" and the material from the McClure book were treated as source material in almost every subsequent book about Edison. . . .

Layer by layer the legends and myths obscured Edison's character, until he was like a magnificent master vanished beneath the encrustations of fiction. As the cynical, knowledgeable, cussing, ruthless, hard-driving, revolutionary, willful, and visionary Al Edison disappeared he was replaced by an Olympian and omniscient genial genius. Yet in the process Edison was not only deprived of his human qualities and turned into a kind of Greco-Roman demigod, a singular once-in-a-millennium phenomenon whom ordinary mortals might only regard in stupefied wonder, but his achievements and his legacy were also overshadowed and diminished.

Edison himself never wavered in his assertion that he was not a wizard or a genius—in fact, he despised the designation. When an acquaintance once referred to his "Godlike genius," Edison snorted; "Godlike nothing! Sticking to it is the genius!"

"Any other bright-minded fellow can accomplish just as much," he proclaimed, "if he will stick like hell and remember nothing that's any good works by itself. You got to *make* the damn thing work."

Edison's talent was not unlimited. Its boundaries were quite well defined. Even in electricity and chemistry, theory and abstractions were beyond his grasp. When he ventured into other fields, such as engineering and mining, the results could be disastrous. He invented best only when his own ingenuity was complemented by the skills of his collaborators. . . .

Batchelor was his most important co-inventor. From 1870 to 1880 there was little Edison did that Batchelor was not involved in; and in such inventions as the mimeograph and the telephone Batchelor probably played the principal role. Jim Adams and Charley Edison made important contributions. Upton's work was essential to the development of the lighting system. At the West Orange laboratory, [Jonas W.] Aylsworth was the key figure in the continuing improvement of phonograph recording and the production of the alkaline storage battery. [William K.L.] Dickson did most of the experimenting on the kinetoscope and the kinetograph.

Edison's character would stand in better light had he been more generous in sharing the credit. Yet it was precisely his need for attention, praise, and justification that drove him on. When writers lacked the energy and perspicacity to look beyond one man, he was not charitable enough to point their error out to them and deprive himself of part of the glory. Only at the golden jubilee did he allude to the conflict in his mind:

"I would be embarrassed at the honors that are being heaped on me on this unforgettable night were it not for the fact that in honoring me you are also honoring that vast army of thinkers and workers of the past without whom my work would have gone for nothing." . . .

EDISON'S INVENTIONS IN CONTEXT

Edison's accomplishments become even more astonishing when compared to those of other leading inventors. James Watt's fame rests on taking an existing machine and perfecting it. Robert Fulton adapted the steam engine to ships (but this was by no means an original concept and he had considerable competition), promoted canal building, and was a pioneer in experimenting with submarines and torpedoes. George Stephenson produced the first practical railroad, but he was simply carrying the work of others to conclusion. Samuel Morse, like Fulton a successful painter, was responsible for one remarkable invention, the telegraph. Cyrus McCormick revolutionized agriculture, but did not venture beyond that field. Charles Goodyear hit upon the process of vulcanizing rubber accidentally. Alexander Graham Bell, after proving that a continuous current was the secret to telephonic transmission, never developed another significant invention. Wilbur and Orville Wright were the first to fly a powered heavier-than-air machine, but were preceded by the near misses of several other men. Guglielmo Marconi took up the theories and experiments of a number of men, among them Edison and Heinrich Hertz, and carried them to a practical conclusion. Henry Ford, who was the world's most ingenious manufacturer and the epitome of the practicality that Edison always aimed for but never achieved, could scarcely be called an inventor at all. Only Michael Faraday, who greatly advanced the sciences of chemistry and metallurgy, was the principal discoverer of the interrelationship between magnetism and electricity, laid the foundation for the generator, made the first transformer, and provided a clue to the existence of the electron, rivaled Edison in diversity.

Edison's inventions are like the building blocks of an obelisk rising out of the history of the world. No other man has ever been responsible for striking the spring of so much wealth, nor had such influence on the lives of so many people.

The mechanism of today's telephone speaker remains essentially the same as that of the carbon-button transmitter of 1878. The microphone is merely an adaptation of the carbon button. The "Edison effect" globe of 1884 laid the basis for the radio vacuum tube. The alkaline battery was an important step forward in the technology of stored electricity. The mutation of the zootrope from a novelty into a commercial instrument was initiated by Edison, and it was at West Orange that the world's first motion-picture studio was established.

The phonograph, for which the kinetoscope was intended as an adjunct, was Edison's most novel and revolutionary invention. Although his belief that a recording and reproducing device would prove valuable in telephone transmission was erroneous, the three different modes with which he experimented proved to be startlingly perspicacious. The disk remains the phonograph of today. The cylinder continues to be used in such dictating machines as are still in operation. The paper band had some similarity to magnetic tape—the underlying idea was comparable even if the technologies are a century apart.

His Major Achievement

Yet quadruplex, telephone transmitter, phonograph, kinetoscope—all pale before Edison's achievement in electric light and power. The incandescent lamp was not so much an invention as the marker of a technological and social revolution. To bring the incandescent light to commercial fruition, Edison had not only to develop a lamp but to produce a generator of far greater capacity than previously conceived, and to design a system of electric distribution. Together with light, he endeavored to bring power to the world—when, early in the fall of 1879, he appeared to have reached a dead end with the lamp, he planned to construct power stations for electric motors.

When Edison launched his quest in 1878, only a few homes, dependent on candles, kerosene lamps, and gas lights, had the illumination of 25 candlepower considered the minimum necessary for reading. Public transportation consisted of horse cars and trains pulled by steam locomotives. The limited power of steam elevators held building heights to a few stories. Dentistry consisted mostly of pulling teeth, since the slow, foot-powered drills made filling cavities excruciating experiences for patients. Factories, dependent on coal and water, were concentrated along waterways, blackened cities with their pollution, and only infrequently operated at night.

Between 1878 and 1882 Edison constructed the prototype for the entire electric light and power industry. The first skyscraper, using electric elevators, was erected in Chicago in 1885. During the next two decades, electric traction systems were built in every major city, and the first electric locomotives came into use. Motors combined with machines and tools increased industrial productivity and lightened household tasks. Electricity revolutionized the factory. The path was cleared for modern medicine and dentistry. Business became more and more dependent upon power; and Edison's early oddity, the electric typewriter, appeared in offices. Home life was transformed because night was no longer a time of darkness—today one house benefits from more candlepower than an entire village in the nineteenth century.

Edison threw open the door through which not only he but a host of scientists and inventors rushed to make discovery after discovery. One hundred years after Menlo Park, Edison's vision of a universe run by electricity has been fulfilled. Blackouts, when they occur, bring life almost to a standstill. It is possible to conceive of a world without automobiles, airplanes, and natural gas, but to revert to an age without electricity would cripple civilization.

Edison was a scientific explorer who discovered new continents where prevailing opinion held that none existed. If sometimes he sailed off the edge of the world, that was part of the risk of exploration. During his career he repeatedly exhibited the amorality of a conqueror; but his conquests were dedicated to progress. . . .

What if there had been no Edison? Would not another man or other men have made the same discoveries? Eventually, in all likelihood, yes. But Edison's enormous impact was due to the uniqueness of his character and his particular approach to life. He was a scientific primitive with talent enough to push ahead, but not the education or sophistication to know that he was, presumably, attempting the impossible. He was the epitome of the practical inventor. At Menlo Park he established and equipped—without conscious intent—the forerunner of the industrial research laboratory. He poured into research and development more money than his enterprises yielded—his ambition for wealth was repeatedly subverted by his passion for invention.

He was inimitable in his time, and it is probable that he

advanced the art of electricity by at least a generation. As for the phonograph, the discovery that sound could be recorded and reproduced was such a rare combination of insight, imagination, and good fortune that it is futile to speculate when someone else might have hit upon the secret.

Edison succeeded, where others failed or never tried, because it was his nature to dare. Moses Farmer, who seemingly had every advantage over Edison, started everything and dropped everything. He lacked the drive and the great vision, he was unwilling to gamble, he looked for a safe nest. Men like Upton and Batchelor didn't have Edison's audacity, his hunger for recognition, his ability to inspire confidence, or the one-sidedness that led Edison to live for his work and by his work. Edison himself recognized that he was an anomaly. "Don't touch this business," he warned an aspiring inventor. "Not one man in a thousand ever succeeds in it."

Edison succeeded because he was an eternal optimist who would not let himself or others consider the possibility of failure; because he was an unconventional thinker, who accumulated the resources that enabled him to transform his ideas into reality; because he charged ahead when others hung back; because he demolished the opposition and bowled over impediments. A child of the rough-and-ready universe of the Industrial Revolution, where many failed but a few succeeded spectacularly, he was the product of a unique conjunction of talent, ambition, and opportunity. There was never anyone like him before. And, in the hundred years since, the world has changed so radically it is highly improbable that there will ever be anyone like him again.

The American Myth of Thomas Edison

Wyn Wachhorst

Wyn Wachhorst, who teaches history at the University of California, Santa Cruz, links the mythology of Thomas Edison as a hero to American cultural values and sheds new light on the origin and cultural function of the myths. Having been crowned a folk hero, Edison's persona as portrayed by various media labels became an unusual blend of Promethean wizard, scientist, inventor, rugged individualist, kindly and democratic benefactor, grandfatherly sage, and technological Santa Claus. As Wachhorst notes, Edison's image changed with the times. For example, when America was suffering from the effects of the Great Depression of 1929, Edison was criticized as a champion of modernization, ignorant that his deeds had helped create a new society that was on the verge of collapse. Later as prosperity returned and America built an atom bomb and entered the space race, science and invention were popular again and Edison became the symbol of American ingenuity. Wachhorst asserts that the varying depictions of Edison have less to do with his true character than with society's fluctuating beliefs about the power of the individual and the potential benefits versus the potential dangers of science.

Almost to the year, his life had spanned that explosion of human energy which transformed America between the 1840s and the 1920s. In his first memory he had seen wagons set out for California during the gold fever of '49; and in his last months he saw the nation sink ever more deeply into depression. Biographers placed his boyhood in the preindustrial innocence of Tom Sawyer's Jacksonian America; his drifting

Excerpted from Wyn Wachhorst, *Thomas Alva Edison: An American Myth.* Copyright © 1981 The Massachusetts Institute of Technology. Reprinted with permission from the MIT Press.

adolescence paralleled civil war, Reconstruction, and the birth of a national economy; and the productivity of his early manhood was indispensable to the urban-industrial transformation. It is understandable that twentieth-century America, imbued with a sense of narrowing options, has looked nostalgically to Edison as the embodiment of a Golden Age of youth, hope, and vitality. . . .

INDIVIDUALISM IN A GOLDEN AGE

In the final analysis it was not technological achievement which placed Edison alongside of Washington and Lincoln. For as twentieth-century America became ever more centralized and interdependent, the Promethean drive which had produced the abstract, impersonal society began to seem less appealing than Edison's raw, unbounded individualism. Yet if he became less the promise of utopia and more the surviving symbol of Paradise lost, it was not the loss of the pastoral itself that was mourned. For individuality was swallowed by "Sleepy Hollow" no less than by the technological society. Rather, Edison survived as a memento from that moment of equilibrium in the historical cycle—characteristic of "golden ages"—when forces cancel and the culture is drawn in all directions. In such transitional times, the cultural mainstream becomes a confusion of eddies and whirlpools in which most people drift erratically and some drown, but many discover unprecedented individual freedom. The resulting explosion of creativity and the fragmentation and decay of the Old Order are experienced as one phenomenon, scattering the seeds of new consensuses. Compared to Periclean Athens or Renaissance Italy, of course, the transformation experienced by nineteenth-century America was less fundamental, proceeding as it did within the larger consensus of rational liberalism. Yet there is more than naiveté in the comparison of Greek sculpture, Renaissance painting, and American invention; for the burst of technological creativity had effects greater than those of all previous upheavals put together.

All of this is simply another perspective on the paradoxical function of all culture heroes and the fact that Edison balanced the machine and the garden, power and innocence, isolation and communion. The shifting emphases within the mythology, from Promethean wizard and erudite scientist to the kindly, venerable, and democratic benefactor and finally to the tinkering, vernacular, unreconstructed individualist, was accelerated, as we have seen, after the turn of the century. By the 1920s Edison had become an incongruous blend of the Promethean and the profane, a kind of grandfatherly, senatorial Santa Claus, who, along with his friend [Henry] Ford, had delivered the modern miracles while America slept—all the trappings of the Jazz Age suddenly discovered by awakened American youth: automobiles, records, telephones, city lights, and silent movies.

CHANGING VIEWS OF EDISON

During the years immediately surrounding Edison's death, a century of unparalleled expansion seemed to reach its limits and collapse. The sense of encroaching boundaries, dating perhaps from the symbolic closing of the frontier in 1890, seemed inherent in the very process of modernization itself. In a larger context, as Walter Webb has argued, the thirties marked the inevitable end of the four-hundred-year boom in Western civilization. But from the perspective of a few Depression-bound Americans, Edison represented the foolish innocence of a late-maturing society. To them it seemed that he [like Prometheus of Greek myth] had stolen the fire but escaped the fate, leaving Everyman himself fastened to the rock with the vulture feeding on his liver. The criticisms of Edison which arose in the thirties completed the humanization process begun decades earlier. It was less the negative comment and more the evolution of the twentieth century itself, however, which eventually caused the image to lose much of its Olympian aura.

In its place, on one hand, was a nostalgic and reactionary vision of Edison as the unrestricted individualist of an earlier and better time. On the other hand, a new view of Edison had begun to emerge in the twenties, though it would not become dominant for almost a half-century. This was the affirmative and energetic human being which the 1970s would see as the antithesis to passivity, defeat, and stagnation. We shall return to this perspective in conclusion; for the moment, we may note that the idea of "service to mankind," which began to develop in the Edison image during World War I, was a nascent aspect of this new dimension. . . .

THE 1920S IMAGE: EDISON THE HUMANITARIAN

The concept of service which emerged in this century differed significantly from that of the nineteenth. By the 1920s, when the shift in orientation from production to consumption—from manufacturing to marketing—was complete, the small-business proprietor on the local level and the top managerial executive on the national level had largely replaced the great manufacturers and inventors as the self-proclaimed symbols of service. The word "service" itself had been used infrequently by the late nineteenth-century titans. In the twentieth century, however, it became so standard as to require a capital "S" for easier handling. Rotary International, founded in Chicago in 1905, built its philosophy around such phrases as "He Profits Most Who Serves Best" and "Service Above Self." As the twentieth century moved toward the "post-industrial society," those engaged in actual services would ultimately outnumber those employed in all areas of production. In an ever more interdependent social organism, success depended less on Edisonian industriousness and perseverance and more on other-directed perception and the ability to project a sincere and self-sacrificing image.

Thus the older and newer heroes of service correspond roughly to the builders and the maintainers, the producers and the managers. Both fit the monomythic pattern in that builders extended the area of freedom in a future-oriented society, while the maintainers hold ground against encroaching limits in a present-oriented society—like [Calvin] Coolidge and Edison, they become surrogate parents who persevere while we play.

This perspective had much to do with the fact that the "humanized" Edison of the twenties still retained an Olympian quality. Such portraits as the Shinn photograph or the Silvette painting made him look like a humanitarian United States senator, provoking descriptions of a venerable and wise old man—"the Nestor of American invention"—and a lover of animals and children. The momentum of this image sometimes led to exaggerated assertions that he "was never angry in his life" or that his protective feelings toward baby mice caused lengthy work stoppages in the laboratory. Most pathetic, perhaps, was one writer's attempt to depict "the human Edison," as he titled his piece, by presenting a series of five incidents, each of which climaxed with Edison crying like a baby; the article, which is saturated with ad-

Throughout his life the public viewed Thomas Edison in a variety of ways, but the description of him as a great thinker and inventor has been the one which continues to describe him today.

jectives, concludes with the alliterated statement that he left the "sad, sobbing old man traduced by the tyranny of tears."

In spite of the fact that Edison himself, as later writers would note, "did not try to imitate the imaginary figure of a cultured, dignified and benevolent gentleman, created by the media," the image was perpetuated in the twenties under the assumption that such figures symbolize empathy with the common man. A strong part of Edison's service image, in fact, was the publicity given to his alleged equalitarian concern for the plain people. (I found no statement of the democratic-egalitarian theme prior to 1909.) Yet Edison himself "never spoke of 'service to humanity' or his 'mission in life,'" said a former assistant; "commercial demand was his measure of need." He "did not care for money but neither did he care for service that much," added another; he was "a compulsive achiever" who craved fame and prestige. Back in Menlo Park, during the struggle to perfect the light, Edison once told a reporter: "I don't care so much for fortune, as I do for getting ahead of the other fellows." . . .

The irony of the stilted stereotypes and shallow criticisms is that, in the end, Edison really *was* at one with the common man. "The birthday interviews, the questionnaires, the an-

nual trips to Florida," said Mary Nerney, who had also been
an Edison employee, "all contributed to a stereotyped impression, as did the hackneyed anecdotes, the 'authorized'
biographies." They "blurred the rough outlines of his individualism." They made him "a conventional figure, exemplary but dull, the victim of the publicity of flat minds. A
great name, a bust in time for the Hall of Fame, but not Edison." The Edison she had in mind was "above everything . . .
human, delightfully, charmingly, naively and utterly human." This was the Edison whom Shaw Desmond depicted
as an innocent child throughout a series of articles in 1922
and who was called "the best beloved man in America" at
the presentation of the Congressional Medal in 1928. It was
the same figure whom Spencer Tracy portrayed in the MGM
film *Edison the Man* (1940) and who, according to the *New
York Times* obituary, was loved for his "fine simplicities and
boyishness" and his "warm human presence."

The "human" Edison, first glimpsed in the success theme,
took more direct form in the human interest interviews after the turn of the century and finally dominated the image
in the 1920s. The human dimension remained incomplete,
however, until after his death. The later descriptions of Edison's raw individualism were based almost entirely on an
article written for *Harper's Monthly* in 1932 by Martin A.
Rosanoff, one of Edison's former assistants. The article,
which radically altered the image of Edison for subsequent
writers, offers a large number of new anecdotes, the most
popular of which occurred during Rosanoff's first day on the
job in 1903:

> I approached him in a humble spirit: "Mr. Edison, please tell
> me what laboratory rules you want me to observe." And right
> then and there I got my first surprise. He spat in the middle
> of the floor and yelled out, "Hell! there *ain't* no rules around
> here! We are tryin' to accomplish somep'n!" . . .

THE MYTH OF THE TINKERING INVENTOR

Some types of criticism, such as that which attacked Edison
as a business baron who posed as champion of the common
man, did not survive the 1930s; his ignorance of [scientific]
theory, however, was the subject of negative comment well
into the post-World War II period. . . .

In the total image, however, we shall find that skepticism
concerning his anti-intellectualism was more than bal-

anced by the degree to which it enhanced his unreconstructed individualism. Edison's attitude was a normal aspect of the nineteenth-century dispute between scientists and inventors—a mutual contempt resolved by the contemporary public in favor of the tinkering inventor. This bias was still evident during World War I when Edison's appointment to the Naval Board was viewed by the press as assurance that the best brains would now be available for the application of science to naval problems. Actually, the one scientist on the Board was put there only because Edison had suggested to the President that "we might have one mathematical fellow in case we have to calculate something out." "As late as 1917," writes James Conant, "it was primarily the inventor, not the scientist, who was looked to by the general public as being the prime mover of technology."

During the interwar period, however, the electrical, chemical, and pharmaceutical industries led the way in bringing science into industry. The great research laboratories of General Electric, Bell Telephone, and DuPont are examples. It is ironic that the inventors, who made possible the increased productive capacity and the means of transportation and communication necessary to national markets, would in turn see their kind swallowed into the impersonal obscurity of the "research team" by the very organizations for which they had paved the way. Edison himself established a model for this nonrecognition, building his own team of assistants and sometimes taking credit for their work in much the same way that corporate organizations now reap the publicity for technological achievement. The difference, in Edison's own case, was best phrased in his answer to a visitor's question about the organization and methods of the laboratory: "Organization! Hell! I'm the organization!"

But Edison's most recent biographer, Robert Conot, suggests that Edison lacked the capacity for supervising; he himself always had to be a part of what was going on:

> Although his ideas and plans were often boundless, he worked best in intimate surroundings, where a few steps could take him from [Charles] Batchelor experimenting with the telephone to [Francis] Upton wrestling with the incandescent light.

> What he could not understand, he was not interested in. Despite the camaraderie of the laboratory and the pleasure he obtained from nocturnal socializing, his deafness acted like an auditory veil—his intake of knowledge was overwhelm-

ingly visual. He had difficulty participating in lengthy conversations or absorbing involved explanations.

Essentially, his was a lonely striving, within a social setting. It was alien to his nature to consider that success might depend on the strength and capabilities of his retainers. He was uneasy with men who were too independent, or whose knowledge challenged his. He was indifferent and even antagonistic toward men who wanted to pursue their own ideas under his aegis. He preferred men of limited talent . . . who he knew were dependent on him.

Consequently, men of real talent, men like Nikola Tesla, Frank Sprague, Edward Acheson, and Samuel Mott, stayed at Menlo Park only a short time and then moved on. The problem was compounded at the West Orange laboratory where Edison assigned projects to people, and tried to make the

LEGACIES OF THE EDISON ARCHIVES

In this article on the Thomas Edison voluminous archives, Seth Shulman paints an accurate picture of the urgency to catalog and microfilm this vast collection (3,500 handwritten notebooks and 5 million papers) of underutilized resources of technical papers written by Edison and his staff.

A massive effort to catalogue [Edison's] voluminous collection of papers and artifacts is yielding fresh clues to account for his phenomenal success.

Leonard DeGraaf, sporting the familiar beige and green uniform of the U.S. National Park Service, leads the way through a narrow subterranean passageway to one of the country's invaluable and rarely viewed wonders . . . the massively thick steel door of an underground bank vault.

Unlike many of his park-ranger colleagues, DeGraaf is neither a forester nor a geologist but a historian of technology. The passageways of his prized grotto, some 15 feet below the barren, paved courtyard of an aging laboratory complex, are human-made and lined floor to ceiling with shelves of papers. DeGraaf pulls open the vault's thick steel portal to reveal a collection of some of technology's most fertile germinations: the 3,500 handwritten notebooks of Thomas Alva Edison. Now administered by the U.S. Park Service, the vault is the heart of the Edison Archives, a bomb-resistant bunker built below the famous inventor's laboratory in West Orange, N.J.

DeGraaf explains that Edison and his colleagues used the notebooks as a daily log of their experiments just as many modern labs do. But Edison also recorded his musings about

rounds of the experimental rooms like a hospital physician. But often he became interested in what was happening in one room, and spent the whole week there. Since he disliked employing people with intelligence and initiative to pursue experiments independently, he left men in other rooms, who were deprived of his direction, floundering about. He continued to measure employees more by their salaries than by their output. He dismissed chemists, but hired hordes of boys with little education on the premise that it was cheaper to train his own workers. . . .

More and more it would become evident that only in those projects in which Edison himself was personally involved was reasonable progress made. Almost never were more than two major projects sustainable simultaneously.

---

cosmology, observations of the natural world, sketches, even occasional poetry. In these pages, for instance, Edison not only details the steps leading to his successful prototype of the incandescent light-bulb but also his forays into everything from x-rays to air travel. Spanning most of his astonishing six-decade career, the vast collection offers an opportunity, rare in its detail and depth, to peer inside the mind of one of history's greatest inventors.

What makes the notebooks all the more fascinating . . . is the fact that the Edison estate, bestowed to the Park Service in 1955, also contains a remarkably diverse collection of related documents and artifacts, including correspondence, legal records, prototypes, and Edison's complete library of books and articles, many scrawled with his wide-ranging and often irreverent marginalia. "We are blessed here with one of the most complete personal archives in the history of technology," DeGraaf says. "A researcher here can trace an idea from its earliest conception through to its full-scale development and production."

Complete as the collection may be, . . . the locked bunker and bank vault serve as an unfortunately apt metaphor for the sequestered archive. As a result of some measure of neglect, underfunding, and incompetence, only a few individuals have ever viewed the bulk of the papers and memorabilia. . . . Roughly half of the lab's 5 million documents and 400,000 artifacts have yet to be catalogued.

Seth Shulman, "Unlocking the Legacies of the Edison Archives," *MIT's Technology Review*, February/March 1997, pp. 42–52.

Edison's view of the laboratory as a creative cornucopia was impracticable.

These realities qualify to some degree the common observation that Edison invented the modern research laboratory.

By World War II, scientists as scientists were being called upon by the government. . . . The man in the street now came to see [said Edwin Layton] "that the scientist is today taking the place of the inventor; that the 'long-haired' professors who were elaborating highly abstruse mathematical theories had been able to play an important part in the extraordinary development of the atomic bomb."

ATOMIC AGE IMAGE: PRODUCER OF SUPERIOR TECHNOLOGY

The impact of the atomic age as such on the Edison image has probably been fourfold. First, the nuclear revolution, being potentially comparable to that of steam and electricity, recharged the aura of magic surrounding science and technology. The layman began to realize that the scientist was playing the same role in other fields that he had in the military; medicine was the prime example. Second, the technological race associated with the Cold War, particularly after the launching of Sputnik I in 1957, stimulated a greater emphasis on careers in science. Not only was attention to science increased in elementary and secondary schools, but television programs such as "Mr. Wizard" and "Science in Action" became extremely popular in the 1950s. In this context Edison remained the symbol of "the miracle of America's productive capacity"—the technological superiority which had won the war, and which made "the genius-hungry Russians fret with envy." "Throughout the world the race of science is on, and the pace is fast," said the president of NBC during a tribute to Edison in 1948. "A nation that is slow to meet this challenge imperils its security." Inevitably, the eighth Polaris atomic submarine, launched in 1961, was christened *Thomas A. Edison.*

Equally predictable was the fact that Edison was credited with anticipating the atomic bomb. Former Postmaster General James Farley, among others, quoted Edison's statement that "there will one day spring from the brain of science a machine of force so fearful in its potentialities, so absolutely terrifying, that even man, the fighter, who will dare torture and death in order to inflict torture and death, will be appalled and so will abandon war forever." . . .

The fact that Edison remained the American symbol of science while interest in the subject increased and the realities of the man himself became ever more anachronistic resulted in the paradox of most culture heroes in this century: appreciation without interest. Thus, in 1957, Edison's birthday was permanently changed to "National Science Youth Day." Referred to as "a nationwide effort by industry, government and education to interest young people in science," the stated purpose was "to focus national attention on the critical shortage of scientists and engineers"—always in the context of the Cold War. . . .

A GROWING DISTRUST OF SCIENCE

Yet to become dated is not always to lose relevance and respect. It it possible that the change in attitudes was as much toward science itself as toward Edison. While he had been associated with a millennial view of science, the new aura of scientific magic after Hiroshima may have seemed more black than white. A 1959 public opinion survey about science and scientists indicated at least a more overt ambivalence. The great majority of Americans (92 percent), the study found, believed that science was "making our lives healthier, easier, and more comfortable" and (87 percent) that it was "the main reason for our rapid progress." Medicine received the greatest praise, followed by contributions to human welfare and the military role of science. A large minority (47 percent), however, also felt that science "makes our way of life change too fast" and (40 percent) that the growth of science meant "that a few people could control our lives" (this group had increased by 25 percent over pre-Sputnik responses). A smaller group (25 percent) felt that science destroyed morals. Most of the developments in atomic science were viewed as an area of threat, and "most of the new advances in space were seen much more in the area of an international race with Russia and the total context of the 'cold war,' than as advances in science per se." In sum, the study found "respect and appreciation, but little real curiosity and interest, and . . . a certain amount of distrust and apprehension."

This ambivalence is the fourth and most significant condition affecting the Edison symbol in the postwar era. "For good or ill, others have let loose the Atomic Age from Pandora's box of uranium," said the *New York Times* in 1947.

"Since Edison's death, science . . . has hurled us, willing or not, into the blind future of a darker world than that in which he lived." At a meeting of the Pioneers on the centenary of his birth—in spite of Mrs. Edison's opening assurances as to "how thrilled he would be if he were here with us today"—the president of Rutgers University, whose speech followed hers, declared that if Edison were alive "he would look with eyes not free from anxiety upon the contemporary scene. He would look out over the international scene in a world shrunk to a hazelnut by the magic of modern science and witness the incredible farce of great nations splitting hairs in the face of potential extinction." "There was a day when the laboratory was not necessarily considered as the birthplace of death-dealing weapons," wrote the editor of the *Los Angeles Times* that same day, "it was the era of Thomas A. Edison." Even Edison's son, former secretary of the navy and governor of New Jersey, Charles Edison, urged an "effort to curb science's power" and avoid catastrophe. By the 1970s, concern for the environment had joined Cold War anxieties as a counterforce to faith in technology. After a blackout of midtown Manhattan in 1971, Charles F. Luce, chairman of the Consolidated Edison Company of New York, told the public that he could not promise that it would not happen again. "Mr. Luce, who used to agree with Mr. Edison and urged increased use of electricity, now does not," said the *Times*.

During the first half of the twentieth century, although there were few abstract, philosophical attacks on either Edison or the technological society, some negative reaction was inevitable, given the style of Edison's pronouncements. His response in 1927, for example, to complaints about automobiles speeding up the world was that "it serves to stir up our sluggish brain cells." Thus one commentator observed that "sometimes it appears that they [Edison and other inventors] have done little except enable us to run around a little more rapidly in our squirrel cage of civilization." In Eugene O'Neill's little-known play, *Dynamo* (1929), the hero worships the dynamo as a religious idol, "a great, dark mother"; inventors, however, are not implicated. . . .

PRODUCTION IS SACRED

In his 1938 memoirs, Edison's secretary, A.O. Tate, attacked the New Deal as a threat to "individual initiative." "The power of government," he said, "must be acquired by subtraction from its original source, the individual. To the same degree that government is strengthened by these accretions, individuals are weakened. The process is like a subtle degenerate disease." In the years which followed, the anecdotes of Edisonian individualism gained the status of scriptural readings in the crusade against government paternalism. In 1947 the Virginia Electrical Power Company ran an ad which called attention to the fact, in reference to the invention of the light, that *"government didn't do the job. Individuals did."* "No human being ever learned to walk by being carried," said a Pennsylvania Chief Justice in 1950, and "at no time in his life did Thomas A. Edison attempt to snuggle in the arms of paternalistic government. No American in those days," he went on, "dreamed that the day would come when the government would subsidize scarcity, foster indolence, discourage industry, and promote general disaster instead of general welfare."

Production, of course, was one of the sacred functions of the machine. Edison's belief in "efficiency"—in the idea that "every effort should be made to speed work up," that "the future of the race depends on quantity production," and that "talk of overproduction is a bugaboo"—was frequently cited by postwar spokesmen who accused their contemporaries of "dodging work" and irresponsibly "restricting production and output." Edison's "life's work and accomplishments challenge us to more intelligent efforts, to greater production, . . . to the end that we may make more things cheaper, sell more things faster, create more and more jobs." . . .

THE EPITOME OF SELF-RELIANT SUCCESS

In the last sentence of his 1938 memoirs, A.O. Tate spoke of "that historic era when, under the inspiration of Individual Initiative and Self-reliance, the foundations of America's great modern Industrial Empire were laid by its courageous Pioneers." But in 1938 that era did not seem quite so distant nor its passing quite so final. "Contemporary philosophers," said Tate, "are straining their intellects to the bursting point in an effort to identify the values which we have lost. They seem to think that something happened in the period following the Great War. They are mistaken. Nothing escaped. We have lost nothing." After the Second World War, however, few denied the loss. The task, said the president of the Southern California Edison Company in 1947, was to "dedicate ourselves anew to the revival of the ideals and moral atmosphere, the freedom and opportunity, which existed in the America which he [Edison] knew, and but for which it is doubtful that his genius could have flowered." It was fitting that in 1951, on the sixtieth anniversary of the invention of the motion picture camera, the person chosen to announce that "Edison's life work stands as a symbol of the spirit of our nation" was none other than Mary Pickford, the silent-film sweetheart of a more innocent time.

The longing for the frontier individualism of a freer and simpler time, which dominated postwar references to Edison, went hand-in-hand with the popularity of the TV western in the fifties. It also suggested comparisons of Edison to Lincoln, who had become the American archetype of self-reliant success, surpassing even Franklin. Edison was often called "the greatest American since Abraham Lincoln." . . .

The individual's conflicting roles and identities in an impersonal yet interdependent society are of course the very condition which has brought the reactionary obsession with individual autonomy. Edison "looked on people as individuals and not as numbers in a file case," said a writer in 1947. And the developer of the radio tube, Lee De Forest, lamented that "the lone inventor will never again have Edison's opportunity for a life work in exploring unknown fields alone. . . . All the seas are charted; all continents, nay islands, are discovered and surveyed. There are no more frontiers for lone La Salles and Coronados. Instead armies of scientists flail the garnered wheat together. This spells wealth for humanity; but never again will solitary names blaze singly in a starless sky." Jonathan Hughes was no less nostalgic when he called Edison "the last great hayseed."

DISCUSSION QUESTIONS

CHAPTER 1

1. Edison was an enterprising teenager. Gene Adair identifies specific instances when Edison showed his entrepreneurial tendencies and quick thinking to leverage two situations to greatly benefit himself. Explain what these were and how he used them to his advantage.

2. The invention of the telegraph by Samuel Morse was the biggest advancement in communications since the carrier pigeons. Neil Baldwin mentions a strange event that gave young Edison the opportunity to learn telegraphy. Describe what happened and what effect it had on Edison's life.

3. Joseph and Frances Gies describe Edison's improvements to the stock ticker and the repercussions that occurred because of them. Discuss what those repercussions were.

CHAPTER 2

1. Thomas P. Hughes comments on Menlo Park being the first American research and development laboratory and that it differed greatly from the R&D labs that would ultimately follow. What were some of the major benefits that Menlo Park offered Edison?

2. According to Andre Millard, the West Orange laboratory that was ten times larger than Menlo Park was created on this grand scale for several reasons. What were they, and did Edison achieve any of these aims?

3. Using the reverse-salient concept used in the metaphor of an advancing military front, Thomas P. Hughes describes the developing of a technological system. Explain how Edison used the reverse-salient technique to launch the incandescent lighting system project and to plot the course of its development.

4. In the 1890s, there was a major shift in the pattern of American inventing. Paul Israel points out some of the practices that caused this. What exactly brought this shift about and why?

211

CHAPTER 3

1. Ira Flatow debunks the myth that Thomas Edison was the sole inventor of the lightbulb but explains that Edison had a single concept that all other lightbulb inventors lacked. Describe what that concept was and how Edison made it work.

2. In describing the war of the electric currents, Robert Silverberg mentions some of the controversies involved. Discuss the pros and cons of each method and explain why the prevailing method won.

3. Paul Israel offers his comments about the specific vision that Edison had for the phonograph. Discuss the unique marketing plan that was ultimately used to promote the phonograph and why this worked so well.

4. Edison often had limited ideas of how particular inventions would best be utilized and made interesting predictions that never came to fruition. Explain what caused Edison to ultimately take a less active role in movie production.

CHAPTER 4

1. Gene Adair gives an overview of some of Edison's less successful inventions. Discuss some of them and why they didn't succeed.

2. William Simonds describes a new process Edison devised to extract pure iron from exhausted mines. Discuss the major factors that contributed to the failure of this and what Edison's attitude was about the outcome.

3. Not all of Edison's ventures beyond the lightbulb, phonograph, and kinetoscope were flops. Matthew Josephson notes several important inventions that share continued success to this day. Discuss what they are and why they succeeded.

CHAPTER 5

1. Auto industrialist Henry Ford believes that Edison's endorsement of his motor car helped to speed up the process of the auto industry. Discuss other reasons why Ford felt everyone owes Edison endless thanks.

2. Robert Conot asks the question "Why Edison?" when he examines how the offspring of such an ordinary family became the most extraordinary inventor in history. Discuss why you think Edison succeeded, even in the face of those who doubted his abilities.

3. Wyn Wachhorst sheds new light on the origin and cultural function of Thomas Edison as a cultural folk hero. Discuss why you think Edison was and still may be considered a hero.

APPENDIX OF DOCUMENTS

DOCUMENT 1: EDISON'S FIRST CHECK

His many improvements to the Wall Street "ticker" machine—a tele-graphic receiving instrument that automatically printed stock quo-tations or news on a paper ribbon—for General Lefferts gave Edison the opportunity of being a specialized inventor. When he was offered the monumental sum of $40,000 for the conclusion of his inventions for Lefferts, for once in his life Edison was almost speechless.

General Lefferts, who was a very prominent man at the time, being colonel of the N.Y. Seventh Regiment, was president of the Gold & Stock Telegraph Company, which supplied tickers to Wall Street and connected with various other companies. He requested me to go to work on improving the ticker he furnishing the money for the work. I made a great many inventions, one was the special ticker used for many years outside of N.Y. in the large cities. This was made exceedingly simple as the outside cities did not have the ex-perts we had in New York to handle anything complicated. The same ticker was used on the London Stock Exchange. After I had made a great number of inventions and obtained patents, the Gen-eral seemed anxious that the matter should be closed up. One day after I had exhibited and worked a successful device, whereby if a ticker should get out of unison in a broker's office and commenced to print wild figures, it could be brought to unison from the central station and which saved the labor of many men and much trouble to the broker. He called me into his office and said, "Now, young man I want to close up the matter of your inventions, how much do you think you should receive?" I had made up my mind that taking in consideration the time and the killing pace I was working that I should be entitled to $5,000, but could get along with $3,000, but when the psychological moment arrived, I hadn't the nerve to name such a large sum, so I said, "Well, General, Suppose you make me an offer." Then he said, "How would forty thousand dol-lars strike you?" This caused me to come as near fainting as I ever got. I was afraid he would hear my heart beat. I managed to say that I thought it was fair. "All right, I will have a contract drawn, come around in three days and sign it, and I will give you the money. I ar-rived on time, but had been doing considerable thinking on the subject, the sum seemed to be very large for the amount of work, for at that time I determined the value by the time and trouble and not what the invention was worth to others. I thought there was something unreal about it. However, the contract was handed to me, I signed without reading it. The General called in the Secretary and told him to fix it up and pay the money. I was then handed a check for $40,000 on the bank of the State of New York, which was at the corner of William and Wall Streets. This was the first check I ever had. I went to the bank and noticed the window marked "Paying Teller," got in line with about a dozen men and a dozen messenger boys and slowly approached the window. When directly in front of the window passed in the check, he looked at it, turned it over and handed it back, making a few short remarks which I could not understand, being at that time as ever since, quite deaf. I passed outside to the large steps to let the cold sweat evaporate and made up my mind that this was another Wall Street game like those I had received over the press wire, that I had signed the contract whatever was in it, that the inventions were gone and I had been skinned out of the money. But when I thought of the General and knowing he had treated me well, I couldn't believe it, and I returned to the office and told the secretary what occurred. He went in and told the General and both had a good laugh. I was told to endorse the check and he would send a young man down with me to identify. We went to the bank, the young man had a short conversation with the Paying Teller, who seemed quite merry over it, I presented the check and the Teller asked me through the young man, how would I have it. I said in any way to please the bank. Then he commenced to pull out bundles of notes until there certainly seemed to be one cubic foot. These were passed out and I had the greatest trouble in finding room in my overcoat and other pockets. They had put a job up on me, but knowing nothing of bank customs in those days, I did not even suspect it. I went to Newark and sat up all night with the money for fear it might be stolen. The next day I went back with it all and told the General about it, and he laughed very greatly, but said to one of his young men—Don't carry this joke on any further, go to the bank with Edison and have him open an account and explain the matter, which I did.

Thomas Alva Edison, *Volume 1: The Papers of Thomas A. Edison, The Making of an Inventor, February 1847–June 1873*. Baltimore: The Johns Hopkins University Press, 1989.

DOCUMENT 2: SOME EDISON EMPLOYEES BECAME FAMOUS IN THEIR OWN RIGHT

Whether Edison knew how to hire the best scientists or these outstanding thinkers were just drawn to him, many brilliant men who partnered with Edison while he invented the incandescent electric lighting system moved on to high positions and great wealth.

There worked at one time along the same bench, several men who in after years became very rich and prominent. One was S. Bergmann, who afterwards, when I invented the incandescent electric lighting system became my partner with E.H. Johnson in the large works, once at Avenue B and 17th Street, and who is now at the head of the great Bergmann Electric Works in Berlin, employing 10,000 men. Mr. Bergmann is many times a millionaire. The next man adjacent was John Kreuzi, who became an engineer of the Works of the General Electric Company at Schenectady, and now deceased. The next was Shuckhart, who left the bench and went back to Nuremberg to settle up his father's estate, remained and started a small electrical works, which grew into the great Shuck-hart Works, the third largest in Germany, employing 7,000 men. Shuckhart died worth several millions. I gave them a good training as to working hours and hustling.

Thomas Alva Edison, *Volume 1: The Papers of Thomas A. Edison, The Making of an Inventor. February 1847–June 1873.* Baltimore: The Johns Hopkins University Press, 1989.

DOCUMENT 3: PERFECTING THE REMINGTON TYPEWRITER

While running four small research and development shops, Edison managed to solve the Automatic Telegraph Company's problem of rapid transmission. D.H. Craig, an agent of the Associated Press, who became interested in the Automatic Telegraph Company, introduced a Milwaukee inventor named Sholes to Edison. Sholes had a machine that Craig was impressed with—a contraption that he felt certain one day all business letters would be written on—a wooden typewriter.

I started an annex shop in Mechanic Street and also in the building occupied by the Richardson Saw Works; also one on R.R. Avenue. While running these shops I was engaged by the Automatic Telegraph Co. of N.Y., who had a line running between N.Y. and Washington to help them out of their trouble. It seems they had organized a company and built a line on the strength of some experiments by an English Inventor. The apparatus worked all right on a short wire in an office, but when put on the actual line, no results could be obtained. Connected with me was E.J. Johnson, who afterwards was associated with me in Electric Lighting and the introduction of the trolley with F.J. Sprague. After experimenting for several weeks, I devised new apparatus and solved the problem of rapid transmission so we succeeded in transmitting and recording 1,000 words per minute between Washington and N.Y. and 3,500 words per minute between Phila. and N.Y. This system was put in commercial operation. These experiments, with running my four shops, made sleep a scarce article with me. Then the Automatic Company wanted to spread out and have devised for them an automatic high speed telegraph, which would print the message in Roman letters instead of dots and dashes, and so they rented a large shop over the Gould factory in Newark, installed

25,000 dollars worth of machinery and gave me full charge. Here I devised and manufactured their instruments for commercial use and also started experiments on the Roman letter systems. I finished this and had a test between Phila. and N.Y., sending and receiving 3,000 words in one minute, and recording the same in large Roman letters. Mr. D.H. Craig, then the agent of the associated press became interested in the Company, of which Mr. J.C. Reiff was Vice President and Manager, and Geo. Harrington, former assistant Secretary U.S. Treasury, the President. Mr. Craig brought on from Milwaukee Mr. Sholes, who had a wooden model of a machine which was called a typewriter. Craig had some arrangement with Sholes and the model was put in my hands to perfect. This typewriter proved a difficult thing to get commercial, the alignment of the letters was awful, one letter would be 1/16 of an inch above the others, and all the letters wanted to wander out of line. I worked on it till the machine gave fair results. Some were made and used in the office of the Automatic Company. Craig was very sanguine that some day all business letters would be written on a typewriter. He died before that took place, but it gradually made its way.

The typewriter I got into commercial shape and is now known as the Remington typewriters.

Thomas Alva Edison, *Volume 1: The Papers of Thomas A. Edison, The Making of an Inventor. February 1847–June 1873.* Baltimore: The Johns Hopkins University Press, 1989.

DOCUMENT 4: DEAFNESS IS DEFINITE ADVANTAGE

For Edison, deafness proved to be such a positive attribute that it spurred him on to new inventions he might never have otherwise pursued. One proof of this is the improvements he made to the telephone transmitter.

This deafness has been of great advantage to me in various ways. When in a telegraph office I could only hear the instrument directly on the table at which I sat, and unlike the other operators, I was not bothered by the other instruments. Again, in experimenting on the telephone, I had to improve the transmitter, so I could hear it. This made the telephone commercial, as the telephone receiver of Bell was too weak to be used as a transmitter commercially.

Thomas Alva Edison, *Volume 2: The Papers of Thomas A. Edison, From Workshop to Laboratory, June 1873–March 1876.* Baltimore: The Johns Hopkins University Press, 1991.

DOCUMENT 5: THE A.B. DICK MIMEOGRAPH MACHINE WAS ORIGINALLY INVENTED BY EDISON

Much to the amazement of many people, the mimeograph machine was invented by Thomas Edison and sold to Mr. A.B. Dick of Chicago, Illinois.

Towards the latter part of 1875 in the Newark shop I invented a device for multiplying copies of letters, which I sold to Mr. A.B. Dick of Chicago, and in the years since it has been universally introduced throughout the world. It is called the Mimeograph. I also invented devices and introduced paraffin paper, now used universally for wrapping up candy, etc.

Thomas Alva Edison, *Volume 2: The Papers of Thomas A. Edison, From Workshop to Laboratory, June 1873–March 1876.* Baltimore: The Johns Hopkins University Press, 1991.

DOCUMENT 6: CLEVER BARGAINING YIELDS BIG BENEFITS

Being a young and innovative inventor, Edison realized the major benefits of being financially "taken care of" by a benefactor. After dropping hints to this affect to Western Union's president William Orton, Edison shrewdly asked Orton to make him an investment offer and wound up with four times the amount of money that he had in mind.

Tests were made between N.Y. and Phila. Also between N.Y. and Washington, using regular W.U. [Western Union] wires. The noises were so great that not a word could be heard with the Bell receiver when used as a transmitter between N.Y. and Newark. Mr. Orton and W. A. Vanderbilt, and the Board of Directors witnessed and took part in the tests. The W.U. then started in to put them on private lines. Mr. Theodore Puskas of Budapest, Hungary was the first man to suggest a telephone exchange and soon after exchanges were established. The telephone department was put in the hands of Hamilton McKay Twombly, Vanderbilt's ablest son-in-law, who made a success of it. The Bell Company in Boston, also started an exchange, and the fight was on the W.U. pirating the Bell receiver and the Boston Co. pirating the W.U. Transmitter. About this time, I wanted to be [financially] taken care of. I threw out hints of this desire. Then Mr. Orton sent for me. He had learned that inventors didn't do business by the regular process and concluded he would close it right up. He asked me how much I wanted. I had made up my mind that it certainly was worth $25,000, if it ever amounted to anything for central station work, so that was the sum I had made up my mind to stick to and get obstinate; still it had been an easy job and only required a few months and I felt a little shaky and uncertain. So I asked him to make me an offer. He promptly said he would give me $100,000. All right I said, it's yours on one condition and that is that you do not pay it all at once, but pay it to me at the rate of $6,000 per year for 17 years—the life of the patent. He seemed only too pleased to do this and it was closed. My ambition was about four sizes too large for my business capacity and I knew that I would soon spend this money experimenting if I got it all at once, so I fixed it so I couldn't. I saved 17 years of worry by this stroke.

Thomas Alva Edison, *Volume 3: The Papers of Thomas A. Edison, Menlo Park: The Early Years, April 1876–December 1877.* Baltimore: The Johns Hopkins University Press, 1991.

DOCUMENT 7: THE SIMPLE PHONOGRAPH

Edison amazed himself when his phonograph invention worked the very first time. He had a machine that would record and reproduce the human voice—a concept everyone was convinced was so complex that no one seemed to understand the process when Edison attempted to explain its simplicity.

In 1877, I invented the phonograph. The invention was brought about in this way. I was experimenting on an automatic method of recording telegraph messages on a disk of paper laid on a revolving platten, exactly the same as the disk talking machine of today. The platten had a volute spiral groove on its surface, like the disk. Over this was placed a circular disk of paper, an electromagnet with an embossing point connected to an arm travelled over the disk and any signals given the magnets was embossed on the disk of paper. If this disk was removed from the machine, and put on another similar machine provided with a contact point, the embossed record would cause the signals to be repeated into another wire. The ordinary speed of telegraphic signals is 35 to 40 words a minute, but with this machine several hundred words were possible. From my experiments on the telephone I knew of the power of a diaphragm to take up sound vibrations, as I had made a little toy which when you recited loudly in the funnel would work a pawl connected to the diaphragm and this engaging in a ratchet wheel served to give continuous rotation to a pulley. This pulley was connected by a cord to a little paper toy representing a man sawing wood. Hence, if one shouted Mary had a little lamb, etc., the paper man would start sawing wood. I reached the conclusion that if I could record the movements of the diaphragm properly I could cause such record to reproduce the original movements imparted to the diaphragm by the voice and thus succeed in recording and reproducing the human voice.

Instead of using a disk, I designed a little machine using a cylinder provided with grooves around the surface. Over this was to be placed tin-foil, which easily received and recorded the movements of the diaphragm. A sketch was made and the piece work price $18 was marked on the sketch. I was in the habit of marking the price I would pay on each sketch. If the workman lost, I would pay his regular wages; if he made more than the wages he kept it. The workman who got the sketch was John Kreuzi, who in after years became Chief Engineer of the General Electric Company. I didn't have much faith that it would work, expecting that I might possibly hear a word or so that would give hope of a future for the idea. Kreuzi, when he had nearly finished it, asked what it was for. I told him that I was going to record talking, and then have the machine talk back. He thought it absurd. However, it was finished, the foil put on; I then shouted Mary had a little lamb, etc. I adjusted the reproducer and the machine reproduced it perfectly. I never was so taken back in my life. Everybody was astonished. I was always afraid of things that worked the first time. Long experiments proved that there was great drawbacks generally found before they could be got commercial, but here was something that there was no doubt of.

I worked at it all night and we fixed it up to get the best results. That morning I took it over to N.Y. and walked into the office of the Scientific American, walked up to Mr. Beech's desk and said I had something new to show him. He asked what it was. I told him I had a machine that would record and reproduce the human voice. I opened the package set up the machine and recited Mary, etc., then I reproduced it so it could be heard all over the room. They kept me at it until the crowds got so great that Mr. Beech was afraid the floor would collapse and we were compelled to stop. The papers next morning contained columns. None of the writers seemed to understand how it was done. I tried to explain it was so very very simple, but the results were so surprising that they probably made up their mind beforehand that they could never understand it, and they didn't.

Thomas Alva Edison, *Volume 3: The Papers of Thomas A. Edison, Menlo Park: The Early Years, April 1876–December 1877.* Baltimore: The Johns Hopkins University Press, 1991.

DOCUMENT 8: A SURE-FIRE BUG REPELLENT

At the request of a farmer, Edison concocted an industrial-strength bug spray that eliminated more than just the pests.

At Menlo Park one day a farmer came in and asked if I knew any way to kill potato bugs; he had 20 acres of potatoes and the vines were being destroyed. I sent men out and culled two quarts of bugs and tried every chemical I had to destroy them. Bisulphide of Carbon was found to do it, instantly. I got a drum and went over to the potato farm and sprinkled it on the vines with a sprinkling pot; every bug dropped dead. The next morning the farmer came in very excited and reported that the stuff had killed the vines as well. I had to pay $300 for not experimenting properly.

Thomas Alva Edison, *Volume 3: The Papers of Thomas A. Edison, Menlo Park: The Early Years, April 1876–December 1877.* Baltimore: The Johns Hopkins University Press, 1991.

DOCUMENT 9: STRAY MUSINGS

Thomas Edison's only diary was written in July of 1885, almost a year after the death of his first wife, Mary Stilwell Edison, and during the first sabbatical ever for 37-year-old Edison. The diary gives glimpses into the human side of the inventor and shows a humorous bent as in the first musing on reading and dandruff, and the second excerpt on a recollected dream.

Menlo Park NJ
Sunday, July 12 1885
    Awakened at 8 15 am. Powerful itching of my head, lots of white dry dandruff—what is this d—— mnable material, Perhaps it's the dust from the dry literary matter I've crowded into my noddle [noodle] lately It's nomadic, gets all over my coat, must read about it in the Encyclopedia. Smoking too much makes me nervous—must lasso my natural tendency to acquire such habits—holding heavy cigar constantly in my mouth has deformed my upper lip, it has a sort of Havana curl. Arose at 9 oclock came down stairs expecting twas too late for breakfast twas'nt. could'nt eat much, nerves of stomach too nicotinny. The roots of tobacco plants must go clear through to hell. Satan's principal agent Dyspepsia must have charge of this branch of the vegetable kingdom.—It has just occurred to me that the brain may digest certain portions of food, say the ethereal part, as well as the stomach—perhaps dandruff is the excreta of the mind—the quantity of this material being directly proportional to the amount of reading one indulges in. A book on German metaphysics would thus easily ruin a dress suit. After breakfast start reading [Nathaniel] Hawthorne's English Note Book dont think much of it.—perhaps I'm a literary barbarian and am not yet educated up to the point of appreciating fine writing—90 per cent of his book is descriptive of old churches and graveyards and coroners— He and Geo Selwyn ought to have been appointed perpetual coroners of London. Two fine things in the book were these. . . .

Woodside
July 21, 1885
    After breakfast laid down on sofa, fell into light draught sleep dreamed that in the depth of space, on a bleak and gigantic planet the solitary soul of the great Napoleon was the sole inhabitant. I saw him as in the pictures, in contemplative aspect with his blue eagle eye, amid the howl of the tempest and the lashing of gigantic waves high up on a jutting promontory gazing out among the worlds and stars that stud the depths of infinity Miles above him circled and swept the sky with ponderous wing the imperial condor bearing in his talons a message. Then the scene gusted—This comes from reading about Napoleon in Madame Recamier's memoirs. Then my dream changed—Thought I was looking out upon the sea, suddenly the air was filled with millions of little cherubs as one sees in Raphael's pictures each I thought was about the size of a fly. They were perfectly formed and seemed semitransparent, each swept down to the surface of the sea, reached out both their tiny hands and grabbed a very small drop of water, and flew upwards where they assembled and appeared to form a cloud. This method of forming clouds was so different from the method described in Ganots Physics that I congratulated myself on having

learned the true method and was thinking how I would gloat over
the chagrin of those cold blooded Savans who would dissect an an-
gel or boil a live baby to study the perturbations of the human lar-
ynx. Then this scheme was wreaked by my awakening.

Thomas Alva Edison, *The Diary of Thomas A. Edison.* Old Greenwich, CT: The
Chatham Press, Inc., 1970, pp. 27–70.

DOCUMENT 10: EDISON VIEWS THE WORLD AT SEVENTY

*In this interview, Edison comments on a variety of topics, from his
diet and smoking habits, musical preferences, to which invention
was the most difficult and which was the easiest for him.*

"Do I still detest the big cities?" asked Mr. Edison. "Indeed yes. I
never go to New York if I can help it. I would not go if I were to be
paid $500 a trip. My organism is built to withstand the demands of
a moderate civilization and my nerves are intact because I don't
hear well. People have to adapt themselves to their environment,
and I guess we'll have to be deaf in time."

Then came the query as to whether Mr. Edison continued to
murder sleep with toil as in past years.

"Yes," he said. "I'm still working eighteen hours a day on the average and sleeping four or five.

"Say," Mr. Edison continued, "I see that a police squad in New
York is trying to see how it feels to live on 25 cents a day. Why, I
have been doing that for years. That is what keeps me so well. For
six weeks at a time I have lived on eleven ounces of food, including
water. I mean the water in food, of course, for I drink lots of it. I
rarely eat more than six ounces. I boil everything except the water;
no lettuce, celery or other raw things. The purpose of that is to
guard me against bacterial invasion. I'm loaded with phagocytes—
the friendly little chaps that fight your battle in the blood against
disease, you know—but I don't want to make their task any harder
than it is. Eating little, but enough food, and having it cooked, is
what keeps my blood in good condition. A while ago I cut my finger and in three days it was completely healed.

"They talk about the danger of working with chemicals, but
chemicals are nowhere near as dangerous as bacteria. I never had
any trouble with chemicals until a week ago, when I breathed
some nitrous acid fumes and it made my lungs smart. There was
something the matter with my nose and my olfactories did not
warn me in time."

Mr. Edison has strong opinions regarding diet, but is no faddist.

"I eat three meals a day," he said, "and never between meals. I
eat everything—whatever I want—but not much of anything. I have
found that I get along best on small quantities. I keep my weight
normal by eating only about one-fourth as much as other men;
that's a good test, isn't it? Eating too much is a habit, just like sleeping too much. If the sun never set men would get out of the habit of

sleeping; they'd get used to going without."

"What do you eat, Mr. Edison?"

"Oh, a red herring, dried beef, a little piece of pie—anything that comes along. Sometimes I have meat, then go without it for a spell."

"And do you Fletcherize it?"

"Fletcherize nothing, bolt. I bolt my food; lower that's the thing. Fletcherized food is too quickly digested. All animals bolt their food. To be sure, the cow chews later at its leisure, but that's because there is so little nutriment in the grass it eats. Our food, on the contrary, is concentrated and requires little mastication."

Noticing that Mr. Edison was not smoking, the interviewer asked him if he still burned twenty cigars a day, as was his habit for many years.

"No," he said, "only one or two, usually after a meal. I don't know of any particular reason for cutting down, but I did. I chew all the time. It's a habit I learned when I was a telegrapher. I had no end of trouble with Mrs. Edison about it and was on the point of quitting when I found out that the Chief Justice of the United States Supreme Court used tobacco in that way. I told Mrs. Edison and that let me out. Used to think that when I got to be as old as I am now I would lay off, but there seems to be no reason for it. I have been waiting for this old age that we hear about, but I can't even seem to feel it approaching. There is one thing I am doing, though. For most of my life I refused to work at any problem unless its solution seemed to be capable of being put to commercial use. I looked forward to the time when I could fiddle around with things I had caught a glimpse of here and there and which would give me personal satisfaction. . . ."

"Mr. Edison, which one of your inventions did you enjoy most while at work upon it?"

"The phonograph; I had a lot of fun with that," was the prompt answer.

"And which did you find the hardest?"

"The incandescent light—that was the hardest and most important. As I say, the development of the phonograph was most interesting, but it took a long time—thirty years."

Which led to the query: What sort of phonograph music does Mr. Edison personally have the greatest fondness for? His face wrinkled with laughter, then shooting a glance at the questioner that seemed to challenge disapproval, he answered:

"Heart songs. Yes, heart songs; they're the real music for me."

"What heart songs?"

"Suwanee River—oh, all of 'em. But I like all kinds of music. I was figuring to-day that I had hear 17,500 pieces played by the phonographs, and I enjoyed most of them. I like all of Verdi, all of Brahms, all of Beethoven, ah there was a composer! I like everything but cubist music, which is hideous.

"One can acquire a taste for almost anything, but I can't stand the type of music that is like a cubist picture. Why, I can turn the phonograph backward and make better music than that. We get curious effects by reversing the phonograph—strange and interesting and sometimes delightful effects.

"You know, there are not more than 250 melodic combinations in music. All comic songs originate in twelve tunes. There are only forty-five waltz movements."

The interviewer did not know it. In fact, those fun-loving eyes of Mr. Edison were dancing so obviously despite the gravity of his face that the visitor faintly suspected he was being spoofed. Let the musical sharps decide. . . .

Mr. Edison directed the conversation back to the matter of a man's habits of living. He would rather discuss that subject any time than his own achievements, which he never mentions unless pressed. He said that he indulged in no physical exercise at all, "except what I get by standing and walking around a laboratory table all day."

"I don't seem to need exercise," he added. "Of course, if a man eats a good deal he has to exercise. That's where I have the advantage of my friends. While they're playing golf I fuss around the laboratory, which to me is much more entertaining.

"But I'm not really working very hard. After a lifetime of pretty steady pegging I am at last in a position to tinker with a few personal hobbies that I've been saving up, and I tell you, young man, it's a luxury for me—luxury."

"Edison Views the World at Seventy," *New York Sun*, February 1917, pp. 14-16 (no byline given). Note: This article is located on the website for the Library of Congress.

CHRONOLOGY

1847

Thomas Alva Edison is born in Milan, Ohio, on February 11.

1859

Edison works as a candy "butcher" on the Grand Trunk Railroad.

1861

The U.S. Civil War begins.

1863

Edison works as an itinerant telegrapher.

1865

The Civil War ends; President Abraham Lincoln is assassinated by John Wilkes Booth.

1868

Edison takes a telegrapher job in the Western Union office in Boston, Massachusetts.

1869

Edison quits Western Union to become a freelance inventor, receives a first patent for an electric vote recorder, moves to New York City, and forms a "General Telegraphic Agency" with Frank Pope and James Ashley.

1871

Edison marries Mary Stilwell.

1874

Edison invents the quadruplex telegraph.

1875

Edison becomes involved in a legal dispute over ownership of the quadruplex.

1876

American novelist Mark Twain publishes *Tom Sawyer;* Edison moves to Menlo Park, New Jersey, and establishes a laboratory.

1877

Edison invents the carbon-button telephone transmitter and the phonograph.

1879

Edison invents a practical incandescent lamp.

1880

Edison perfects a system of electrical distribution.

1881

U.S. president John Garfield is assassinated by a disgruntled office seeker; Edison moves the bulk of his operations to New York City and begins installation of an electrical distribution system.

1882

The Pearl Street central lighting station in New York begins operation.

1884

Mary Stilwell Edison dies.

1886

Edison marries Mina Miller and moves to West Orange, New Jersey.

1887

The new laboratory complex in West Orange is completed and Edison resumes work on the phonograph.

1888

Edison begins ore-milling experiments and mounts a campaign against alternating current promoted by George Westinghouse.

1889

Edison begins developing motion picture devices (the kinetograph and kinetoscope) and starts production of an improved phonograph; Edison General Electric is formed.

1890

Edison constructs an ore-milling plant in Ogden, New Jersey.

1892

General Electric is formed; Edison's ties to the electric industry start to weaken.

1893

The first movie studio, the Black Maria, is built at West Orange labs.

1894

Edison forms the National Phonograph Company.

1896

The U.S. Supreme Court approves segregation in *Plessy v. Ferguson*; Edison introduces a new spring-motor phonograph.

1900

Edison closes the ore-milling plant.

1903

The Great Train Robbery movie is released.

1905

Edison reintroduces a dictating machine.

1908

The Motion Picture Patents Company is formed.

1909

Edison perfects a practical nickel-iron storage battery.

1910

Edison reorganizes his companies as Thomas A. Edison, Inc.

1912

The ocean liner *Titanic* sinks on its maiden voyage; Edison attempts to develop an auto ignition system for Henry Ford.

1914

Fire destroys a portion of the West Orange complex.

1915

Edison is named chairman of the Naval Consulting Board.

1917

The United States enters World War I.

1918

Edison ends his involvement in motion pictures; World War I ends.

1926

Edison retires as head of Thomas A. Edison, Inc.

1927

Edison undertakes a search for a domestic source of rubber.

1929

The U.S. stock market crashes; the Light Bulb's Golden Jubilee is held in Dearborn, Michigan.

1931

Thomas Edison dies at home in West Orange, New Jersey, on October 18.

FOR FURTHER RESEARCH

THE WRITINGS OF THOMAS EDISON

Thomas A. Edison, *The Papers of Thomas A. Edison. Vol. 1: The Making of an Inventor, February 1847–June 1873.* Ed. Reese V. Jenkins et al. Baltimore: Johns Hopkins University Press, 1989.

——, *The Papers of Thomas A. Edison. Vol. 2: From Workshop to Laboratory, June 1873–March 1876.* Ed. Robert A. Rosenberg et al. Baltimore: Johns Hopkins University Press, 1992.

——, *The Papers of Thomas A. Edison. Vol. 3: Menlo Park, the Early Years, April 1876–December 1877.* Ed. Robert A. Rosenberg et al. Baltimore: Johns Hopkins University Press, 1994.

Thomas Alva Edison, *The Diary and Sundry Observations of Thomas Alva Edison.* New York: Greenwood Press, 1948.

BIOGRAPHIES OF EDISON

Gene Adair, *Thomas Alva Edison: Inventing the Electric Age.* New York: Oxford University Press, 1996.

Neil Baldwin, *Edison: Inventing the Century.* New York: Hyperion, 1995.

Ronald W. Clark, *Edison: The Man Who Made the Future.* New York: Putnam, 1977.

Robert Conot, *A Streak of Luck: The Life and Legend of Thomas Alva Edison.* New York: Da Capo Press, 1986.

Henry Ford, *Edison as I Know Him.* New York: Cosmopolitan Book Corporation, 1930.

Lawrence A. Frost, *The Edison Album: A Pictorial Biography of Thomas Alva Edison.* Seattle: Superior, 1969.

H. Gordon Garbedian, *Thomas Alva Edison: Builder of Civi-*

lization. New York: Julian Messner, 1994.

Paul Israel, *Edison: A Life of Invention.* New York: John Wiley & Sons, 1998.

Matthew Josephson, *Edison: A Biography.* New York: John Wiley, 1992.

William H. Meadowcroft, *The Boys' Life of Edison.* New York: Harper & Brothers, 1911.

Andre Millard, *Edison and the Business of Innovation.* Baltimore: Johns Hopkins University Press, 1990.

William S. Pretzer, ed., *Working at Inventing: Thomas A. Edison and the Menlo Park Experience.* Introduction by William A. Pretzer. Dearborn, MI: Henry Ford Museum, 1989.

William A. Simonds, *Edison: His Life, His Work, His Genius.* Indianapolis, NY: The Bobbs-Merrill Company, 1943.

Byron M. Vanderbilt, *Thomas Edison, Chemist.* Washington, DC: American Chemical Society, 1971.

Wyn Wachhorst, *Thomas Alva Edison: An American Myth.* Cambridge, MA: MIT Press, 1981.

ABOUT EDISON'S INVENTIONS

C.L. Boltz, *How Electricity Is Made.* New York: FactsOnFile, 1985.

Robert Friedel and Paul Israel, with Bernard S. Finn. *Edison's Electric Light: Biography of an Invention.* New Brunswick, NJ: Rutgers University Press, 1986.

Roland Gelatt, *The Fabulous Phonograph, 1877–1977.* New York: Macmillan, 1977.

Francis Jehl, *Menlo Park Reminiscences.* Dearborn, MI: Edison Institute, 1937.

Charles Musser, *Thomas A. Edison and His Kinetographic Motion Pictures.* New Brunswick, NJ: Rutgers University Press, 1995.

David Robinson, *From Peep Show to Palace: The Birth of American Film.* New York: Columbia University Press, 1995.

Harold I. Sharlin, *The Making of the Electrical Age: From the Telegraph to Automation.* New York: Abelard-Schuman, 1963.

Robert Silverberg, *Light for the World: Edison and the Power Industry*. Princeton, NJ: D. Van Nostrand, 1967.

Alfred O. Tate, *Edison's Open Door*. New York: E.P. Dutton, 1938.

Walter L. Welch and Leah Stenzel Burt, *From Tinfoil to Stereo: The Acoustic Years of the Recording Industry*. Gainesville: University Press of Florida, 1994.

ON INVENTING AND INVENTORS

Ira Flatow, *They All Laughed . . . : From Light Bulbs to Lasers, the Fascinating Stories Behind the Great Inventions That Have Changed Our Lives*. New York: Harper-Collins, 1992.

Joseph and Frances Gies, *The Ingenious Yankees: The Men, Ideas, and Machines That Transformed a Nation, 1776–1876*. New York: Thomas Y. Crowell, 1976.

Thomas Parkes Hughes, *American Genesis*. New York: Viking, 1989.

——, *Technology in America: Thomas Alva Edison and the Rise of Electricity*. Ed. Carroll W. Pursell Jr. Cambridge, MA: MIT Press, 1981.

Paul Israel, *From Machine Shop to Industrial Laboratory: Telegraphy and the Changing Context of American Invention, 1830–1920*. Baltimore: Johns Hopkins University Press, 1992.

David Lindsay, *Madness in the Making: The Triumphant Rise and Untimely Fall of America's Show Inventors*. Kodansha International, 1997.

Geoffrey J. Noonan, *Nineteenth-Century Inventors*. New York: FactsOnFile, 1991.

Robert Pool, *Beyond Engineering: How Society Shapes Technology*. New York and Oxford: Oxford University Press, 1997.

Rebecca Weaver and Rodney Dale, *Home Entertainment*. New York: Oxford University Press, 1993.

Trevor I. Williams, *The History of Invention: From Stone Axes to Silicon Chips*. New York: FactsOnFile, 1987.

EDISON HISTORIC SITES

Con-Edison Energy Museum
(www.greatcollegetown.com/museums.html)
145 East 14th St.
New York, NY 10011
(212) 460-6244

Exhibits on the early electric lighting are some of the attractions at this museum, which is run by the New York City power company that still bears Edison's name.

Edison Birthplace Museum
(www.tomedison.org)
9 Edison Dr.
Milan, OH 44846
(419) 499-2135

This house where Edison was born is now maintained as a museum and overlooks what remains of the historic Milan canal basin. It features furniture from the period, as well as family memorabilia. It also contains an exhibit of Edison's inventions, among them a model of the original phonograph and an early electric lightbulb.

Edison National Historic Site
(www.nps.gov/edis/home.htm)
Main St. and Lakeside Ave.
West Orange, NJ 07052
(973) 736-5050 (recorded information)
(973) 736-0550 (reservations, group rates)

The National Park Service preserves Edison's research laboratory as it was in the inventor's day. The archive that houses Edison's large collection of papers and records is maintained here. Visitors can see the library, machine shop, chemical lab, a replica of the Black Maria movie studio, and demonstrations of the early phonograph. Glenmont, the nearby Edison estate, is open for tours. The house contains the original furnishings used by Thomas and Mina Edison, who are buried on the grounds.

Henry Ford Museum and Greenfield Village
(http://edison-ford-estate.com and www.hfmgv.org/)
20900 Oakwood Blvd.
Dearborn, MI 48121
(313) 271-1620

This estate was the location of "Light's Golden Jubilee" in 1929. Greenfield Village includes reconstructions of the

Menlo Park laboratory and the nearby boardinghouse where Edison's staff stayed, and many other historic buildings such as Orville Wright's bicycle shop and a courthouse where Abraham Lincoln once practiced law. The museum exhibits everything from farm equipment and automobiles to household items, including devices that originated with Edison.

Menlo Park Memorial Tower and Menlo Park Museum

(www.edisonnj.org/menlopark/)
Route 27
Edison, NJ 08817
(732) 248-7298

This 131-foot tower is topped with a 14-foot high lightbulb and commemorates the site of Edison's Menlo Park laboratory.

Thomas Edison Winter Home and Botanical Gardens

(www.msu.edu/msu/imp/mod70/70000054.html and
www.coconet.com/fortmyers/museum.html)
2350 McGregor Blvd.
Fort Myers, FL 33901
(941) 334-7419

This site was willed to the city of Fort Myers by Mina Edison. The fourteen-acre Edison winter estate includes a botanical garden where the inventor cultivated various plants used in his research, such as bamboo for lamp filaments and goldenrod for rubber production. Among the buildings are the main house, a honeymoon cottage, a chemical laboratory, and a museum that exhibits a collection of Edison inventions. The winter home of Edison's close friend Henry Ford is also located in Fort Myers.

INDEX

Thomas Edison

Clark, Ronald W., 13, 26
Columbia Phonograph Company,
134
Conant, James, 203
Conot, Robert, 183, 203–204
De Forest, Lee
characteristics of, 67
on Edison, 210
and General Motors, 66
and reverse salients, 94
and telegraphy, 91, 92
DeGraaf, Leonard, 204–205
Delany, Patrick, 70
Desmond, Shaw, 202
de Tocqueville, Alexis, 37
Detroit Free Press (newspaper),
34
Dickson, William K.L., 21, 192
dictating machines, 24
Dow, Alexander, 162
Dudley, Charles, 87
Dynamo (O'Neill), 208

Eastman, George, 143
Eckert, Thomas, 65–66
economy, 123
Ediphone, 24
Edison, Charles (son)
birth of, 20
and Edison enterprises, 24, 151
importance of, 192
on scientific discoveries, 208
Edison, Madeleine (daughter), 20
Edison, Marian "Dot" (daughter),
15, 20
Edison, Mary Stilwell (wife), 15,
20, 49, 60
Edison, Mina Miller (wife), 20,
60, 77
Edison, Nancy Elliott (mother)
and education of Edison, 12, 30
health of, 44
and religion, 32
Edison, Samuel (father)
background of, 12
as businessman, 30, 44
characteristics of, 24
Edison, Tannie (sister), 40
Edison, Theodore (son), 20
Edison, Thomas Alva
appearance of, 166, 172
awards received, 26, 202
Black Friday, 47
characteristics of

ambition, 46, 184, 185
creativity, 151, 185
curiosity, 12
decision-making ability, 191
egotism, 132, 185, 190, 192,
203, 204
inflexibility, 121
optimism, 24, 25, 50, 151, 153,
169, 196
perseverance, 24, 39–40, 105,
148–49, 151, 166, 171–72,
185, 190–92
prankster, 61
pride, 170
rebelliousness, 184, 185
self-confidence, 50, 104,
151–52, 184–85
sense of humor, 45
short tempered, 166, 171
solitariness, 39–40
storyteller, 61
childhood of, 12–13, 29–31, 36
children of, 15, 20, 151, 192, 208
death of, 25
education of, 12, 29–30, 43, 62,
188–89
as entrepreneur, 11, 14
boyhood, 12–13, 29–31, 33, 36,
38
and electric lighting, 57
and employees, 150, 154,
203–206
and labor unions, 67
financing of, 102
marketing abilities of, 189
and ore milling losses, 153,
157, 159
partnership with Pope and
Ashley, 47
and phonograph, 134
and storage battery, 160,
168–70
success, 22
fame of, 26
on Faraday, 14, 45–46
health of, 25, 44, 77, 171
hearing loss, 12–14, 32, 38,
184, 203–204
on human nature, 41
images of
evolution of, 187, 191–92,
198–99
as humanitarian, 200–202
as rugged individualist, 185,
199, 202, 209–10